The Family Guide to Colorado's National Parks and Monuments

by Carolyn Sutton

WESTCLIFFE PUBLISHERS

westcliffepublishers.com

International Standard Book Numbers:
ISBN-10: 1-56579-536-9
ISBN-13: 978-1-56579-536-5

Editor: Kelly Kordes Anton
Designer: Angie Lee, Grindstone Graphics, Inc.
Production Manager: Craig Keyzer

Published by:
Westcliffe Publishers, Inc.
P.O. Box 1261
Englewood, CO 80150

Printed in China by: C & C Offset Printing Co., Ltd.

Library of Congress Cataloging-in-Publication Data:
Sutton, Carolyn.
  The family guide to Colorado's national parks and monuments / by Carolyn Sutton.
     p. cm.
  Includes bibliographical references and index.
  ISBN-13: 978-1-56579-536-5
  ISBN-10: 1-56579-536-9
  1. National parks and reserves--Colorado--Guidebooks. 2. Family recreation--Colorado--Guidebooks. 3. Colorado--Guidebooks. I. Title.
  F774.3.S88 2006
  917.880434--dc22   2006004910

For more information about other fine books and calendars from Westcliffe Publishers, please contact your local bookstore, call us at 1-800-523-3692, or visit us on the Web at westcliffepublishers.com.

Please Note: Risk is always a factor in backcountry and high-mountain travel. Many of the activities described in this book can be dangerous, especially when weather is adverse or unpredictable, and when unforeseen events or conditions create a hazardous situation. The author has done her best to provide the reader with accurate information about backcountry travel, as well as to point out some of its potential hazards. It is the responsibility of the users of this guide to learn the necessary skills for safe backcountry travel, and to exercise caution in potentially hazardous areas, especially on glaciers and avalanche-prone terrain. The author and publisher disclaim any liability for injury or other damage caused by backcountry traveling or performing any other activity described in this book.

The author and publisher of this book have made every effort to ensure the accuracy and currency of its information. Nevertheless, books can require revisions. Please feel free to let us know if you find information in this book that needs to be updated, and we will be glad to correct it for the next printing. Your comments and suggestions are always welcome.

Cover: *Kids will love exploring the unusual landscape of Great Sand Dunes National Park.*
Previous page: *The Pine Creek Trail in Curecanti National Recreation Area leads to freedom and adventure.*

Acknowledgments

I may not have as much money as some, but I consider myself very wealthy. You see, from the time I was tiny, my folks explored Colorado with me. They gave me the riches of scenery, history, and nature that are Colorado's heritage for all Americans. As a little girl I hiked, picnicked, camped, went sightseeing, threw rocks into streams, climbed trees, and played in our national parks and monuments.

My parents sweated up trails with my sister and me, stopping at overlooks to share take-your-breath-away views. As we snuggled into our sleeping bags, Mom read us wildflower guides as bedtime stories. Later, she rose from her warm bed to take me to the outhouse in the frosty night, and stood with me, stunned by the blizzard of stars overhead.

My Dad bravely held the tent stake while I swung the mallet to pound it into the ground. He skewered hapless worms and showed me how to cast my fishing line way out into the pond. He taught me to pack my own gear, carry my own gear, and read a map. He used his belt to cinch the poncho around my young waist and then sent me into the rain to play in the mud. I can still hear the emotion in his voice when he looked out over the spread of a jagged mountain range and murmured in my ear, "Isn't that beautiful, Honey? Just gorgeous!"

The author, her sister, and her Mom camping at Dinosaur National Monument in 1971

A book of this size and scope is a big project. I am grateful to my own husband and boys for letting me drag them—frequently—to each and every national park and monument in Colorado. They exhibited extreme good nature as I asked them over and over to "turn a little more this way" for a picture.

And to the park service rangers and volunteers who were so patient with my endless questions, I am indebted to you. I don't know how you do so much with so little. John, Linda, Jenna, Craig, and Barrett at Westcliffe Publishers: I appreciate your support and confidence in me.

But it was Carla and Joe who started it all when they took the trouble to pack the lunches and the car and headed out on another adventure. It is to them that I dedicate this book. Thanks, Mom and Dad!

Hiking the Desert Voices Trail in Dinosaur National Monument

Contents

Colorado State Map 6

Preface
    The Gift 8

Introduction
    Is This Book for You? 9
    How to Use This Guide 10

Adventuring with Munchkins
    Keys for Success 11
    Kitchen Sink? Check! 12
    Safety in the Outdoors 12

Park Wise
    A Monumental Mission 14
    Services for Families 15
    Park Manners 15
    BLM National Monuments: A Different Drummer 19

Desert Canyons 20
    1. Dinosaur National Monument 22
    2. Colorado National Monument 40
    3. Canyons of the Ancients National Monument 52
    4. Hovenweep National Monument 66
    5. Mesa Verde National Park 80
    6. Yucca House National Monument 96

Mountains 104
    7. Rocky Mountain National Park 106
    8. Florissant Fossil Beds National Monument 132
    9. Black Canyon of the Gunnison National Park 144
    10. Curecanti National Recreation Area 158
    11. Great Sand Dunes National Park and Preserve 176

Prairie 198
    12. Sand Creek Massacre National Historic Site 200
    13. Bent's Old Fort National Historic Site 208

Trip Log 216
Leave No Trace Principles 218
Essential Gear for Family Hiking 220
Guides and Outfitters 221
Recommended Reading 225
Index 226

Colorado State Map

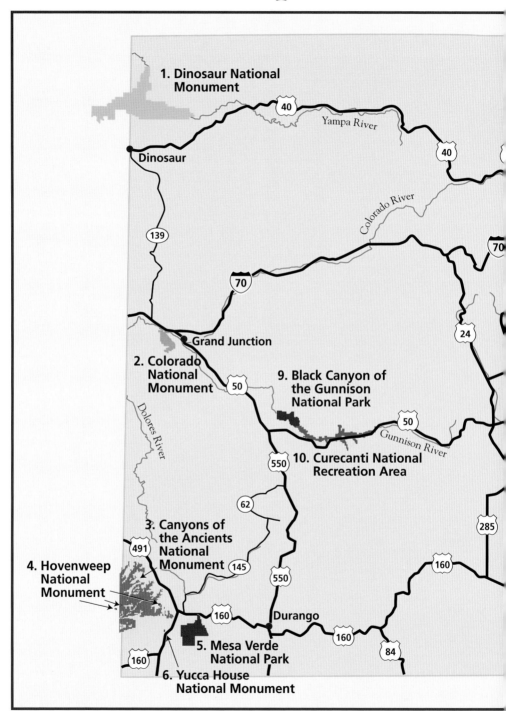

1. Dinosaur National Monument

40

Yampa River

40

Dinosaur

Colorado River

139

70

70

70

Grand Junction

24

2. Colorado National Monument

50

9. Black Canyon of the Gunnison National Park

50

Gunnison River

Dolores River

550

10. Curecanti National Recreation Area

62

285

3. Canyons of the Ancients National Monument

491

145

4. Hovenweep National Monument

160

550

160

Durango

160

5. Mesa Verde National Park

160

84

6. Yucca House National Monument

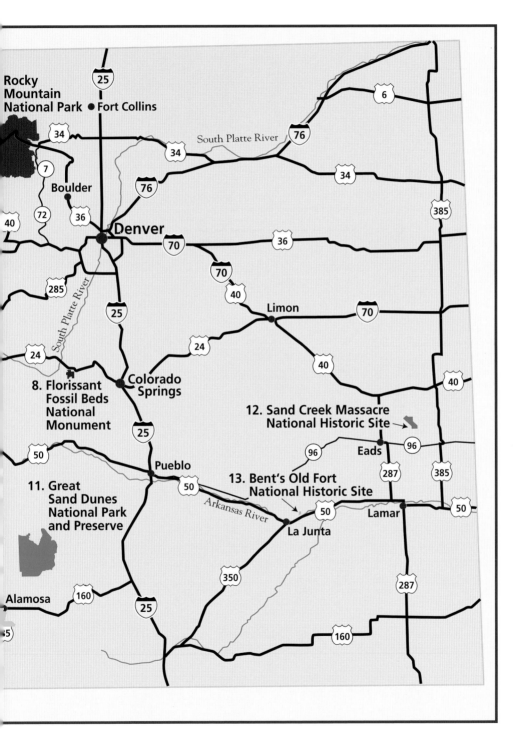

Rocky Mountain National Park ● Fort Collins

Boulder

Denver

Colorado Springs

8. Florissant Fossil Beds National Monument

11. Great Sand Dunes National Park and Preserve

Alamosa

Pueblo

Limon

Eads

12. Sand Creek Massacre National Historic Site

13. Bent's Old Fort National Historic Site

La Junta

Lamar

South Platte River

Arkansas River

25, 34, 7, 76, 72, 36, 40, 285, 70, 24, 50, 160, 6, 385, 96, 287, 350

Preface

The Gift

It's a long story, but the upshot is that at the tender age of 3, I ended up camping out at the Great Sand Dunes National Monument with my family, a car full of borrowed gear, and no tent.

That evening while my Mom fixed dinner, my Dad spread the sleeping bags on the ground. Curious campers stopped by to ask what we were sleeping in.

"Our sleeping bags," Dad said.

"But what are you going to sleep under?" they persisted.

"The stars," Mom replied.

The author, her sister, and her Mom at a Colorado roadside viewpoint

As darkness fell, my family nestled into bed while sparkles filled the inky sky. And then, as a special treat for our intrepid family lying on the ground, the stars began to dance. First one shot across the sky, and then another. Every few seconds a shooting star sliced the heavens, sending a thrill down my wee spine.

This was my first experience in Colorado's national parks. Lucky us, we had bumbled into one of nature's best shows, the Perseid meteor showers, which occur every year in mid-August.

And my family was hooked. Dad bought a tent-trailer and every summer we plastered it with stickers reminding us of our adventures—Dinosaur National Monument, Rocky Mountain National Park, Mesa Verde. By the time I was 7, I had seen most of the national parks and monuments now listed for Colorado.

Colorado's national parks are a gift. The people who fought to have them set aside gave them to us. The parks preserve natural and cultural wonders for future generations of Americans. In fact, we are one of those generations. Colorado's national parks are a gift to us and a gift for our heritage.

Yet, visiting our national parks and monuments offers more than a taste of nature and different cultures. These trips allow you to have uninterrupted time with your family—undistracted by phone calls or television or housework. They give you the chance to discover new places and learn new things together. And the variety of Colorado's national parks and monuments will give you the state in all its moods. And the more you get to know it, the more you'll fall in love with it.

Introduction

Is This Book for You?

This book is for you if you have kids and you want to get motivated to take the vacations of a lifetime—plenty of them. It is for you if you want to get the family out of the house and exploring new places and learning new things. It is for you if you want to build relationships with your kids based on positive experiences, and you know you need information to make that happen.

The author as a little girl, on a hike with her Dad and sister

The information in this book is tailored for families in two ways. It highlights the features of Colorado's national parks and monuments that are particularly entertaining and educational for kids, and it includes the nitty-gritty details to make adventuring as easy as possible on parents. The book tells you where the diaper-changing stations are, if there is a snack bar, and the best trails for little boots. And when you've had enough of nature, it tells you where the closest hotel is.

This book is for you if you want to connect with your kids and your place in the world. Colorado's national parks and monuments were designated because folks saw something so remarkable that they fought, sometimes for more than a century, to have a place set aside for future generations. You are one of those generations, and so are your kids.

When you visit a park, monument, recreation area, or historic site with your children, you are becoming part of something that makes Colorado what it is—and makes America what it is. In some cases, you'll be visiting a Biosphere Reserve or a World Heritage Site, indicating international recognition of the park's worth. A family is hard put to explore such a place and come away unaffected.

The author and her Dad climbing a ladder at Mesa Verde's Balcony House in 1966

9

How to Use This Guide

If nothing else, use this book to inspire you to get out and see Colorado. Whether you need rest, solace, excitement, or just a breath of fresh air, head to a national park or monument. Smell the vast, windswept prairies, feel the burning in your thighs as you climb around in the mountains, and hear the dribbling notes of a canyon wren's voice in the desert. Here is the motivation to lock the front door behind you and get going.

Then use the information in this book to make the trip as much of a success as you can. Plan ahead using the specifics in the "At a Glance" sections at the beginning of each chapter. Read up on the natural history and human history of the place so you can appreciate the parks and monuments more deeply. Explain to your kids what they are seeing and they'll think you are really smart—and you are. You have done what it takes to make a trip interesting and fun.

A young hiker soaks in the view at Black Canyon of the Gunnison National Park.

At every visitor center, you can find an ink pad and a stamp with the date and the name of the national park unit. You can either purchase a National Parks passport at the bookstore or stamp the box at the beginning of each chapter in this book to mark when you've visited a park or monument. Make a copy of the "Trip Log" on p. 216–217 and help or encourage your kids to fill it out to document your visit and preserve the memories.

In the process, you will make learning interesting and fun for your kids. They will come to appreciate the value of seeing a place firsthand. They will know that nature isn't something far away and only on the Discovery Channel, but a part of their own experience.

With this experience, your kids may develop a sense of responsibility for the national parks and monuments that belong to them. They may keep a closer eye on the government officials in charge of protecting those treasures for the generations to come. And isn't that how better citizens are made? Then, eventually, when your kids want to give the gifts of Colorado's national parks and monuments to their own children, the places will be there still, and still be in good shape.

But first you have to pack up the kids and head out. Pick a park or monument and go. Then try another. See as much of Colorado as you can, then send us a postcard and tell us what you think. We'd love to hear from you.

Bon Voyage!

Adventuring with Munchkins

Keys for Success

As any parent will tell you, traveling with kids has its opportunities and its limitations. On the one hand, you and your children will get to share some pretty special experiences. On the other hand, kids make hitting the road a bit more complicated.

By and large, Colorado's national parks and monuments are family-friendly places. Still, before you leave, it helps to keep in mind four keys to successful outings:

Plan: Research and strategize, taking into account the ages and number of kids, your family's comfort level with the outdoors, the season, the length of your trip, your goals for going on this particular outing, and individual interests of the family members.

Pack: Taking a close look at your day-by-day plan, list everything you might need, and add special items for emergencies. Include things such as snacks and toys for entertaining the little tigers in the car, first aid and medications, and surprises to spring on the kids when emotional storm clouds loom and they need a good distraction.

Daily Activities: Be prepared to modify activities as necessary. Bored of hanging around camp? Whip out some ideas for an impromptu short hike. Worn out from too much sightseeing? Hang out at a picnic area and do spur-of-the-moment nature crafts or just let the kids have free time to mess around in the woods. Keeping tabs on the ebb and flow of the family's energy and then varying activities to match will make the trip much more enjoyable for all.

Say "Uncle": When the weather is crummy, someone gets sick, or you've all just had enough, know when to call it quits. Head into town to that motel with a swimming pool and room service and give everyone a break. You may be disappointed that you didn't do all you planned, but it is better than teaching your kids to hate the national parks. This is, after all, a family vacation, not boot camp.

Visiting remote areas like Canyons of the Ancients National Monument requires planning and preparation ahead of time.

Kitchen Sink? Check!

Knowing what to bring and what to leave home is unfortunately largely a function of trial and error. Nonetheless, certain items will be needed by all families while visiting nearly every site in Colorado. These include guidebooks and maps; water bottles; lunch, snacks, and extra food; jackets, raingear, and extra clothing; sunblock, lip balm, sunhat and sunglasses; camera and film; first aid kit; bug repellant; and toys to play with in the car.

Whether you are camping, staying in a hotel, or taking a day trip, it always makes sense to plan your activities in advance, listing items needed for each event. For example, on a trip to the Great Sand Dunes, jeans and boots with heels are a good idea if you plan to go horseback riding. On the other hand, if all you want to do is play in the creek, bathing suits and beach towels may be on your list. If you're planning to hike, see "Essential Gear for Family Hiking" on page 220 for a list of additional items to pack.

Safety in the Outdoors

Every single national park, monument, recreation area, preserve, and historic site in Colorado has major outdoor attractions. That means you and your crew will be exposed to the elements any time you visit. So dress for an audience with Mother Nature, and be prepared to look her in the eye when you meet her. Keep in mind the following factors:

Kids love to learn new things from park rangers.

Altitude: Colorado's position in the atmosphere affects everything from the intensity of the sun to kids' energy. Know the symptoms of altitude sickness (fatigue, weakness, shortness of breath, headache, loss of appetite, nausea, vomiting) and know what to do for it (rest, fluids, light diet, avoid alcohol and caffeine).

Solar Intensity: For every 1,000 feet of elevation gain, solar intensity increases by 5 percent. Think of the sun as a great big thermonuclear explosion and a tan or sunburn as a sign of radiation exposure. The atmosphere offers some protection, but not enough in Colorado. Slather exposed skin with sunblock several times each day, protect eyes with sunglasses, and make sure everyone dons a brim. Use lip balm with an SPF of at least 15.

Dry Air: Partly due to its altitude and partly due to its position on the continent, Colorado is a dry place. It can be 90 degrees out and you might not even break a sweat. Truth is, you are sweating, but it dries so fast, you don't notice it. Even in cold weather, the air is stealing your body's moisture right out of your lungs. Replace it with plenty of water. We add a bit of drink mix powder to water bottles to make the liquids go down easier. Kids should be peeing several times a day, and urine should be the color of straw. Otherwise, up the fluid ante!

Temperature: For every 1,000 feet in elevation you gain, plan on the temperature dropping about 3.6 degrees. The higher you go, the greater the chances are that it will be windy, so plan on a chill factor, too. In other words, what may start out as a pleasant, springlike day in the valley may turn out to be a downright wintry one on a nearby ridge. On the other hand, beware of high summer in the canyon country and on the plains. Avoid the blast furnace by visiting in the fall or spring, or hike in the early morning or evening.

Rough Ground: Who named them the Rocky Mountains, anyway? No matter where you are, unless you plan to spend your entire visit in the car or the visitor center, you'll likely be on a trail. Especially if you've only been walking for a few years, it's easy to trip, twist an ankle, or skin a knee. It sure is great when Mom or Dad whips out the antiseptic, Band-Aids, and kisses for those boo-boos. Bring a well-stocked first aid kit.

Wildlife: Tromp around in the wilds much and you are bound to come in contact with creatures living the wild life. Let them. Don't feed the animals—and that includes the mosquitoes. Animals carry fleas and ticks, which may enjoy a bite of human for a change of pace. Wear insect repellant to protect against diseases such as bubonic plague, West Nile virus, Colorado tick fever, Rocky Mountain tick fever, and Lyme disease. Also, remember that those peaceful deer and elk practice their kicking and stomping techniques on tougher customers than you. If you get too close, they'll think you are an enemy—and you may suffer painful, if not fatal, consequences. In mountain lion country, keep close tabs on your kids. The kids should stay between adults when hiking, and never run off by themselves. Mountain lions can resist a running child like a house cat can resist a bouncing ping-pong ball. It's best to stay in a group to discourage the cats from hunting people. And watch for rattlesnakes on the trail. They prefer not to meet you, and it is best to respect their wishes. Use binoculars, a spotting scope, or a camera with a long lens to enjoy the wildlife from a distance. For more tips on wildlife encounters, see "Park Manners" on page 15.

Road Trip: It's hard to get to just about any national park or monument in Colorado without driving there. And sometimes, it's a really long drive. Keep your car well maintained, full of gas, and equipped with a healthy spare tire and the tools needed to change it. Pay attention to speed limits (rangers give speeding tickets, too!) and watch the road for obstacles, hazards, and wildlife. Bring little toys, coloring books, maps, and other entertainment for the kids, so drivers can do their job without being distracted.

In other words, take care of the nitty-gritty—the practical stuff—so you can relax and enjoy nature's magic. When the pressure is off because the family's basic needs are met, your mind can ease up and wander a bit. It can linger on the sound of that hummingbird as it dips and soars overhead and the lovely shadow pattern those aspen leaves make in the breeze. Then nature can seep into your heart and into your kids as well, and you'll know the enchantment of Colorado's national parks and monuments.

Park Wise

A Monumental Mission

Pull off onto a scenic overlook to survey all of Colorado's national parks and monuments and you'll see a crazy quilt of places. What with high windblown prairies, toothy peaks, and deep canyons hiding mysterious vanished cultures, the National Park Service has a complicated job.

The National Park Service aims: "…to conserve the scenery and the natural and historic objects and the wildlife therein and to provide for the enjoyment of the same…as will leave them unimpaired for the enjoyment of future generations." In other words, it wants your grandkids to experience the same great park or monument that delighted you when you were little.

To reach that goal, the National Park Service adheres to a list of guiding principles, including excellent service, outstanding employees, effective park management, and education about our common heritage, among other things. In addition, the National Park Service fills the roles of guardian of our cultural and recreational resources, advocate for the environment, and leader in open space protection. The United States, through the National Park Service, has been a guiding influence in the worldwide national park movement. It all began with Yellowstone's establishment in 1872. Since then, more than 100 nations around the world have created nearly 1,200 national parks or preserves. Within the National Park Service in Colorado, several designations exist.

National Parks are large, natural areas with a wide variety of attributes; mining, hunting, and other activities that would consume the resources of the place are prohibited. It takes an act of Congress to designate a national park. Colorado currently has four national parks: Black Canyon of the Gunnison, Mesa Verde, Great Sand Dunes, and Rocky Mountain.

National Monuments can be declared by the president without the involvement of Congress, and include structures and other objects of historic or scientific interest on lands owned or controlled by the government. In Colorado, national monuments include Colorado National Monument, Dinosaur, Florissant Fossil Beds, and Yucca House. Canyons of the Ancients is a national monument managed by the Bureau of Land Management.

National Preserves are similar to national parks, but they permit public hunting, trapping, and oil and gas exploration and extraction. Currently, Great Sand Dunes National Park and Preserve is the only national preserve in Colorado.

National Historic Sites usually contain a single historical feature. Bent's Old Fort and the Sand Creek Massacre National Historic Sites are in Colorado.

National Recreation Areas are large reservoirs that emphasize water-based recreation. They combine open space with natural and historic resource preservation and recreation. Colorado has Curecanti National Recreation Area.

Services for Families

From diaper-changing stations to junior ranger badges, the National Park Service has a great focus on children. Many websites for the various Colorado units have a "For Kids" button to click. Depending on the park, offerings include a junior ranger program, special exhibits in park museums, special programs, and ranger talks for kids. Frequently, units have outreach classes with detailed lesson plans meeting Colorado state educational standards for preschool through college level. Without exception, the rangers working the information desks at the visitor centers were helpful at directing us to kid-friendly activities and attractions in their area. Frequently, they took time to come out from behind the counter and look at bird or flower guidebooks with the kids, to show them their equipment, or point out an endangered falcon soaring overhead. On the whole, park service personnel delight in sharing a great treasure with youngsters.

Park Manners

Congress established the National Park Service to conserve the parks "unimpaired for the enjoyment of future generations." And the National Park Service relies on the public to help it further that mission. When you visit a park or monument, even your presence has an impact. We must all take care that our impact doesn't mess up the experience for our grandkids or their grandkids.

Each park service unit across Colorado has a different resource to protect, and sometimes several very different types of resources. These might include scenery, historic buildings, wildlife, archaeological sites, fragile life zones, or fossils. It is your responsibility to abide by the laws and regulations within each unit. Check in at the visitor center when you arrive to get a feel for what is important at that park or monument. Certain points of etiquette stand for all the national parks, monuments, preserves, recreation areas, and historic sites in Colorado:

The Great Sand Dunes put smiles on the faces of Colorado kids.

When you visit someone, it is polite to knock on their door before you tromp around in their backyard. Stop in at the visitor center before you head into the park. You can gather maps and informative brochures, plus you can get valuable insider tips from a person who lives there and loves the place. They'll let you know where moose were last sighted or if the wildflowers are particularly pretty in a certain meadow. You can also pick up sunblock, bottles of water, and other necessities.

Take only photos. It's illegal to remove anything from a National Park Service unit. Found a pretty rock? Leave it for others to enjoy. Same with that cool stick and the wildflowers. If your kids want a souvenir of their trip, pick up a postcard at the visitor center, or promise them the map and brochure after your visit.

Leave only footprints, and in some cases, not even those.

Don't be a litterbug. Also, please pick up after folks who have failed to pack out their own trash. It's always a good idea to leave a place better than you found it.

Watch your step and keep your feet on the established trails. Some fragile places, such as the tundra areas in Rocky Mountain National Park and the cryptobiotic crust in Colorado National Monument, will be destroyed for years if even a few boots tread on them. Trailblaze only where appropriate. Check at the visitor center for information.

Adhere to Leave No Trace Principles when exploring and camping in the back-country (see page 218).

If you discover a fossil or ancient artifact, leave it exactly as you find it. Report your find to the visitor center or a ranger. In Colorado's national park lands, it isn't unusual for visitors to happen upon ancient sites. For example, in Dinosaur National Monument, the canyons were home to some of the very last Fremont culture sites to be inhabited—but less than 10 percent of the land has been archaeologically surveyed.

Paleontologists and archaeologists often learn as much—or even more—from the context an item is found in than from the item itself. The soil type surrounding the object, its orientation in the ground and in relation to other items, and its distance from other important features of the site are all important information for a researcher. If you ever notice those pictures of Indiana Jones types at a dig, they aren't just prying stuff from the ground. They use soft paintbrushes to dust away the soil. There is a reason they do that—to protect and learn—not just because it's fun.

Pothunters and fossil collectors, on the other hand, don't take such loving care of a site, and they don't give much thought to the information about the culture they are wrecking. They just want the artifacts, or the parts of them they can pry loose, to sell on the black market. The National Park Service counts on the public to keep their eyes open and to partner with the rangers to help protect America's heritage.

Leave your dog at home, or at least at the kennel in town. With a very few exceptions, dogs are not allowed on trails in the national parks and monuments, in visitor centers, or in museums. And you cannot leave dogs in the car. In the camp-grounds, dogs must always be kept on a leash. Take your dog to a national park, and everyone ends up disappointed. Unfortunately, necessity wrote this rule—rangers don't want visitors bitten, wildlife chased, or hikers stepping in nasty surprises.

Give wildlife space. The neat thing about the wildlife in our parks and monuments is that it is truly wild. The only way the animals will stay wild—and healthy—is if we humans respect nature and leave them alone. It is very possible to enjoy wildlife, from a cute little chipmunk to a bugling bull elk, without getting too close. If an animal stops what it is doing and looks at you, you are too close and harassing it. Back off and enjoy it from farther away.

Don't feed wildlife. Lots of times people food isn't that good for people. It can be deadly for wildlife. Even if you feed the birds or rodents "healthy" food, it creates a host of problems. First of all, if they get used to being close to people, they won't be careful if a mean person comes along. In addition, they lose their natural foraging skills. They forget where food is found in nature, and they don't teach these skills to their babies.

Or, they don't store food for the winter as they should. Then, when the crowds leave, the animals starve. Also, fleas and ticks often hang out on animals—and they can jump to humans, possibly passing on nasty diseases such as plague or Lyme disease. It's best to just let them find their own dinner while you eat yours.

Mule deer are common at Mesa Verde National Park.

Speaking of not feeding the wildlife—this also includes not feeding yourself to the wildlife! Most of our parks and monuments are home to mountain lions. They generally like to eat deer, but don't object to a person once in a while. When in lion country, hike in groups. Keep the kids between the adults. Also, make sure they walk—not run—as something about running makes a mountain lion want to pounce. If you see a lion, pick up the kids in your arms. It makes you look bigger and keeps the kids from running. Look in the general direction of the lion, but don't look one in the eye. Back away and walk to safety. Be sure to talk to rangers and pick up information about staying safe in lion country.

Mountain lions aren't the only dangerous animals in Colorado's parks. Those big, lurking cats make the deer feel jumpy. Deer can get defensive as a result, and they carry a mean kick and can jab with their antlers. Moose are great stompers. Ground squirrels aren't averse to sinking those long front teeth into the hand that feeds them. And folks who test the limits and approach an elk are likely to witness a set of antlers backed by 700 pounds of muscle and hoof bearing down on them. Colorado's wildlife is often beautiful, but it is also wild. It's best to keep your eyes open and keep your distance.

Don't get lost while losing yourself in nature. In just about every one of Colorado's national park units, it is easy to get disoriented. It is your responsibility to carry a map, follow your progress on it, and keep track of where you are and how to get back. Before you leave, use the map to show someone where you plan to go and tell them when you should be back. You can register at the visitor center or at some trailheads. Don't hike alone.

Be self-sufficient. National parks are not urban parks and they are not theme parks. The lightning is real, not made by strobe lights. The animals aren't mechanized. There is no exit in case of emergency. Hospitals and even clinics are usually a long way away.

Make memories with your family at Colorado's diverse national parks and monuments.

Rangers are often off covering the range, and may not be around when you need them. Unfortunately, even experienced outdoorspeople—including rangers—can get into trouble and have even lost their lives while hiking alone in Colorado.

Be prepared to take care of yourself and your family, even in the most adverse of circumstances. Know the risks and know how to avoid them. Know how to handle the situation if something bad should happen. Remember that much of the time, you are on your own out there.

A hole in a rock face provides a window view of McElmo Canyon in Canyons of the Ancients National Monument.

BLM National Monuments: A Different Drummer

Canyons of the Ancients National Monument is Colorado's only national monument that isn't run by the National Park Service. And you will notice it in subtle and not-so-subtle ways. Whereas the Park Service grew from the conservation movement of the late 19th and early 20th centuries, the Bureau of Land Management (BLM) came out of an older movement to settle and develop the resources of the land. Congress charged the Bureau of Land Management with managing its lands for multiple uses, including grazing, mineral extraction, and recreation.

Starting in 1996, the Bureau of Land Management started to manage national monuments, and conservation became a part of its multiple-use mandate. At Canyons of the Ancients, the agency takes conservation very seriously.

As I traveled around with my family to research this book, the National Park Service personnel were always visitor-focused. Clearly, our positive experience in their unit was a priority for most everyone we met. On the other hand, at Canyons of the Ancients, the employees seemed not to care much about our recreation. At first I was put off until I realized their focus is protection and preservation. They are managing an area with the highest known density of archaeological sites in the nation. While they are happy to educate visitors about it, they don't necessarily want you to go tromping around all over the place. Although the approach seems a bit unfriendly at first, in the end, we had one of our most memorable and soul-stirring trips at Colorado's Bureau of Land Management–run national monument.

*Visitors enjoy the scenery and solitude at remote Painted Hand Pueblo
in Canyons of the Ancients National Monument.*

Desert Canyons

Long ago, when titanic forces shoved the Rocky Mountains up into the sky, the lands just to the west were also pushed up. But the lands didn't tilt like the mountains. Instead, the rock layers remained relatively horizontal as the huge region—spanning most of Utah, half of Arizona, and large swaths of Colorado and New Mexico—was heaved thousands of feet into the air. This extensive, uplifted province of horizontal rocks is known as the Colorado Plateau.

Rivers of snowmelt gathered speed as they plunged out of the high peaks. When the waters reached the Colorado Plateau, they began to gouge away at the layers of rock. Smaller streams joined them, together forming gullies and ravines, sometimes thousands of feet deep. These canyons of the Colorado Plateau possess spectacular scenery, fascinating geology, unusual communities of wildlife, and a great number of national parks and monuments.

The eastern edge of this geographical province covers western Colorado. This is home to Dinosaur National Monument, Colorado National Monument, Canyons of the Ancients National Monument, Hovenweep National Monument, Mesa Verde National Park, and Yucca House National Monument.

The sites were designated for their remarkable geology (as were those at Colorado National Monument and Dinosaur National Monument) or for the mysterious remnants of bygone cultures (as at Mesa Verde and Hovenweep). The topography and the ruins are haunting, and visitors must take care lest they fall under the spell of these sinuous Western lands.

Rugged desert canyons in Colorado National Monument
© John Fielder

Dinosaur National Monument

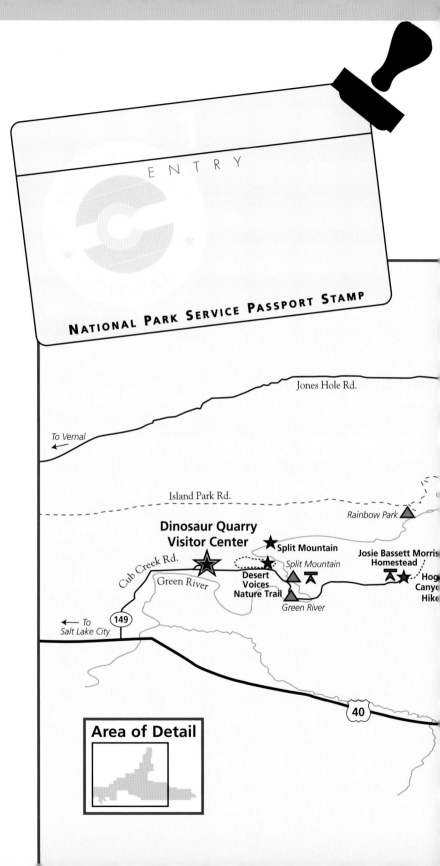

ENTRY

NATIONAL PARK SERVICE PASSPORT STAMP

Jones Hole Rd.

To Vernal

Island Park Rd.

Rainbow Park

**Dinosaur Quarry
Visitor Center**

Split Mountain

Cub Creek Rd.

Split Mountain

**Josie Bassett Morris
Homestead**

Green River

**Desert
Voices
Nature Trail**

Hog
Canyon
Hike

Green River

← To
Salt Lake City

149

40

Area of Detail

Bird's-Eye View: Multiple Personalities

In the far northwest corner of the state, Dinosaur National Monument stretches like an upside-down T over 210,000 jumbled acres, crossing the border into Utah. The Yampa and Green Rivers create its shape. These linear oases ripple like verdant ribbons through red and yellow desert canyons.

Dinosaur suffers (or is blessed with) multiple personalities. Its first personality—broken, deeply wrinkled landscape—overwhelms visitors when they first arrive. Scary and acutely beautiful at the same time, the ruggedness cries out to be explored. If you take care to follow safety guidelines, carry essential equipment, and stay on the trails, you'll have a hiking or driving adventure to remember.

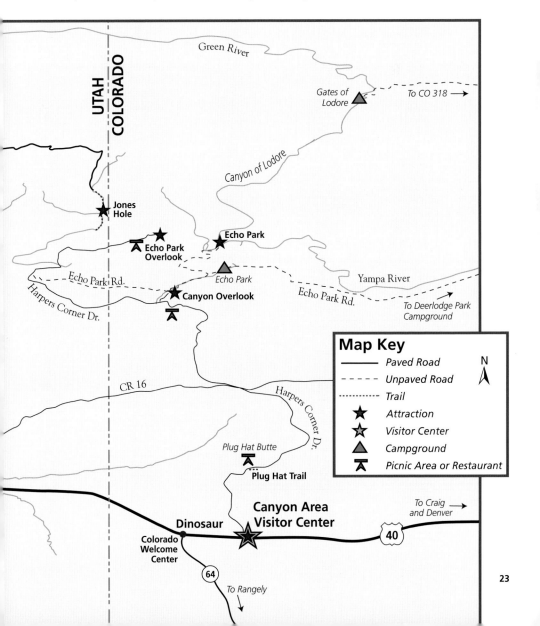

Map Key

——	Paved Road
- - - -	Unpaved Road
··········	Trail
★	Attraction
☆	Visitor Center
▲	Campground
⊼	Picnic Area or Restaurant

N

Dinosaur's name comes from its second personality, and is the reason that most folks visit the place. Studying ancient life is easy here. Everywhere you turn, your eyes run smack into cliffs made of tinted rock layers. Those rust- and sulfur-colored stone bands reveal a billion years' worth of accumulated dirt. Erosion exposes the lives and deaths of creatures lying in the dirt, including dinosaurs. More than 1,500 of their bones can be seen in the quarry exhibit. It's a budding paleontologist's dream.

Dinosaur's third personality is all wet. The isolation, topography, rapids, wildlife, and soulful beauty of the rivers here are legend. Many visitors sign up with commercial rafting companies to experience some of the best river running in the world. Private boaters who wish to raft or kayak the Yampa and Green Rivers must apply to be included in a park service lottery. Usually fewer than one in 25 applicants get a permit to run Dinosaur's rivers. But hundreds of people still send in their fees to be included in the lottery.

The upside-down T's western branch is home to the dinosaur quarry, museum, and visitor center. Almost entirely over the state line in Utah, this end of the monument also has the biggest and most accessible campground.

The monument's northern branch follows the powerful Green River as it flows south through the remote and very wild Canyon of Lodore. One dirt road ventures to a campground on the northern end. Rafting and kayaking is the best way—indeed the only practical way—to explore this section of Dinosaur.

Dinosaur's eastern branch stretches along the Yampa River from a small campground called Deerlodge Park to its confluence with the Green River. Explore this neck of the monument on a rough four-wheel-drive road running roughly parallel to the Yampa River canyon or by floating the river, either with a permit from the National Park Service or on an outfitted trip.

Access Dinosaur's center and Echo Park via the Journey Through Time Auto Tour. This 31-mile paved road runs from the monument headquarters through the twisted land to Harpers Corner, which overlooks the rivers' junction and Echo Park. A 13-mile spur road takes you to the confluence itself.

The Canyon Overlook stop on Harpers Corner Drive offers views of a deeply wrinkled landscape.

OUR EXPERIENCE:
OUTSIDE VOICES

Long dry roads, empty save for jackrabbits and coyotes, stretch behind us. Dust covers our sunbaked car. Deep in northwestern Colorado's canyon country, cliff walls soar all around us, their tops nearly 1,000 feet above our heads.

In the remote heart of Dinosaur National Monument hides an oasis, Echo Park. Only river runners see it, plus a few tourists who venture down the steep, squiggling track that wanders here through sagebrush and (mostly) dry washes. Two major Western rivers, the Yampa and the Green, meet like old friends here in the canyon depths. Heat, hypnotic and buzzing with insects, settles on the bottomlands.

A path curves through grandfather cottonwood groves to the rivers' confluence, and the boys are eager to get out of the car. About 0.5 mile up the trail, my 4-year-old mentions casually, "There's a beaver." Sure enough, the furry fellow appraises us from his swimming spot in the Green River, not 15 feet away. Then with a flip, he disappears under the olive-colored water's surface.

A wide, sandy beach, powdery-soft under bare toes, slopes down near the trail's end. We drop our shoes and shuffle to the river. The damp ground at the water's edge oozes like pudding between our toes, and soon we find spots where we sink in up to our ankles. Lumpy river rocks, buried in the muck, make walking a precarious balancing game as we slide and scramble to the cool water to wash off. Our laughter echoes back to us.

Pudding mud on the banks of the Green River in Echo Park

Directly across the river Steamboat Rock, an icon of Dinosaur National Monument, soars more than 700 feet into the sky. Its sheer wall is perfect for bouncing off shouts and giggles. We begin using our "outside voices" with wild abandon and listen with delight to our ricocheting hoots.

Grubby, tired, and hungry, we wander back to the campground, still issuing an occasional yell to check the rock's acoustics. A river otter, native to the monument, though almost never sighted by humans, ripples and splashes on the far bank, seemingly unaffected by our voices.

Dinosaur National Monument's fame comes from its paleontology and the opportunity kids have to learn about and actually touch fossilized bones. But for our family, the best part of this national monument has nothing to do with *Tyrannosaurus rex*.

Attractions

Dinosaur Quarry Visitor Center

Steel, glass, and concrete shape the geometry of this building, constructed in 1957. Its asymmetrical butterfly roof angles like the folded rock strata surrounding it. A wall of windows connects the natural world outside to the displays inside the building. The structure both harmonizes with its natural setting and makes visitors feel a bit like the Jetsons.

The Dinosaur Quarry Visitor Center houses the monument's most visited resource —the place where its dinosaur bones were unearthed. Here, families can listen to informative ranger talks, study exhibits, and actually rub fossilized dinosaur bones suspended in stone. If you are lucky enough to be there when the paleontologists are working in their lab, you can watch them wiggle bones from the surrounding rocks.

During the crowded summer months, park in the lower parking lot and use the restrooms and drinking fountains near the interpretive displays there. Then, catch the shuttle to the visitor center itself.

River Running

Except for paying respects to the deceased lizards at the quarry, there is no activity more popular with Dinosaur's visitors than seeing the monument by river raft. And with good reason. As in the days of the first European explorers of the region, water routes are often an easy way to get around this rough territory.

Rangers give informative talks on a regular basis at the Dinosaur Quarry Visitor Center.

Of all the major tributaries to the Colorado River, only the Yampa River still flows freely for its entire course, unimpeded by dams. Surging in the spring with the Rocky Mountain snowmelt, it dwindles to a lazy trickle in late summer. Peak river running times are May through early July. Not recommended for kids under 8 years old, the four or five day trip through Dinosaur includes Class IV rapids with turbulent currents, raft-flipping holes, and lots of rocks. Recover from and relive the experience in riverside campsites with picnic tables and views of cliffs that glow rose-colored at sunset.

The Green River, carving through the ancient stone of Lodore Canyon, offers passage through exceptional geology, even by Colorado standards. And that geology makes travel there next to impossible unless you are floating the river. Consequently, this stretch sports some of the most remote camping in the state. The river offers a series of rapids, including the colorfully named Hell's Half Mile, which can reach Class III difficulty.

Dinosaur National Monument at a Glance

Location: The far northwest corner of Colorado

Address: 4545 E. Highway 40, Dinosaur, CO 81610-9724

Telephone: 970-374-3000

Website: www.nps.gov/dino

Size: 210,278 acres

Elevation: From 4,800 feet to just over 9,000 feet above sea level

Major Activities: Dinosaur quarry and museum, river running, scenic drives, camping, hiking, and photography

Weather: Highly variable with time of day and location; summer highs average 95 degrees; winter days range from 20 to 30 degrees with light to moderate snow.

Best Seasons: Spring and fall

Hours: The Canyon Area Visitor Center is open from 8 a.m. to 4:30 p.m. daily, Memorial Day weekend through Labor Day, and weekdays through the fall and spring. The Dinosaur Quarry Visitor Center is open from 9 a.m. to 6 p.m. daily, Memorial Day through Labor Day, and 8 a.m. to 4 p.m. daily the rest of the year.

Closures: The Canyon Area Visitor Center is closed from November through February; the Dinosaur Quarry Visitor Center is closed Mondays and Tuesdays in the winter; both visitor centers are closed Thanksgiving, Christmas, and New Year's Days; Harpers Corner Road is closed mid-December through Easter.

Cost: The costs are $10 per non-commercial vehicle (good for seven days) and $8 to $12 per night for camping.

Facilities: Both visitor centers have restrooms with diaper-changing stations, bookstores, and exhibits. The Canyon Area Visitor Center shows a short film in its auditorium. Ranger stations are located at the Canyon Area and Dinosaur Quarry Visitor Centers, and in the summer at Echo Park, Gates of Lodore, and Deerlodge Park. The Dinosaur Quarry Visitor Center has an excellent museum devoted to paleontology, while the headquarters has a small one with exhibits about the deep canyons of the region. Shuttle buses provide transportation from a lower parking lot to the dinosaur quarry in the summer.

Accessibility: The Canyon Area Visitor Center is fully wheelchair accessible; the Dinosaur Quarry Visitor Center is minimally so, because the ramp was not designed for wheelchairs. One site in the Green River Campground and its restroom are accessible. The vault toilets at the Deerlodge Park, Echo Park, Gates of Lodore, and Rainbow Park campgrounds are somewhat accessible, as is the vault toilet at the end of Harpers Corner Road. The Plug Hat self-guided nature trail is accessible to wheelchairs and strollers.

A family begins their river trip by floating through the Gates of Lodore.

Expect to ride high waves, navigate tricky currents through the rocks, and get wet. Outfitters recommend this trip only for families with kids older than the age of 8.

After the Yampa joins the Green, the waters pass through swirling Whirlpool Canyon, flat Rainbow and Island Parks, and into the dramatic chasm through Split Mountain. Many river runners opt for a trip from Rainbow Park through Split Mountain, which takes one day to complete.

Check the monument's website or the "Guides and Outfitters List" on page 221 for the names of outfitters who run these sections of river. If you are planning a private trip, get directions for entering the lottery on the website or call the river office at 970-374-2468.

Tour of the Tilted Rocks and the Josie Bassett Morris Homestead

Slanting cliff faces, dinosaur tracks, and prehistoric rock art treat explorers of the 12-mile long Cub Creek Road. Pick up a pamphlet and a "Dinosaur National Monument Junior Ranger Activity Book" at the Dinosaur Quarry Visitor Center and read descriptions of each point of interest along the way. The drive ends at the Josie Bassett Morris Homestead, a spring-fed patch of emerald shade in the desert. Kids who complete the investigations in the activity book can earn their Junior Ranger patch and gain deeper insight into the land they are surveying.

Desert Voices Nature Trail

The paradox of the Desert Voices Nature Trail is its silence. Starting near the Split Mountain boat ramp, the path winds along a streambed, past a prehistoric stone shelter, and out onto open rocky desert. There, a sign informs visitors that the ambient sound level of Dinosaur National Monument is less than 20 decibels—quieter than a recording studio.

At each point of interest along the route, hikers find two plaques. The first describes geology and wildlife. The next sign displays poetry and artwork, drawn by children and inspired by the landscape. More than just a listing of facts about the area, the signs express the attraction and intangible importance of wild places to children. Hiking the trail's spectacular landscape, with its giant wrinkles and jumbles of rock, exercises your body. The poetry of the interpretive signs moves your soul.

Hog Canyon Hike

The relentless summer sun can often turn Dinosaur National Monument into a blast furnace and kids into cranky sweat monsters. Need a magic spell to tame the grouches? Try a hike up Hog Canyon. Grab hats, snacks, and at least a quart of drinking water per person (more for adults). Then, head out past the historic chicken coop at the Josie Bassett Morris Homestead. The trail winds for about 1 mile into a steep-walled box canyon. Frequent spots of thick vegetation offer shade for resting and sipping from water bottles. At the end of the canyon, a natural sandbox hides beneath a sandstone wall. Here, kids can dig and sift to their hearts' content while their parents lounge on the cool stone of the canyon walls.

Canyon Area Visitor Center

Rangers in this low, stone building can give you an overview of the monument's offerings and help you plan your visit. A large relief map provides a great way for kids to get a feel for the various parts of Dinosaur and its layout. A small theater allows families to view an orientation film and the bookstore has a decent collection of kids' books and other educational tools about the area. The Canyon Area Visitor Center is a good place to stop for information, especially if you plan to explore the scenic canyons either by car, on foot, or by river.

Harpers Corner Drive and Trail

Pullouts, picnic areas, and short hikes to cliff-top viewpoints dot this 62-mile, paved round trip into the center of Dinosaur National Monument. The park service recommends two to four hours to cover the ground, but we started early in the morning and returned well after dark, and still didn't see everything we wanted to see. Pick up a pamphlet describing points of interest and a "Dinosaur National Monument Junior Ranger Activity Book" at the monument headquarters before you head out. Make sure the car is gassed up and bring plenty of drinking water, sunblock, extra picnic food, and film or memory chips for your digital camera. There are no services along this road, although several picnic areas have pit toilets. You can get drinking water and camp in Echo Park, if your vehicle can make it down the 13-mile dirt road from Harpers Corner Drive.

If at all possible, hike out to the viewpoint at Harpers Corner, which perches on a cliff top overlooking some of the most convoluted terrain in the nation. The 2-mile round trip will make your heart pound, although it isn't very strenuous!

Echo Park

When hermit Patrick Lynch chose Echo Park for his homestead in 1883, he wasn't messing around. Nearly as isolated today as it was then, this bottomland in the middle of Dinosaur National Monument bursts with wildlife, scenery, and opportunities for exploration. From fallen logs to balance on, to squishy mud along cool rivers, to ancient Indian petroglyphs (not to mention one of the world's best sound-bouncing walls), Echo Park holds an amazing variety of activities for kids in a deeply quiet, slow-paced setting.

Jones Hole

Slicing through 2,000 feet of solid rock, Jones Hole Creek sparkles and laughs to itself. Lush vegetation lines its trough, providing visitors with soothing respite from the desert's intensity. An easy, 4-mile hiking trail follows the creek between Whirlpool Canyon of the Green River and the stream's birthplace, a spring emerging from the rock layers. Watch for wildlife and prehistoric rock art along the way. Reach the trail either by driving the Jones Hole Road (46 miles from the quarry) to the trailhead at the Jones Hole Fish Hatchery, or by rafting the Green River through Whirlpool Canyon (by permit only).

Programs and Activities

Quarry talks about the dinosaur fossils are held several times a day when the Dinosaur Quarry Visitor Center is open. Fossil Activities for Kids appeals to families with little ones who need an air-conditioned escape from the desert's summer heat.

Ranger walks, such as the 0.75-mile Fossil Discovery Walk, leave from the Dinosaur Quarry Visitor Center. Stop in at the monument headquarters or the Dinosaur Quarry Visitor Center for a schedule of programs.

Evening campfire programs were once held on Fridays and Saturdays during the summer at the Echo Park Campground, and daily at the Green River Campground. Depending on budget constraints, these programs may or may not be available. Check at a visitor center or with a ranger.

Two different **Junior Ranger Program** booklets are available at the visitor centers. Children who complete a "Dinosaur National Monument Junior Ranger Activity Book" driving tour and accompanying questions, and pass the oral exam given by a ranger, will earn an official Dinosaur National Monument patch and be added to the ranks of Junior Rangers. If kids prefer, they can pursue a Junior Paleontologist patch by following the Dinosaur Quarry Exploration Route around the quarry parking lot. If they fill out their booklet and answer the questions correctly, they will be designated an official Junior Paleontologist. Either booklet can be purchased for $2 at a visitor center.

Ranger guided activities for educational groups offer students the opportunity to pursue several different themes. With a park service interpreter, students can explore dinosaurs and fossils, the desert environment, the river systems and water issues, geology, Native American culture, and homesteading. The courses are keyed to Colorado curriculum content standards and can be adjusted for different age ranges. Leaders must book in advance to reserve a time and topic for their educational group.

Natural History

Geology: Pulled Taffy

Colorado's oldest rocks lie in the faulted anticline that forms the Uinta Mountains to the west and the Yampa Plateau of Dinosaur National Monument. These rocks may be 2.3 billion years old, but they are still essentially sedimentary rocks. They never melted and bent like other very old Colorado rocks. Deeply slicing rivers, especially the Green River in the Canyon of Lodore, exposed them for inspection.

A billion years of Earth's history lie open for inspection in Dinosaur National Monument.

At various points throughout the monument, the rock layers bunched up along fault lines, adding as much as a thousand feet to the depth of the canyons. In these places, you can see how slow uplift along a fault can gradually bend solid rock layers, causing them to form huge, sweeping curves, reminiscent of pulled taffy.

Dinosaur is home to as many as 26 different rock formations, each with its own chemistry, erosion patterns, and permeability to moisture. These formations and their orientation to prevailing winds and the sun create a wide variety of habitats for the plants and animals that live in the region. The variation in available water adds to the diversity of life here as well.

Plants and Wildlife: Free Flowing

Four physiographic provinces overlap in Dinosaur National Monument. Here live creatures typical of the Wyoming Basin, the Colorado Plateau, the Great Basin, and the Rocky Mountains. In addition, the rivers act as conduits for immigrants from far away. Seeds, plant cuttings, pollen, birds, aquatic animals, and overland travelers find their way along these wet highways and into the monument.

More than 600 species of plants live in Dinosaur. On the high mountains of the monument you can see ponderosa pines and Douglas fir trees growing. On the northern slopes of Stuntz Ridge, along the Harpers Corner Road, you'll even find drifts of aspen trees. Oregon grapes are common in these montane communities, as are mountain mahogany, snowberry, mountain sage, and bitterbrush.

At lower elevations, scrubby plants dominate the landscape. The conifer trees give way to rabbitbrush, sagebrush, Mormon tea, serviceberry, chokecherry, and mountain mahogany. Lupine grow among a variety of grasses, including needle-and-thread grass. Piñon and juniper forests begin to dominate as you drop in elevation. In the higher temperatures and infrequent precipitation of lower elevations, piñon-juniper forests yield to desert shrub communities of sagebrush, greasewood, saltbush, grasses, and cactus.

A HiKE FoR LiTTLE LEGS

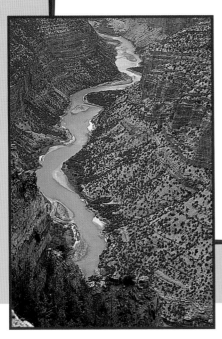

Several trails wander through the monument, varying in length from the easy 0.25-mile Plug Hat Trail to the 8-mile round trip Jones Hole Trail. Although it is a heck of a drive to the trailhead, we loved the easy, 2-mile round trip Harpers Corner Trail. Its views rank as some of the most awe inspiring in the national park system.

Whirlpool Canyon drops right under the viewpoint at the end of the Harpers Corner Trail.

Then, cutting through the arid landscape, are the verdant communities of the riversides. Currants, elderberry, chokecherry, mock-orange, horsetails, box elders, willows, and cottonwoods all live along the waterways.

Native and endangered fish swim in the rivers and creeks of Dinosaur, in addition to several introduced species. The Flaming Gorge Dam on the Green River has changed the waterway's environment, making the stream flow much more consistently throughout the year than it normally would. Also, the water released from the dam is clearer and colder than the flow from the Yampa, which has no dams. Thus, the free-flowing nature of the Yampa creates one of the last areas where native fish can live comfortably. On a July river trip, when the river was low, slow, and warm, we were fortunate enough to spot a few humpback chub swimming near the glassy surface of the Yampa. Other native species seen in Dinosaur's rivers include the Colorado squawfish, bonytail chub, and the speckled dace. Introduced species include bluegill, smallmouth and largemouth bass, northern pike, channel catfish, and walleye, along with brown, rainbow, and cutthroat trout.

The dramatic differences in elevation, water availability, and soil type, coupled with influences from surrounding mountains and deserts, make for a huge variety of biological neighborhoods in Dinosaur. Consequently, the monument's extensive bird list includes well over 200 species.

The waterways and their attendant foliage support large populations of birds. Along the rivers, look for mallards, goldeneyes, and Canada geese, as well as killdeer, spotted sandpipers, and great blue herons. Occasionally, you might see a snowy egret, a belted kingfisher, a coot, or a snipe. In the streams, such as Jones Creek, look for water ouzels (dippers), flying in and out of the water, and yellow warblers, northern orioles, and lazuli buntings in the surrounding trees. If you are particularly lucky, you may spot a threatened bald eagle resting in a cottonwood or an osprey fishing in a river.

Canyon wrens trill from the cliff walls, and violet-green swallows, particularly fetching when seen from above, swoop through the spaces looking for insects. Cliff swallows peer with beady eyes and pointy beaks from their mud nests plastered on stone walls, overhanging the rivers. Rock doves (which sure look like pigeons) roost everywhere, it seems, in the canyons, too.

Watch for birds of prey soaring over the canyons and scrublands, including northern harriers, American kestrels, rough-legged and red-tailed hawks, and golden eagles. Turkey vultures are abundant while peregrine falcons, nesting on the canyon cliffs, are endangered.

Visitors often see mule deer and elk in all environs within Dinosaur. Bighorn sheep and beaver are common in riparian areas. In the mixed desert shrub you might spot pronghorn antelope, cottontails, jackrabbits, and ground squirrels. Deer mice (with the species name *maniculatus*, meaning "small hands") are abundant throughout the monument and guaranteed to try their best to steal your unsecured trail mix at night. Fortunately, coyotes are common and help keep the little rodents in check, as do great horned owls. Both hunters haunt campers with their songs at night. Mountain lions, though common, are reclusive, and humans rarely see them.

Bighorn sheep © Wendy Shattil/Bob Rozinski

Human History

According to Wayne Prokopetz, Chief of Resource Management for the monument, the prehistoric sites in Dinosaur represent "one of the most complete records of human occupation and development in North America known anywhere." Yet still the story is sketchy.

Extremely old stone artifacts, Folsom and Plano projectile points, have been found both on the surface and in an archaeological dig site in Dinosaur National Monument. These indicate that, near the end of the Ice Age, hunting and gathering groups of Paleo-Indians traveled through and perhaps camped in the area. According to the National Park Service, some of the evidence may be 12,000 years old and represents some of the oldest finds in North America.

As the huge animals of the Ice Age died out, hunters and gatherers began to rely on smaller game such as deer and beaver and more plants for sustenance. Archaeologists characterize these people as living in the Archaic times, and this way of life seems to have lasted for thousands of years.

About 1,500 years ago, a new culture emerged in the area now covered by Dinosaur National Monument and the Uinta Basin to the west. Known as the Uinta Fremont and later the San Rafael Fremont, this lifestyle incorporated the use of pottery, shallow pithouses, and extensive rock art. The Fremont people were at least semisedentary, and raised corn to supplement their hunting and gathering. The San Rafael Fremont built stone structures to store corn and other food as well as for shelter.

Rock art along the Tour of the Tilted Rocks captures visitors' attention.

While the Fremont culture spread over large swaths of what is now eastern Utah as well as into this corner of Colorado, it seems to have faded out 800 to 1,000 years ago, except in and near what is now Dinosaur National Monument. Here, archaeologists have found evidence that the Fremont culture lasted until the 1500s, when Europeans were busy "discovering" the Americas. Archaeologists still debate why the Fremont way of life was abandoned and where the people went. All that is left are ghostly artifacts left in the dust.

Archaeological evidence suggests that around 1,000 years ago, Ute people were immigrating into the region. Some speculate that the Ute mixed with the Fremont at that time. The Ute were living in the Dinosaur area when the first Europeans arrived in 1776, with the De Anza expedition.

In 1824, an adventurer named William Ashley and his crew of "enterprising young men" journeyed down the Green River, past an area near the Gates of Lodore, where he noted that "several thousand Indians had wintered the past season." The group ran and portaged around the rapids of the Canyon of Lodore, through Echo Park, Whirlpool Canyon, and on into Island Park, all in handmade boats not particularly well-suited for running such rough water.

Sometime before 1849, an unnamed party ran the Green River as far as Disaster Falls, where it abandoned its boat and some heavy cooking gear. The folks left a note saying they were leaving the river and heading to Salt Lake on foot. The identity of the river runners remains a mystery today. In 1849, William Manly and a group of six hardy volunteers ran the river in high spirits, in spite of their own mishaps.

Twenty years later, a well-funded scientific expedition, led by the one-armed Major John Wesley Powell, ventured down the canyons of what is now Dinosaur. Powell and his men gave many of the places the names we use today. In 1936, Bus Hatch began leading the first commercial guided trips down the Green River. The end of World War II provided surplus inflatable rafts, which Hatch used to build his business. Dinosaur National Monument awarded its first river concession permit to Bus Hatch in 1953; and the Hatch family still outfits trips through the monument today.

At the beginning of the 20th century, a paleontologist named Earl Douglass was searching the area for specimens to collect for the Carnegie Museum of Pittsburgh, Pennsylvania. In 1909, he discovered hundreds of fossilized dinosaur bones here in the Morrison Formation. In the following years, he shipped nearly 700,000 bones to the Carnegie Museum and other institutions. By 1915, President Woodrow Wilson recognized the area as the richest late Jurassic paleontological site in the world, and designated it a national monument. Douglass proposed a shelter to protect the quarry, itself, plus its scientists and visitors. The structure, now the Dinosaur Quarry Visitor Center, was completed in 1957.

Meanwhile, the 1950s saw one of the country's biggest environmental battles play out over the canyons of the Green and Yampa Rivers. The Bureau of Reclamation proposed a huge dam to be built in Whirlpool Canyon. The resulting reservoir would flood Echo Park, the Canyon of Lodore, and the Yampa for 44 miles. Although every member of Congress from the surrounding states supported the project, the Sierra Club, then headed by David Brower, was able to generate enough public opposition to stop the dam. Boundary changes were instituted in 1960, 1963, 1964, and 1978, adding the canyons and creating the current outline of the national monument.

Restaurants and Picnic Areas

There are **no restaurants** within the monument.

Several **picnic areas** offer lunch spots, and the Harpers Corner Drive sports four of them. At the **Canyon Area Visitor Center** picnic grounds, elm trees shade tables in the parking lot's island. The building offers drinking water and flush toilets. The **Plug Hat Butte Picnic Area** is worth the 4-mile drive from the Canyon Area Visitor Center. Here, picnic tables, fire grates, and a vault toilet perch on top of a wooded mesa. A path runs along the edge of the mesa, offering picnickers vast panoramas of the surrounding country. Situated on the edge of a fault, the **Canyon Overlook Picnic Area** is high enough in elevation to provide relief from the desert's heat. Ponderosa pines frame views of convoluted gullies that bottom out 2,600 feet below. From the **Echo Park Overlook** you can survey the heart of Dinosaur National Monument and the river canyons leading to it. The pullout has a vault toilet. Its picnic tables lie exposed to the elements.

Just over 3 miles from the Dinosaur Quarry Visitor Center in Utah, the **Split Mountain Picnic Area** is a sun-blasted section of picnic tables adjacent to the campground. Drinking water and vault toilets are available. Far more pleasant, although not marked on the brochure, is the lunch spot at the **Josie Bassett Morris Homestead,** just over 11 miles from the Dinosaur Quarry Visitor Center at the end of Cub Creek Road. Here, tables rest beneath arching cottonwood trees near a burbling, spring-fed creek.

American Indians camped near this spot just upstream of the Gates of Lodore.

Lodging and Camping

No hotel lodging is available inside the monument.

All campgrounds in Dinosaur National Monument have picnic tables, fire grates, and at least vault toilets. The **Green River Campground,** located in the Utah side of the park, has 88 sites. During the summer months, drinking water, flush toilets, a ranger station, and ranger talks are available. Dotted with shady cottonwood trees and seeming a bit worn out, the Green River Campground has sites for tents and RVs up to 35 feet in length.

The sunnier **Split Mountain Group Campground** is open year-round. In the summer, only groups can camp there and its four sprawling sites are only for tents.

Rainbow Park has two tents-only campsites, vault toilets, picnic tables, fire grates, and a boat ramp.

Near the end of the Harpers Corner Drive, drop down to the **Echo Park Campground** on a steep, narrow, 13-mile-long dirt road that becomes impassable when it is wet. Trailers and motor homes should not attempt this road. Picnic tables, tent pads, drinking water, vault toilets, and a knock-your-socks-off view are available at Echo Park.

The seven sites at **Deerlodge Park Campground,** situated in a cottonwood forest, offer a quiet retreat and good fishing when river-running season is over. Drinking water and a ranger station are available in the summer.

The **Gates of Lodore Campground** has 17 sites for both tents and RVs, although rain or snow turn its access road into a slimy, impassable mess. The campground has vault toilets, and in the summer the drinking water faucet is on and a ranger patrols the area. The river access point for the Canyon of Lodore river trip is here.

Backcountry **primitive camping** permits can be obtained at the visitor center. Jones Hole at **Ely Creek** has the only designated backcountry campsite. Parties camping at Ely Creek should number eight or fewer. If you're planning to visit, it is a good idea to call in advance to check availability and make a reservation.

Group campers find a place to bed down at Split Mountain Campground.

Nearby Towns

About 90 miles to the east of Dinosaur's headquarters is **Craig,** the county seat for Moffat County. Home to about 9,500 people, the town has more than a dozen motels and bed-and-breakfast homes to choose from and about twice as many restaurants. Its city park has restrooms, picnic tables, a playground, tennis courts, and an outdoor swimming pool and wave pool. South of Craig, on the banks of the Yampa River, Loudy Simpson Park has picnic and restroom facilities, a playground, fishing, hiking trails, and a canoe/raft launch area. The town has one KOA campground and an RV/trailer park. Contact the Craig Chamber of Commerce at 970-824-5689.

Rangely, a dusty ranching-turned-oil town lies about 20 miles south of the monument's headquarters. Its history museum (970-675-2612) tells its story from the time the ancient Fremont people lived in the area. The Elks Park in the southwest part of town has restrooms, picnic shelters, a playground, a basketball court, and shade trees. A handful of hotels and a rooming house provide travelers with lodging, and you can choose from seven or so locally owned restaurants for chow. The Rangely Camper Park on the northeast side of town has some sites with electrical hookups, restrooms, showers, a dump station, and cottonwood trees. Reach the Rangely Chamber of Commerce by calling 970-675-5290.

Dinosaur National Monument's main gateway town is **Vernal, Utah.** With around 7,700 people, a Super Wal-Mart, and the Utah Field House of Natural History State Park Museum (435-789-3799), Vernal is a local focus of activity. It takes about 20 minutes to drive from the Dinosaur Quarry Visitor Center into Vernal, where you will find hotel chains, restaurants, and gas stations. The town has a few parks, the largest of which is Ashley Valley Park, with sprawling lawns, two playgrounds, a horseshoe pit, a gazebo, and two pavilions. The Ashley Valley Medical Center is a Joint Commission Accredited acute-care facility with an emergency room, ICU, and obstetrical and pediatric departments. It is located at 151 West 200 North, in Vernal. The Chamber of Commerce can be reached at 435-789-1352.

Tiny **Dinosaur** is located just 2 miles from the Dinosaur National Monument Head-quarters, on US 40. It has two gas station/convenience stores; two small, locally owned motels; two full service cafes; and a deli-sandwich/ice cream/gift shop. A Colorado Welcome Center is located in Dinosaur. You can get a cup of coffee there, use the restrooms, and pick up maps and brochures for the surrounding area. Call the welcome center for information at 970-374-2205.

Special Considerations for Families

Dinosaur National Monument lies in sparsely populated Moffat County in the far northwestern corner of the state. It's a long drive from any major towns. Distances within the monument stretch out as well. In other words, be prepared for an epic road trip. Fortunately, once you get there, the great outdoors beckons and it feels great to leave the car behind.

Then again, the great outdoors in Dinosaur can be kind of harsh. The dry air sucks the water out of visitors in every season. It is a good idea to bring (and drink) gallons of water while you are there. The high elevation also creates a greater risk of sunburn. Slather everyone up with sunblock and don't forget the lip balm. Shade hats are definitely essential equipment here. When the temperature soars, seek shade in the canyon bottoms and take another swig from your water bottle.

In the canyons, steep drops, loose rocks, and rough ground can be dangerous. Parents must supervise their children closely. Also watch for various wildlife hazards from prickly pear cactus spines to rattlesnakes to mountain lions.

While travel brochures make whitewater rafting seem like a smile a minute, the power of the water must be taken very seriously. River outfitters don't require their customers to know how to swim, but my personal opinion is that every member of a river trip should be a strong enough

Echo Rock soars over the confluence of the Yampa and Green Rivers in Echo Park.

swimmer to self-rescue. That means being comfortable enough in the water to be able to withstand shocking cold, repeated dunking, and turbulent currents, all the while maintaining enough presence of mind to steer clear of obstacles and navigate toward safety. Private boaters should be experienced at river rescue techniques and commercial trip participants must listen carefully to the safety talk at the beginning of the trip. A healthy respect for the river contributes tremendously toward the pleasure of the voyage.

What Makes Dinosaur National Monument Special

Dinosaur National Monument has a lot to offer. Whether you are a bookish, scientific type, a rough-and-tumble rapids buster, an archaeologist searching for missing links, or a pioneer-history buff, this monument has an attraction for you. But for me, Dinosaur is special because it is so doggone far away from anywhere. Very few places in Colorado still feel as remote and uncivilized as this. It makes me feel independent and self-reliant, and a little bit nervous. This is what I love about the West.

ENTRY

NATIONAL PARK SERVICE PASSPORT STAMP

Bird's-Eye View: Escarpment

Just off I-70 west of Grand Junction, the vivid geology and spectacular erosional features set Colorado National Monument apart. It is a perfect sample of the slickrock canyons and mesas typical of the Colorado Plateau.

Shaped like a rough triangle with a crooked tail, one side of the monument parallels the Colorado River and I-70 from Grand Junction to the town of Fruita. As you drive this section of highway, look to the giant red cliffs looming up in the west. These form the eastern boundary of Colorado National Monument.

Colorado National Monument is a hiker's monument. While its scenic drive is pretty, only scrambling around in the canyons will give you and your kids a sense of the enormous scale of the landforms. Let your children clamber over boulders at the bottom of an escarpment and rub their fingers along the base of huge sandstone walls. Or wander a dry streambed and listen to the magical, musical trill of a canyon wren. Rest in a cottonwood tree's rattling green shade. Then your family will know why the original boosters of the national monument wanted it saved for future generations to experience.

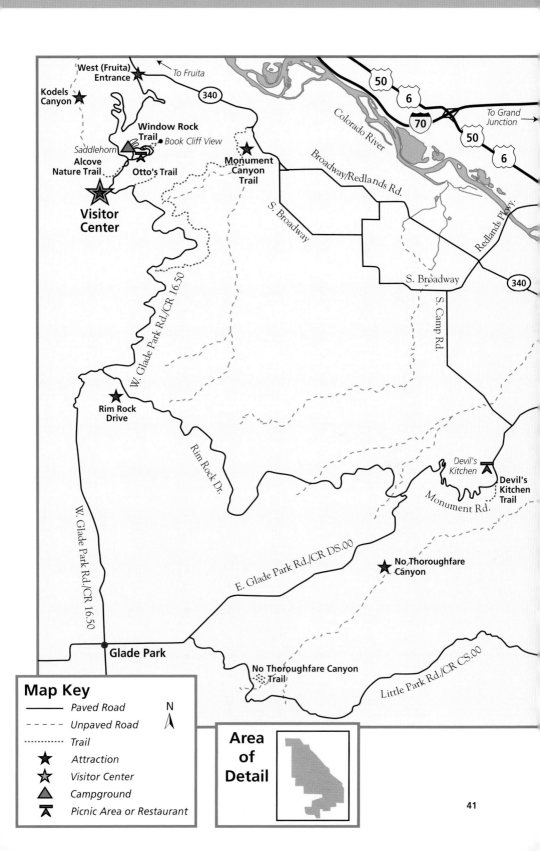

Map Key

- ——— Paved Road
- - - - - Unpaved Road
- ·········· Trail
- ★ Attraction
- ☆ Visitor Center
- ▲ Campground
- ⊤ Picnic Area or Restaurant

N

Area of Detail

West (Fruita) Entrance
To Fruita
Kodels Canyon
340
Window Rock Trail
Book Cliff View
Saddlehorn
Alcove Nature Trail
Otto's Trail
Monument Canyon Trail
Visitor Center
Colorado River
50
6
70
To Grand Junction
50
6
Broadway/Redlands Rd.
S. Broadway
S. Broadway
340
Redlands Pkwy.
S. Camp Rd.
W. Glade Park Rd./CR 16.50
Rim Rock Drive
Rim Rock Dr.
Devil's Kitchen
Devil's Kitchen Trail
Monument Rd.
E. Glade Park Rd./CR DS.00
No Thoroughfare Canyon
W. Glade Park Rd./CR 16.50
Glade Park
No Thoroughfare Canyon Trail
Little Park Rd./CR CS.00

OUR EXPERiENCE:
DROPS
iN A BUCKET

All night rain patters on the fiberglass roof of our tent-trailer. When we finally poke our heads out, drizzle kisses our faces good morning. A bucket left out overnight holds an inch of water—one-twelfth of the annual precipitation for the year in this area. Piñon trees are phantoms in the fog.

We bundle the kids up against the wet and prepare to head into town. But when our family clambers outside, the rainy desert insists we go exploring. We set out on the Window Rock Trail, right from the campground.

On the slick red clay trail, the boys have fun jumping from rock to rock as we head to the viewpoint. And there, beneath our muddy toes and the safety railing, Monument Canyon falls away before us. Clouds drift quietly around the chunky rock spires rising from its depths. The valley floor lies hidden in mist, and then the hiss of waterfalls reaches our ears.

Normally parched and bone dry, Colorado National Monument feels dreamy in the rain. By noon, a weak sun shines on our picnic and bright wildflowers pop from their buds. At nightfall, a sky full of stars wheels overhead. Moody weather, to be sure, but truly characteristic of the monument's springtime personality.

Window Rock Nature Trail in the fog

Attractions

Rim Rock Drive

This road winds along the mesa-tops through the main part of the monument. Seventeen pullouts with interpretive signs offer visitors the opportunity to get out of their cars and gaze into the canyons and at vast vistas of the Grand Valley and the Book Cliffs beyond. Several trailheads dive into the landscape from the road's edge. Plan extra time to explore some of the paths that lead into the depths below the pavement.

Visitor Center

Recently listed in the National Register of Historic Places, the visitor center is a fine example of the modern architecture that was becoming popular in the national parks in the early 1960s when it was built. Its low, horizontal profile helps the building blend beautifully with the layered rock formations of the monument. Updated interpretive displays inside help families understand the forces, both immense and tiny, that created the views outside the door.

Canyons, Rock Formations, Wildlife, and Boundless Views

The monument's wild country, itself, makes up the real attraction of this place. Take the time to leave your car and explore rocketing spires, humped rock sculptures, twisted trees, and canyon labyrinths. The monument is best when you become a part of the scene.

Alcove Nature Trail

Right across the road from the visitor center is the Alcove Nature Trail. Running for 1 mile atop the Kayenta Bench, this self-guided nature trail is a great introduction to the plants and animals living in this beautiful, severe landscape. Be sure to pick up the Junior Ranger brochure (as opposed to the one written for adults) with information for each stop on the trail. It enhances kids' understanding—and therefore their enjoyment—of canyon country.

Plan enough time to walk the full distance. The path leads past low cliffs that narrow and deepen into a mini-canyon, and the surprise ending is the best part of the trail.

Monument Canyon Trail (from the bottom up)

The Monument Canyon Trail is 6 miles in length, one way. If you hike from the trailhead on Rim Rock Drive, be prepared to drop more than 600 feet in the first 0.5 mile. The trail switches back and forth along steep drop-offs. It is a risky proposition for families with little kids.

A better bet is to exit the monument at the West (Fruita) Entrance. Then turn right immediately and drive southeast on the Broadway/Redlands road. Look for a small sign marking the Monument Canyon Trail on the west side of the road, near a new, upscale housing development. Walk less than 0.5 mile up a gentle slope around the houses to the bottom of a 600-foot-high mesa inside the monument boundary. The trail skirts the edge of the mesa for another 0.5 mile to the frequently dry streambed at the bottom of Monument Canyon. Families can follow the rugged trail for as long as they like past massive walls and soaring rock pinnacles.

Programs and Activities

Evening campfire programs were once held every evening from Memorial Day through Labor Day. Budget cuts forced staff reductions and now campfire talks have been eliminated. Ask at the visitor center if programs have been reinstated.

Ranger walks are not held in the monument due to the lack of funds for even one interpretive position. Occasionally, and on an intermittent basis, Back Porch Talks may be held at the visitor center when staffing allows. Ask at the visitor center if these programs have been reinstated.

Junior Ranger Program booklets are available at the visitor center for 95 cents. Activities include Monument Bingo, Monumental Match, and drawing a picture of

Rock formations rise from the depths of Monument Canyon.

Colorado National Monument at a Glance

Location: West-central Colorado, about 5 miles west of Grand Junction

Address: Fruita, CO 81521-0001

Telephone: 970-858-3617

Website: www.nps.gov/colm

Size: 20,534 acres

Elevation: From 4,800 feet to just over 7,000 feet above sea level

Major Activities: Camping, hiking, photography, scenic drive, and picnicking

Weather: Summer highs range from 80 to 100 degrees; winter days range from 20 to 45 degrees; precipitation is rare.

Best Seasons: April and May, mid-September through October

Hours: The visitor center is open from 8 a.m. to 6 p.m. in the summer months, and 9 a.m. to 5 p.m. in the winter.

Closures: The monument is closed on Christmas Day.

Cost: The costs are $5 per noncommercial vehicle (good for seven days) and $10 per night for camping.

Facilities: The visitor center has a ranger station, a bookstore, and exhibits. A slide presentation is shown every 30 minutes. Flush toilets are located at both picnic grounds, and in the campground. Diaper-changing stations are available in the restrooms at the visitor center. The scenic drive has several pullouts with interpretive signs.

Accessibility: The visitor center is wheelchair accessible, although the trail leading from the back porch to a nearby lookout is not. A wheelchair-friendly picnic area with a ramada and tables lies just outside the visitor center door. One site in the campground and its restroom are accessible, as is the Devil's Kitchen Picnic Ground during the spring, summer, and fall seasons. Some of the pullouts along the Rim Rock Drive are accessible to wheelchairs.

something in the monument. Youngsters must also take a small number of hikes to earn Junior Ranger status. After the ranger reviews their booklet and quizzes them on their work, kids get a certificate and a pretty Colorado National Monument pin.

Teacher's guides, corresponding to Colorado curriculum guidelines, are available for local teachers who are interested in taking their classes to the monument for field trips. Teacher's guides are also for sale in the bookstore for families who wish to enrich their visits.

A HiKE FoR LiTTLE LEGS

Several trails clamber in and out of the canyons from the scenic Rim Rock Drive. Maps are available from the bookstore in the visitor center. The USGS 7.5-minute topographic map, the Colorado National Monument Quadrangle map, is quite helpful. The map and guide brochure the ranger hands you when you pay your entrance fee has excellent trail descriptions. Otto's Trail is an easy 1-mile round-trip featuring jaw-dropping views. It is a bit exposed in some places, so use care and hold hands at the narrow spots. We also love the hike up No Thoroughfare Canyon. The trail isn't official—you just walk up the streambed as far as the first waterfall. In late spring and early summer, the water flows and enchants little desert hikers. Canyon bottoms can reach temperatures well above 100 degrees in summer, so drinking water, a hat, and sunblock are absolute necessities if you plan to hike then.

Columbus Canyon stretches beneath Cold Shivers Point along Rim Rock Drive.

Natural History

Geology: Great Block

The monument perches on of part of the Uncompahgre Uplift, a great block of land that dammed the mighty Colorado River and forced it to change its course. Now the river flows to the north, around the Uncompahgre Uplift, before continuing on west into Utah.

Small streams cart dirt and sand from the top of the Uncompahgre Plateau as they flow to the Colorado River. Little by little they have dug deep, narrow canyons in the uplifted block of land. As they reached bedrock, they began to carve wider gaps in the mesas. Now their beautiful, undulating sculptures wind through the monument.

Plants and Wildlife: Extremes

Relentless trickles of water, restless puffs of air, a pebble bouncing, a boulder crashing— all are erosion's tools. In due course, the elements build a grand, rocky backdrop to the drama of life in the desert. And what a story the animals, plants, and microbes play out on this fantastic set. You've got to admire the survival strategies of creatures that make a home in this extreme environment.

One late December day when we visited, the thermometer read just 12 degrees, and a bitter wind blew. In the summer, the furnace blasts over 100 degrees. And always it is dry, dry, dry—except when it is flooding, like after a big afternoon thunderstorm.

Coyote © Wendy Shattil/Bob Rozinski

After these events, when potholes in the rock are full and water soaks the ground, you may be lucky enough to hear frogs and toads calling in the evening air. Amphibians such as the canyon tree frog or the red-spotted toad burrow into the desert ground to wait out the dry periods in a dormant state that sometimes lasts more than a year. They come to the surface to reproduce as quickly as possible after a rain, while conditions are optimal. Families who visit the small perennial streams in No Thoroughfare Canyon and Ute Canyon in the late spring and early summer may be lucky enough to see and hear frogs and toads, or the one, rarely seen species of salamander that lives in the monument. Please take care not to disturb or pollute water resources and be sure to report any amphibian sightings to the visitor center staff.

If you visit between March and late October, you are more likely to see some of the monument's reptiles, including lizards like the yellow-headed collared, side-blotched, or sagebrush lizard. Most active in May and June, they dart about on the rocks and tree trunks, doing push-ups and flickering their forked tongues at curious folks. Look for them as they sun themselves to warm up in the early morning. Midget faded rattlesnakes are rarely seen, but do inhabit the monument. Bullsnakes are common.

Endangered peregrine falcons nest in the cliffs, and turkey vultures are common from April to September. Golden eagles often soar over the canyons, hunting for food, as do red-tailed hawks. White-throated swifts and violet-green swallows dive and arc between the sheer walls. Watch for Gambel's quail in the canyon bottoms and for scrub and piñon jays and magpies scolding visitors on the forest-covered mesa tops.

Campers may see mule deer and occasionally elk near the visitor center. Coyotes, foxes, and bobcats hunt deer mice, ground squirrels, and desert cottontail rabbits throughout the monument. Desert bighorn sheep scramble in the rocks and scrub in Kodels Canyon, which lies north of the West Entrance, but is still within the monument boundary. It requires a backcountry hike to reach this ravine. And mountain lions, though elusive, do find homes, search for groceries, and raise their families throughout the area. Watch for their tracks and signs near streams in the canyon bottoms.

Violet-green swallow
© Wendy Shattil/Bob Rozinski

Families who hike the canyons or mesa tops will notice another wonder of high desert adaptation: cactus and other succulents. These plants, with their waxy skin, are excellent at soaking up the intermittent rainfall and storing the water in their bodies. Yet here at Colorado National Monument, where the temperatures drop to freezing and below in the winter, all that water can form crystals inside the plant's tissues. The damage from the freezing can be severe enough to kill the plant. So in the wintertime, the cacti here are able to reduce their water to the point that the moisture left is in a solution that doesn't freeze. They shrivel up, go limp, and in some cases even shrink back into the ground. When spring warmth and moisture return, the cacti soak up more water and puff out their chests, proud of being all big and juicy again. Look for Missouri pincushion and spineless hedgehogs in the southeastern part of the monument, while mountain ball cactus may be found at higher elevations. At least three kinds of prickly pear cactus live in Colorado National Monument, as do claret cup and eagle claw cactus. You can see showy cactus blooms from mid-April to early July, depending on the elevation.

In the higher elevations of the monument, the rocky hillsides are home to shade-loving snowberry, which grows under serviceberry bushes there. Also common are sagebrush and mountain mahogany along with Gambel's oak thickets. Relic stands of Douglas fir trees cluster in shady north-facing drainages. The mesas are forested with piñon and juniper trees, interspersed with sage flats that support rabbitbrush and native grasses. Look for Indian rice grass, galleta, and needle-and-thread grass. Indian paintbrush, desert four o'clocks, and hairy goldenasters are common, and evening primrose bloom after dusk along Rim Rock Drive. Wildflowers will be most abundant during wetter springs.

In the canyon bottoms, Fremont cottonwood trees, coyote willows, and tamarisk grow along the streambeds. The region's only native broadleaf tree, the single-leaf ash, digs its roots in around the rocks in areas that collect a bit of extra moisture.

Along the perennial streams, sedges and rushes live beneath the cottonwoods and hikers will happen upon an occasional stand of cattails in a marshy area. Springs seep from the canyon walls and the moisture creates surprise fairylands of ferns with Apache plume (a member of the clematis family) and wild roses blooming below.

Take the time to notice where desert life *isn't* flourishing. If a deposit of soil accumulates in a crack or hole, and a rock protects it from the drying winds, something, it seems, is growing. If you look closely, even exposed patches of soil are held in place by a layer of black-and-gray fungus and algae, known as cryptobiotic ("mysterious life") crusts. These organisms fix nitrogen into the soil and keep the dirt from blowing away. Only very bare rocks, the bottoms of dry streambeds, and trails made by the feet of people and animals show a lack of its growth. Up close, the cryptobiotic crusts have shapes that mirror the huge rock walls and towers around you.

Cryptobiotic soil forms mysterious gardens in the desert.

Human History

Some evidence exists that the people of the prehistoric Fremont culture ventured into the area now within Colorado National Monument. Historically, the Utes used the area as well. However, signs of any human habitation are scanty to nonexistent.

In the late 1800s, shortly after European-Americans settled in the Grand Valley, they recognized these canyons and mesas for their unusual scenery, as early photographs show. In the early 1900s, John Otto, the monument's first caretaker, was a strong voice among many who campaigned for the area to be set aside as a national park. On May 24, 1911, the monument was established, making it the first national monument in Colorado. Since then, visitor numbers have steadily increased to more than 350,000 each year.

Restaurants and Picnic Areas

There are **no restaurants** within the monument.

Two **picnic areas** offer lunch spots with gorgeous views. Both have picnic tables, water, restrooms, and charcoal grills. The **Devil's Kitchen Picnic Area** also offers a large picnic shelter for shade when the summer sun is blasting down. The **Saddlehorn Picnic Area** is closer to the visitor center.

Lodging and Camping

No hotel lodging is available inside the park.

The **Saddlehorn Campground** is open year-round, although reservations are not accepted. Sites are closely placed among low piñon and juniper trees. Many, especially in loop B, have fantastic views of the Grand Valley and Book Cliffs beyond. However, these

A Junior Ranger answers questions along the Alcove Nature Trail.

sites also get traffic noise drifting up from the city. Fees are $10 per night, and include a charcoal-only grill and picnic table. Drinking water, flush toilets, and trash removal are available. Wood fires are not permitted. Sites will accommodate RVs and tents, and a few are pull-through. There is no dump station at the campground.

Backcountry **primitive camping** permits can be obtained at the visitor center. No water is available in Colorado National Monument backcountry, so plan to bring plenty (at least one gallon of drinking water per person per day) with you.

Nearby Towns

Fruita, a community of about 30,000 people, lies just 2 miles from the monument's west entrance. It has grocery stores, sporting goods stores, gas stations, motels, restaurants, and a peaceful town park with a playground and restrooms. It is also home to the Dinosaur Journey Museum, where kids enjoy interactive exhibits about dinosaurs and paleontology.

Grand Junction is 4 miles from the monument's east entrance. Canyon View Park, off I-70 at exit 28, has a large, modern playground, restrooms, picnic shelters, baseball diamonds, and an in-line skate rink. Several restaurants and hotels are located just off the freeway on Horizon Drive. The city is home to St. Mary's Hospital, a regional trauma center, which treats patients from western Colorado and much of eastern Utah. The new Bananas Fun Park offers family entertainment with 18 holes of miniature golf, batting cages, water bumper cars, and a restaurant. Contact the Grand Junction Chamber of Commerce at www.visitgrandjunction.com or 800-962-2547.

Special Considerations for Families

While the monument is a beautiful and exciting place to visit with children, its steep drop-offs and cliffs can be dangerous. Parents must be extremely vigilant along the trails that are exposed to heights. Also, it is only natural that kids (and their big people) want to throw rocks over the edges of the cliffs. Please don't. Trails wind down the canyon faces and through the bottoms, and frequently there are people down there who you can't see. You don't want your child to be the one who threw a rock that hit someone on the head.

A hiker checks to see if Indian paintbrush smells good along the Alcove Nature Trail.

Temperatures in the bottom of the canyons can reach well over 100 degrees in the summer, so plan accordingly. Hike early in the morning, late in the late afternoon, or evening when the weather calls for it. Rangers recommend lugging along one gallon of drinking water per person. Be watchful for rattlesnakes and scorpions, which are sometimes spotted in the monument.

That said, hazards are part of the canyon experience. If parents are properly prepared for them, they add to the adventure and allure of Colorado National Monument.

What Makes Colorado National Monument Special

One monument employee confided that her favorite thing about where she works is that, even during the busiest weekends, there are still places where she can go to find solitude. And that is truly one of the most special things about Colorado National Monument. Even with metropolitan Grand Junction and Fruita minutes away, and suburban sprawl growing like a fungus on the monument's boundaries, you only need to hike into a canyon a short ways, round a bend, and you are truly out of sight and sound of civilization.

ENTRY

NATIONAL PARK SERVICE PASSPORT STAMP

Bird's-Eye View: Solitude of Spirits

Prolific author of Western novels, Zane Gray, is said to have coined the term, "Great Sage Plain." This wide expanse of semiarid hills and mesas stretches across the Four Corners region from Cortez, Colorado, to Monticello, Utah. Gullies and canyons crease its face, looking like the weathered wrinkles on an old cowhand's cheek.

Canyons of the Ancients National Monument sprawls across the Great Sage Plain along the Utah border, just north and west of Mesa Verde National Park. US 491 (formerly 666) curves around it to the east and north, and McElmo Canyon borders it on the south. A few parcels spill over into Utah.

The Bureau of Land Management (BLM) runs this monument, unlike all the others in Colorado, which are under the jurisdiction of the National Park Service. Canyons of the Ancients is a patchwork of remote, jumbled tracts of land with the highest density of archaeological sites in America. A very few of the sites are developed or have interpretive displays; these are accessible mostly by unpaved county roads. The rest of the monument is open for exploring via a network of poorly marked trails. Navigating here is truly a test of your orienteering skills.

All in all, the remote, wild beauty of the place and a solitude peopled with ancient spirits makes this a family adventure like no other.

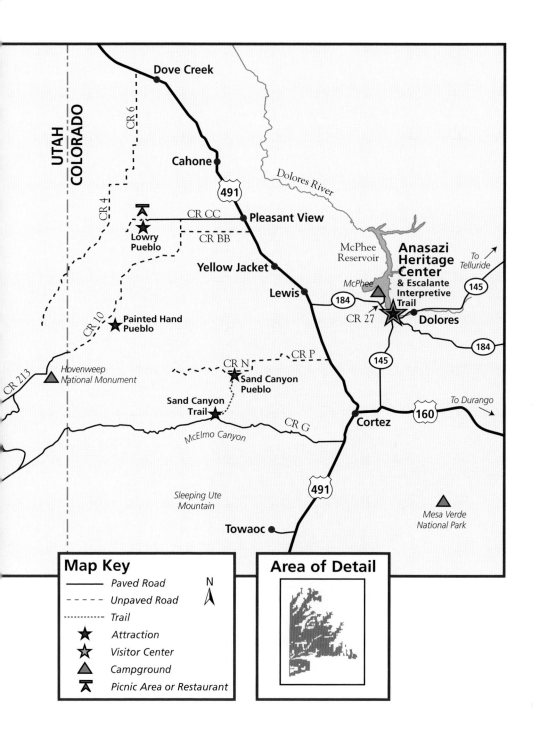

Dove Creek

UTAH
COLORADO

CR 6

Cahone

491

Dolores River

CR 4

CR CC   **Pleasant View**

★ Lowry
Pueblo

CR BB

Yellow Jacket

McPhee
Reservoir

**Anasazi
Heritage
Center**
*To
Telluride*

Lewis

McPhee

184

& Escalante
Interpretive
Trail

145

CR 10

★ **Painted Hand
Pueblo**

CR 27

★ **Dolores**

184

CR N   CR P

145

CR 213

▲ *Hovenweep
National Monument*

★ **Sand Canyon
Pueblo**

**Sand Canyon
Trail**

★

CR G

McElmo Canyon

Cortez

160   *To Durango*

491

*Sleeping Ute
Mountain*

▲ *Mesa Verde
National Park*

Towaoc

Map Key

—— *Paved Road*   N ⋀

- - - - *Unpaved Road*

·········· *Trail*

★ *Attraction*

☆ *Visitor Center*

▲ *Campground*

⊼ *Picnic Area or Restaurant*

Area of Detail

Attractions

Anasazi Heritage Center

Every visit to Canyons of the Ancients should begin with a visit to the Anasazi Heritage Center parking lot. From this vantage point on a hill overlooking the Montezuma Valley and Sleeping Ute Mountain, you can give your kids a great overview of the Canyons of the Ancients. The national monument drapes the McElmo Dome, which looms up in a great dark green mound to the north. This geologic feature hides the vestiges of a people who once outnumbered the region's modern population.

Painted Hand Pueblo lies in a remote section of Canyons of the Ancients National Monument.

Inside the Anasazi Heritage Center, you will find valuable information about the monument. Maps and directions will help out as you navigate the difficult landscape. Interactive exhibits impart an understanding of the area's ancient peoples so that children will both respect and appreciate the prehistoric sites. With movies and microscopes, corn to grind, and cloth to weave, this is a place that no family should miss.

Escalante Interpretive Trail and Pueblo

A paved trail winds to the top of a hill that is right behind the Anasazi Heritage Center. This 0.5-mile trail is dotted with interpretive signs about the plants and landscape and their significance in the lives of the Ancestral Puebloan (Anasazi) people. At the top, the straggly piñon forest opens to a wide view of the surrounding countryside. Here, the ruins of the Escalante Pueblo lie silently under the sun's glare. With only a couple of signs to explain what you are looking at, your intellectual brain begins to take a backseat to your intuition. All you can do is walk around the crumbling, rust-colored walls and try to feel what it must have been like to be one of the Ancestral Puebloans. It is a good way to begin to understand the people who lived here—and left here—so long ago.

OUR EXPERIENCE:
TIGHTLIPPED

As each member of our family reaches the high point of our hike, we stop and look around. To the north and east, the Dolores River Canyon plummets to the blue surface of McPhee Reservoir, which fills the bottom of the ravine. Beyond it, the snowy, jagged peaks of the San Juans scrape the sky's dome. To the south rises the dark massif of Mesa Verde and to the southwest of us is the clear outline of a giant Indian slumbering on his back (Sleeping Ute Mountain). In between these two high points sinks the Montezuma Valley, which runs down Navajo Wash all the way to the Four Corners. To the northwest, the McElmo Dome heaves up along the horizon.

The ruins of Escalante Pueblo crumble at our feet. Grasses and prickly pear cactus poke out along the humpy outline of this structure first built by prehistoric stonemasons. Outlined in melted mortar and sandy block rectangles, the ruin is tightlipped.

Sunshine bakes us and the wind dries our skin and as we gaze at the same views they saw, and we have to wonder, why were they building a heavy stone structure way up here? What were they thinking? The question will arise frequently in the days to come.

As we breathe in the surrounding vistas, understanding tickles at the back of our skulls. This ancient land begins to seep through our cracks. It is getting under our skin.

Winds whistle through the lonely Ancestral Puebloan structures that overlook Canyons of the Ancients National Monument and Sleeping Ute Mountain.

Lowry Pueblo

Most of the Ancestral Puebloan sites and cliff dwellings in Canyons of the Ancients National Monument are unexcavated, unimproved, and in the backcountry. The Lowry Pueblo, however, is easier to get to and more developed. From Pleasant View on US 491, go west on County Road CC about 9 miles. The road is paved most of the way.

Excavated in 1936 by Paul Martin of Chicago's Field Museum of Natural History, Lowry shows a different architectural style from the famous cliff dwellings of nearby Mesa Verde. Located on a plain, rather than in a canyon wall, it included as many as 40 rooms and a Great Kiva, in addition to several smaller kivas. This has led some archaeologists to theorize that Chaco Canyon's structures influenced its builders. Indeed, the ruins are classified as a Chaco outlier.

Visitors survey the Great Sage Plain from the Lowry Pueblo site.

The walls of the Lowry ruin, rising from the scrubby grasses, have been stabilized and are designated a National Historic Landmark. Interpretive signs and brochures help parents understand the structure and explain it to their kids. The trail around the ruin is wheelchair accessible, and picnic tables offer places to have lunch beneath a relentlessly sunny sky. Scrubby desert trees offer some shade. Drinking water is available from a spigot in the parking lot, and a vault toilet sits off to one side.

Painted Hand Pueblo

Just southwest of Pleasant View on US 491, County Road BB takes off to the west. After 6 miles, it crosses County Road 10. If you drive southwest on CR 10 for just over 11 miles, you'll see a rutted, rocky track snaking away through a piñon-juniper forest. That's BLM Road 4531, and your path to one of the neatest little ruins in Canyons of the Ancients.

Road 4531 heaves and bounces for about 1 mile before it circles around on some uneven slickrock at the rim of a small canyon. A rough wooden sign lets you know you're in the right spot. It also counsels that, "Impacts from visitation pose the biggest threat to the cultural and natural resources of the Canyons of the Ancients." They want you to take care of the ancient sites here.

If you squint out along the edge of the cliff, you can make out the ruin, tucked under the protective rock face. The 0.25- to 0.5-mile trail is a puzzle. You have to crouch

Canyons of the Ancients National Monument at a Glance

Location: Southwest Colorado, on the Utah border

Address: 27501 Colorado State Highway 184, Dolores, CO 81323

Telephone: 970-882-5600

Website: www.co.blm.gov/canm
or www.co.blm.gov/ahc

Size: About 164,000 acres

Elevation: From 4,900 feet to just over 7,000 feet above sea level

Major Activities: Hands-on discovery area in the museum, educational programs on archaeology and Native American cultures, hiking, photography, scenic drives, and picnicking

Sand Canyon is a great hike for kids.

Weather: In the summer, temperatures fluctuate widely with daytime highs often exceeding 100 degrees; summertime violent storms bring flash floods; biting gnats arrive in spring and early summer; winter temperatures swing between lows as cold as 0 and highs of 50 degrees.

Best Seasons: September and October are best, followed by May and June.

Hours: The Anasazi Heritage Center is open from 9 a.m. to 5 p.m. from March through October, and 9 a.m. to 4 p.m. from November through February.

Closures: The monument is closed Thanksgiving, Christmas, and New Year's Days.

Cost: The Anasazi Heritage Center admission is $3 per person from March through October and free the remainder of the year. Kids under 18 and Golden Pass holders are free.

Facilities: The Anasazi Heritage Center is a modern, well-thought-out museum with films, interactive exhibits, and a pithouse replica. The gift shop offers a wide range of books, replicas, fine crafts, posters, and cards. Restrooms with a diaper-changing station are available at the Anasazi Heritage Center. Law enforcement rangers and trail volunteers patrol the monument itself.

Accessibility: The Anasazi Heritage Center is wheelchair accessible, as is the trail leading to two nearby archeological sites. The Lowry Pueblo also has an accessible trail, picnic area, and vault toilets.

and stretch to scramble through this canyon-edge path. My son's favorite spot was the "skinny-dude place," where hikers squeeze through a spot about 18 inches wide for 3 or 4 feet. The trail offers panoramic views, with New Mexico's Shiprock jutting up in the distance.

A masonry tower stands on a big rock, but the ruin itself has never been excavated. Beneath it is a place where the ancient ones put handprints on a stone surface. This pictograph gives the site its name.

Sand Canyon Pueblo

For an Ancestral Puebloan site, this pueblo at the head of Sand Canyon is a doozy. It has 420 rooms, 100 kivas, and more than a dozen towers. But if you take your kids there, you won't see much of it. When archaeologists were finished digging in Sand Canyon Pueblo and studying it, they covered it all back up with dirt. That way, all the walls and hearths and other features that are still in one piece will stay protected and the site will be preserved from further weathering and deterioration.

Even though the pueblo itself now looks like a mound of sand with stony outlines of walls poking up through the grass and cactus, plaques show how the place was laid out and what archaeologists think life was like there for the Ancestral Puebloans.

To get to the Sand Canyon Pueblo, take US Highway 491 northwest of Cortez about 5 miles to County Road P. Drive west on CR P about 1.5 miles past the Hovenweep National Monument's Goodman site to County Road 16. Go 1 mile south on CR 16 to County Road N and go west again. The parking lot is about 1 mile west of the intersection of CR 16 and CR N.

Sand Canyon Trail

This trail winds for 6.5 miles between the Sand Canyon Pueblo at its head and McElmo Canyon on the south. A gorgeous hike through orange slickrock and piñon-juniper country lies in between. Along the way, sneaky little cliff dwellings peek

from the canyon walls and surprise you as you come round the bends.

Walking the length requires a car shuttle, unless your kids are long-legged teens who can cover the 13-mile round-trip in one day. Plus, the top of the canyon is steep and rough. Families with

Families can hike right up to ancient structures on the Sand Canyon Trail.

younger children are better off driving to the lower parking lot in McElmo Canyon. The trail here is moderately easy, and you will encounter your first ruin, Castle Rock Pueblo, right after you cross the large slickrock expanse that rises up from the trailhead. Families on this trail can wander as far into the Canyons of the Ancients as they like, playing "I Spy a Ruin" along the way. Most of the archaeological sites are 1 or 2 miles in.

To reach the lower trailhead of Sand Canyon, take US 491 south from Cortez to County Road G. Go west about 12 miles (paved all the way) to the trailhead on the north side of the road. Portable toilets are sometimes available at the trailhead.

Programs and Activities

Docent-led walks to Escalante Pueblo and other sites are held during the summer months. Check at the Anasazi Heritage Center for a schedule. Most walks begin at 1:45 p.m. and 3:10 p.m.

The monument's **Junior Explorer Program** is an excellent introduction to archaeology in the southwest. Kids who complete the Junior Explorer activities earn a pin and a door hanger. The program's content is best suited to fourth graders and up; for children in the lower elementary grades, an adult will need to help them solve the puzzles and answer the questions. The activities are based mostly on

Students weave at an interactive exhibit at the Anasazi Heritage Center.

the Dominguez Pueblo, an actual archaeological site located right in front of the Anasazi Heritage Center. Pick up a booklet at the front desk.

Curriculum guides, "Getting to Know Canyons of the Ancients," corresponding to Colorado educational guidelines, are available for local teachers who are interested in taking their classes to the monument for field trips. For sale in the bookstore, it is a worthwhile read even if you aren't teaching a class.

Natural History

Geology: Carving Gullies

Canyons of the Ancients rests upon a geographical province known as the Colorado Plateau. Here, it seems as if a giant preschooler made a dozen big Play-Doh pancakes of different colors, stacked them up, pressed them together, and then dug out gulches with chubby fingers. The result is a gorgeous, lumpy, striped landscape with a maze of canyons to explore.

The layers of rock under Canyons of the Ancients National Monument were shoved together a little, causing them to fold gently upward. This is known as the McElmo Dome, and because the ground is slightly elevated, runoff water got a little boost and was able to carve some really deep gullies in the surface. In some areas, these gullies are as much as a thousand feet deep.

Plants and Wildlife: *Chee-Chee!*

Between the gullies are mesas of grasslands and piñon-juniper forests. During the Ice Age, glaciers eroded the mountains to the west, and the resulting dust blew over the mesas of McElmo Dome, creating a layer of topsoil.

Sagebrush, serviceberry, saltbush, Mormon tea, rabbitbrush, and yucca grow throughout the monument. If you are lucky, you may see the sky-blue blooms of the narrowleaf beardstongue (a variety of penstemon) or its cousin, the bright orange desert paintbrush. Evening primrose occur occasionally in Canyons of the Ancients, and larkspurs, with their dainty white or blue flowers, bloom in the spring. Watch for sego, or mariposa, lilies growing in sunny spots. Cactus varieties include fishhook, hedgehog, and prickly pear.

Mule deer   © Wendy Shattil/Bob Rozinski

Cottonwood trees, with their lovely dappled shade, are common in the canyon bottoms and single-leaf ash trees sometimes grow in dry washes as well. The seeds of the single-leaf ash are a favorite food source for the rodents such as deer mice and grasshopper mice, woodrats, antelope squirrels, and pocket mice. Beaver have been known to venture up streams of Yellow Jacket Wash and McElmo Canyon. As the shadows fall, several species of bats begin their hunt for flying bugs above the canyons.

The bird list for Canyons of the Ancients is quite long, including golden eagles, which you may see hunting in the wintertime. Peregrine falcons nest in the high canyon walls, and white-throated swifts swoop through the spaces looking for insects in the summertime. Look for flycatchers, phoebes, and kingbirds in the canyons as well. You may be treated to

Great blue heron
© Wendy Shattil/Bob Rozinski

a canyon wren's beautiful trill or the *chee-chee* of scolding jays. Magpies and crows are easy to spot. Streams may host great blue herons, ducks, red-winged blackbirds, and mountain bluebirds. Great horned owls are common and wild turkeys have also been sighted inside the monument. Gambel's quail, mourning doves, and other game birds are hunted in Canyons of the Ancients.

Among the jumbled rocks, rattlesnakes and scorpions are common, so choose your path and seat with care. Other reptiles include the twin-spotted spiny lizard, the long-nosed leopard lizard, and the Mesa Verde nightsnake.

Deer, elk, black-tailed jackrabbits, and desert cottontail rabbits are prey for coyotes, kit and gray foxes, and bobcats. Mountain lions also hunt among the mesas and ravines, but are rarely seen; still, their presence is a good reason for kids to stay close to adults when hiking.

Great horned owls
© Wendy Shattil/Bob Rozinski

Human History

A human presence in the area goes back for many thousands of years, but the first Basketmaker culture appeared on the McElmo Dome about 1500 BC. These folks farmed the topsoil of the mesas, planting corn. As our name for them implies, they were very skilled in weaving baskets, which they used even for cooking. As their culture developed, they settled in year-round and began to build pithouses. In the year AD 750 or so, they began moving together to create small settlements

A HiKE FoR
LiTTLE LEGS

At Canyons of the Ancients, recreation takes a backseat to preservation. The number and quality of archaeological sites in the monument make protection of this fragile resource a priority. So while you may visit any part of the monument with your family, the only established hiking trail is in Sand Canyon and it suits young trekkers just fine. If you are bent on traveling off trail through rough country near delicate and uninterpreted ruins of Ancestral Puebloan homes, pick up a BLM Land Status Map. This handy map can be obtained at the Anasazi Heritage Center, and you can also ask the staff there for suggestions.

A Denver family explores nature on the Sand Canyon Trail.

or pueblos consisting of a cluster of pithouses. Their skills as clay workers developed and pottery use replaced most of the functions of baskets. Their architecture changed, too, and they began to construct their pueblos out of cut stone. They still made pithouses, but these became more ceremonial in nature.

By AD 1100 they were part of a trade network that brought shells from the Pacific and cotton from the south. They kept domesticated turkeys and dogs, and they farmed corn, beans, and squash on the mesas. The artistry of their pottery is still appreciated today. Population increased and the people of the area began to cluster their homes in larger towns, usually sited at the upper ends of canyons. Eventually they were building multi-storied buildings of cut stone, kivas, plazas, and reservoirs for storing water. This is known as the Pueblo III, or classic period.

Around the turn of the 13th century, many of Ancestral Puebloans began to build homes in the shallow caves of the canyon walls, moving off the mesas. Then, even though their cliff dwellings and mesa-top pueblos were well-constructed and built with great labor, they abandoned them and the entire region. By 1300, thousands of people were gone, moving to northern Arizona and the Rio Grande Valley in New Mexico. The huge exodus left the pueblos of the Great Sage Plain deserted.

Today, the archaeological community hotly debates why the cliff dwellings were developed and eventually abandoned. It is a story, as of yet, incompletely told.

More than 100 years after the last Ancestral Puebloans left, nomadic Athapascans, ancestors to the Navajo, had a presence in the area. The Ute people followed some-time later. Evidence of their early occupation includes remnants of wickiups.

In 1765, the Spanish expedition of Juan Maria Antonio Rivera recorded seeing ancient ruins in the region, but made no specific mention of cliff dwellings of the McElmo area. In 1776, Friars Antanasio Dominguez and Silvestre Velez de Escalante described several ruins, including the ones in front of and on the bluff behind the Anasazi Heritage Center. These sites now bear the explorers' names. The first archaeo-logical discoveries in the Canyons of the Ancients National Monument area were recorded by a Mormon expedition led by W. D. Huntington in 1854 near Hovenweep.

In 1923, the few, small, scattered sites of Hovenweep were proclaimed a national monument and interest in the surrounding area continued throughout the 20th century. In May of 2000, Canyons of the Ancients was designated a national monument by President Clinton.

Restaurants and Picnic Areas

There are **no restaurants** within the monument.

The **Anasazi Heritage Center** has a lovely courtyard with benches and about five sheltered tables on the path to Escalante Pueblo.

The **Lowry Pueblo** offers drinking water and has a wheelchair-accessible picnic table and toilets.

Lodging and Camping

No hotel lodging is available within Canyons of the Ancients, but Dolores and Cortez offer a choice of many inns.

There are **no established campgrounds** at Canyons of the Ancients National Monument. However, **McPhee Campground,** overlooking McPhee Reservoir and run by the National Forest Service, is less than 5 miles from the Anasazi Heritage Center. **Hovenweep National Monument** has a campground just outside Canyons of the Ancients to the west.

Primitive camping is allowed in Canyons of the Ancients National Monument, with the exception of a few locations, and vehicles must stay on established roads. Check at the information desk at the Anasazi Heritage Center for details about the best areas for sleeping out.

Nearby Towns

Dolores, a community of 1,200 people, is just 3 miles from the Anasazi Heritage Center, about 10 miles east of Sand Canyon Pueblo, and about 15 miles east of Lowry Pueblo. It sits on the upstream edge of McPhee Reservoir and the Dolores River runs through town on its way to fill the lake. There are gas stations, hotels, restaurants, a sporting goods store, and a hardware store in town. You can pick up groceries at the Dolores Food Market at 400 Railroad Avenue. Three of the community's four parks are situated on the river, and the Kid's World playground is a welcome relief for little tigers who have been cooped up in their car seats too long. The Rio Grande Southern Railroad Museum is in a picturesque replica of a Victorian depot. Contact the Dolores Chamber of Commerce at 800-807-4712 or www.doloreschamber.com. Also check out www.mesaverdecountry.com for more information.

Cortez is about 10 miles from the Anasazi Heritage Center and about 2 miles from the easternmost sections of the monument. The Colorado Welcome Center for southwest Colorado is located in Cortez, and offers a full array of maps and brochures for nearby services and activities. The town boasts more than 160 acres in parks, all right off Main Street behind the Colorado Welcome Center. They include duck ponds, skateboard tracks, ball fields, and a swimming pool. The new $7.5 million recreation center has an indoor swimming pool with a water slide, gymnasium, racquetball courts, climbing wall, fitness area, and a hot tub as well as showers.

Several chain and independent hotels and motels offer family lodging, and some have their own swimming pools. There are many restaurants to choose from, as well. Southwest Memorial Hospital is located at 1311 North Mildred Road, in the southwest part of town, and it offers a Level IV trauma center as well as acute-care beds, surgery, orthopedics, and obstetrics.

The Cortez Cultural Center museum offers interpretive displays about the Ancestral Puebloans who lived in the area in the past and the Ute people who live there today. Open year-round, the Cortez Cultural Center has an art gallery displaying the work of local artists and a gift shop. Native American dances are held there during the summer. Visit www.mesaverdecountry.com or call 800-253-1616 for more information.

Special Considerations for Families

The brochure for Canyons of the Ancients National Monuments describes it as lying in rugged and remote country—and they aren't kidding. When your family heads out to explore this place, you'll feel a bit like Indiana Jones preparing for an expedition. It is important that you have a vehicle with high enough clearance to navigate the roads, which are often rutted and rocky. When it rains or snows, the dirt roads can turn into slippery bogs of clay, becoming impassable. Be sure to have good maps and extra supplies of food and water when driving through the monument. Carry a first aid kit.

The desert weather can be extremely hot and dry, and the sun is intense at all times of year. Protect little explorers by bringing at least one gallon of drinking water per person per day. It is also absolutely necessary to defend tender skin from the sun with wide-brimmed hats, sunblock, and lip balm. Long sleeves and pants are a good idea for both sun protection and to ward off sharp cactus spines, jagged rocks, and biting insects. Feet, both little and big, should be covered in good socks and hiking boots.

If you are traveling in May or June, bring insect repellent and apply it to your kids' clothes. Biting gnats at that time of year leave itchy, stinging welts.

This is mountain lion country, so hike in a group, with the kids walking with adults in front of and behind them. Warn children to walk along the trails, as running can urge lions to pounce. It is very unlikely that you will see a mountain lion; they are rare and shy around humans. Their favorite food is deer. However, if you do spot one, pick your children up and carry them to look larger and prevent the kids from running. Make noise, don't look the lion in the eye, and walk back to your car.

Keep your eyes open for rattlesnakes sunning themselves on open spaces during the cooler hours and hiding in the shade during warmer times. Make noise when you walk to warn the reptiles and give them a chance to slither away.

When at an archaeological site, behave with the utmost respect for the physical ruins themselves and for the spiritual significance they carry. Keep your feet and those of your children on the ground in front of the structures. Don't climb, lean on, or push the walls. Crumbs and sugary juice from a snack or lunch attract ants and small rodents, which dig around in the ruins and undermine their foundations. So picnic away from the archaeological sites. And keep your fingers off the rock art, because the fresh oil from our skin can deteriorate pictographs that have been there for centuries. You wouldn't go up and rub the surface of the "Mona Lisa" to see what it felt like, would you? Same idea here. On paper, it sounds like a bunch of draconian rules, but when you visit the sites, it is easy to be awed by their antiquity and respect comes naturally. Honor that instinct and be cautious by the ruins.

What Makes Canyons of the Ancients National Monument Special

Canyons of the Ancients National Monument is rough around the edges. It doesn't wear quite the visitor-friendly smile that other national parks and monuments do. The staff isn't as welcoming of tourists, but as long as you are there, they'll show you their state-of-the-art museum and let you touch some of their prehistoric artifacts. Then they'll get out the maps and point you to a phenomenal field site or two, but they won't encourage you to go traipsing about all over the place. You get the distinct feeling that if you got in trouble out there and they had to come get you, they'd be pretty annoyed.

You get mixed messages everywhere you go here, and it kind of puts you in your place. I mean, who are we to go snooping around in folks' ancestors' homes? But the people who work at Canyons of the Ancients also know they are sitting on top of something pretty special, and they are secretly proud of it. The staff doesn't actually mean to be unwelcoming —they want to teach visitors the right way to visit this type of place. In addition, they emphasize that Canyons of the Ancients is a place that people can explore on their own, and on their own terms. Besides, maybe the ancient ones have lessons of their own for those nosy tourists, and who are they to get in the way of that?

ENTRY

NATIONAL PARK SERVICE PASSPORT STAMP

Bird's-Eye View: Isolated

Just about 15 miles northwest of Mesa Verde as the crow flies, the McElmo Dome rises and then slopes gently toward the Utah-Colorado border. As at Mesa Verde, ancestors of today's Pueblo Indians thought the uplifted McElmo area would make a good place to settle and farm. Eventually, their culture developed to the point that they built communities of fine stone structures, which have lasted for centuries. But while Mesa Verde is synonymous with cliff dwelling, Hovenweep is known for its towers.

Hovenweep National Monument, a smattering of archaeological sites about 25 miles north of Four Corners, preserves superb examples of these towers—the most accomplished of Ancestral Puebloan architecture. The six sites, isolated from each other but connected by a network of trails and rough county roads, lie in both Colorado and Utah. The monument headquarters lies in Utah, but four of the sites are in Colorado, surrounded by Canyons of the Ancients National Monument.

The main complex of trails, ruins, and interpretive displays is in the Square Tower group near the headquarters. This is also where the visitor center, campground, and established picnic areas are. Just inside Colorado to the east is the Holly group or village, and at the heads of the next two small canyons is the Horseshoe/Hackberry group. About 3.5 miles northeast of that is the Cutthroat Castle village. Fifteen miles farther east yet is the Goodman Point group of ruins. The last site, Cajon, is southwest of Square Tower in Utah.

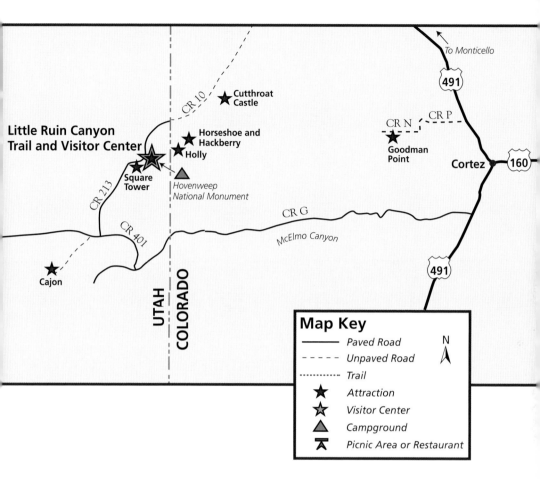

With the exception of Goodman Point, it is easiest to access the Colorado pieces of Hovenweep by heading south out of Cortez on US 160, and turning west on County Road G, which follows McElmo Creek into Utah. Then follow the marked roads north and slightly east to the monument headquarters.

Attractions

Little Ruin Canyon Trail

Right outside the front door of Hovenweep's visitor center, you can walk down a path that leads to the rim of Little Ruin Canyon. Although it's a little canyon, it is chock-full of ruins. A small spring seeps from rock layers near the canyon's head. Large hackberry trees take advantage of the moisture now, but in times past it was the water source for an Ancestral Puebloan farm town of 200 to 300 people. A tall, slightly spiraling square tower rises over the spring like a sentinel. Hence the other name for this trail—the Square Tower Ruins Trail.

The kids descended into the quiet of their nighttime worlds, tucked in sleeping bags, breathing gently. Their eyelids fluttered with dreams. A tiny slip of a pull-through camp-space on the mesa's edge was barely big enough to hold our tent-trailer. The kids' dad and I sat on campstools, snuggled together against the evening chill, and watched the silhouette of Sleeping Ute Mountain, looming black against the emerging stars.

A nighthawk cried and plunged over the canyon at our feet. When it flared its wings at the bottom of a dive, air vibrated in its feathers with a buzz that made my skin itch. Something big rustled once in the scrub down below. My first thought was a mountain lion, but then we reasoned that a cat would probably be silent. We never did know what it was.

The dry air held a top note of sagebrush with lingering dust, and we thought of the parents who had sat on this mesa's rim, listening to the same sounds, breathing the same air, and loving their children, whom they tucked in nearly 800 years ago.

Hiking the 2-mile loop is an exercise in mixed emotions. The scenery and easy slickrock path lift your spirits, but the remnants of homes and religious structures are a bit spooky. Again and again you wonder why these folks worked so hard just to leave their fine stone houses shortly after. The question is unsettling. Nonetheless, with the park service pamphlet to guide you—and plenty of spots for exploring and resting in turn—this is a perfect day hike for stumpy little legs.

Outliers

Hovenweep's visitor center and campground lie in the midst of what was once much more heavily populated country. During the time the Ancestral Puebloans were building their towers in Little Ruin Canyon, similar communities pockmarked the whole McElmo Dome area. The national monument preserves five of these sites, in addition to the Square Tower complex of Little Ruin Canyon. Four of them lie within 10 miles of the visitor center. Now the area is all but empty of human habitation. In addition, the roads to the outliers are not marked and can be a good

Opposite: Ancient vestiges at Hovenweep National Monument
© John Fielder

place to get your vehicle stuck. Before heading to these sites lying out in the boonies—hence the name outliers—it's absolutely necessary to check in at the visitor center for information and directions. That said, the paths to the various sites make short hikes, perfect for stretching little legs. And the intrigue of finding long-abandoned buildings helps keep kids motivated to push on.

Cutthroat Castle is the site farthest north along County Road 213, which turns into County Road 10 at the Colorado border. From CR 10, a rutted, two-track pathway

leads nearly 2 miles through the juniper and piñon trees and over slickrock to a parking area. The trail from the parking area to the ruins is about 0.6 mile and quite manageable for children. Four towers rise up from the uneven boulders at the mesa's edge. Several kivas are associated with the towers, and one unusual kiva was built above ground. Back at the car, the view stretches over most of the Great Sage Plain and beyond.

Horseshoe and Hackberry can both be reached along a 1-mile round-trip trail. As kids walk across the mesa top, this is a good place to play "Who can spot the ruins first?" The Horseshoe site offers a beautiful view down a length of the canyon at its feet.

Little Ruin Canyon, with its Square Tower Ruins Trail, is a fascinating tour of an Ancestral Puebloan neighborhood.

Holly is reached either by driving past the Horseshoe-Hackberry parking area on the dusty, rough road or by hiking a 4-mile trail from the main Square Tower area of Hovenweep. The trail to the Holly ruins undulates through scrubby forest to a ruin called Tilted Tower. It stood straight when the ancient people first constructed it, but after they left, the boulder supporting it cracked and the top of the tower tumbled into the canyon below. A rectangular tower at Holly is impressively built on a very uneven boulder top. Handholds and toeholds were pecked into the solid rock so people could climb up to the tower's entrance.

Cajon lies farther into Utah, about 9 miles from the Square Tower complex. Like the other Hovenweep outliers, it has stone towers at the head of a small canyon. The complex is a few steps from the parking lot, which has views of the Four Corners area as far away as Monument Valley in Arizona and Shiprock in New Mexico.

Hovenweep National Monument at a Glance

Location: Southeastern Utah and southwestern Colorado

Address: McElmo Route, Cortez, CO 81321-8901

Telephone: 970-562-4282

Website: www.nps.gov/hove

Size: 785 acres

Elevation: From 5,080 to 6,600 feet above sea level

Major Activities: Archaeology, hiking, photography, picnicking, and stargazing

Weather: Temperatures fluctuate wildly with summer daytime highs often exceeding 100 degrees and winter temperatures swinging between lows as cold as 0 and highs of 50 degrees; summertime violent storms bring flash floods; biting gnats are a nuisance from mid-May to mid-June.

Best Seasons: Autumn, especially September and October

Hours: The visitor center is open 8 a.m. to 5 p.m.

Closures: The visitor center is closed Thanksgiving, Christmas, and New Year's Days.

Cost: Fees are $6 per car (for seven days) and $10 per night for camping.

Facilities: The visitor center offers interpretive displays, a bookstore, and restrooms with diaper-changing stations in both the women's and men's restrooms. The only ranger station is at the monument headquarters. Restrooms are also available at the campground, but they do not have diaper-changing stations.

Accessibility: The visitor center and its restrooms are wheelchair accessible, as are the restrooms in the campground. Wheelchairs can navigate part of the paved portion of the Square Tower Group Trail with assistance. All other trails in the monument are rough.

Start exploring Hovenweep at the headquarters building.

A HiKE FoR
LiTTLE LEGS

There might be a trail at Hovenweep that isn't a good hike for children, but we didn't find it. The terrain is relatively gentle, with just enough rock scrambling to keep it interesting for adults and make it really fun for kids. The distances are manageable—even for very young hikers or a parent lugging a baby in the backpack carrier. Follow the precautions about sunblock, hats, drinking water, and sturdy boots, and Hovenweep is a family hiking paradise. Our favorite? Little Ruin Canyon, right outside the visitor center.

Easy hiking on the rim of Little Ruin Canyon

Goodman Point Ruins group is a cluster of buildings on the east side of the McElmo Dome, about 12 miles west of Cortez. It differs from the other Hovenweep sites in both the architectural style and the longevity of its occupation. Inhabited for as long as 700 years, it is considered a major Ancestral Puebloan community center for the region. Although it was the first group of ruins in America to be given federal protection, it has been the subject of almost no research or scientific testing—until now.

In April of 2005, the Crow Canyon Archaeological Center, in conjunction with the National Park Service, commenced a six-year excavation and study of the site. Evidence suggests that the Goodman Point ruins are the single best location in the central Mesa Verde region to investigate major trends in the prehistory of the Ancestral Puebloans. The hope is that findings there will shed light on some of the major unanswered questions about the ancient culture.

That said, Goodman Point is not very exciting to visit. Unlike the other Hovenweep outliers, this ruin is just a pile of dust and stone rubble with trees and cactus growing up through it. Although the National Park Service doesn't discourage visitors, there is not much for the untrained eye to look at. It is a good idea to check in at the Hovenweep visitor center before heading out to Goodman Point.

Programs and Activities

Evening campfire talks are held from late May through September, usually on Friday, Saturday, and Sunday evenings. Rangers present their programs right in the campground, where the backdrop of Sleeping Ute Mountain reflecting the setting sun makes it hard to concentrate on the excellent information offered. Check in the visitor center for schedules.

Hovenweep's visitor center offers books and maps to get families started.

Back porch and overlook talks occur throughout the spring, summer, and fall months at various times. Ask at the visitor center for a schedule. Groups can arrange ahead for **ranger-led walks** to the sites. In addition, an 18-minute **video program** is available at the visitor center upon your request.

Hovenweep has a **Junior Ranger Program** for kids 6 to 12 years old. A fun activities book helps kids learn about the people who built the towers and lived in the canyons and mesas. Plus, it adds to their understanding of the desert environment. When they have completed the required activities, they can show their book to a ranger at the headquarters, answer questions about their work, and receive a badge and a gorgeous, full-color certificate that designates them a Junior Ranger of Hovenweep National Monument.

For kids too young for the Junior Ranger Program, Hovenweep offers a **free activity sheet** for them to work on. It is actually quite informative and fun for younger kids.

Natural History

Geology: Running Uphill

Hovenweep's misty story is based on events that happened long before the ascendance of the Ancestral Puebloans and their exquisite architecture. McElmo Canyon slices deeply between Sleeping Ute Mountain on the south and the high ground around Hovenweep to the north. Streams draining the elevations on either side of the canyon help the creek to run year-round through the dry land.

There is something odd about the tributaries that come from the north. If they were to establish their courses today, they would have to run *uphill* before reaching McElmo

Golden eagle
© Wendy Shattil/Bob Rozinski

Creek. This evidence suggests that the streams were already entrenched when the ground under them began to ever-so-slowly rise. This upward bend in the rock layers, or anticline, is the McElmo Dome. It appears to be younger in geologic terms than the waterways that run across it. Its uplift made the little streams cut deep canyons through the rock as they followed their paths to the creek.

The rock itself is Dakota Sandstone, which is fairly porous. Water from rain and melting snow can soak down through it until it runs into the next layer, the Burro Canyon formation. When the water hits the Burro Canyon shale, it doesn't soak in, but rather runs sideways until it meets a spot where a canyon has been carved down through the rock layers. Then the water leaks out onto the canyon wall as a damp spot or even a spring.

In Ice Age times, glaciers ground high mountain rocks into fine silt, which was picked up by the wind and spread in a thick layer over the Dakota sandstone of the McElmo Dome. The silt is great for growing some crops, especially beans. The town of Dove Creek, near Hovenweep, claims to be the "Pinto Bean Capital of the World" and it owes its fame to this silt. In fact, the earliest farmers in the area were attracted to the good topsoil of windblown silt as well. Eventually, they built their communities around springs at the heads of the deep canyons that cut south through the McElmo Dome.

Plants and Wildlife: Falling Trill

Piñon-juniper forests fill much of the high ground around the Hovenweep sites. You will also see sagebrush, saltbush, rabbitbrush, and serviceberry. Green Mormon tea, a variety of ephedra, also grows within the boundaries of many of the sites. Look for yucca and several varieties of cactus, including prickly pear, fishhook, and hedgehog cactus.

Fremont cottonwood trees rustle their leaves in the streambeds. At Square Tower, Horseshoe, and Hackberry, you can see Colorado's only native ash, the single-leaf ash, in the canyons as well. Wildflowers include goldenasters, larkspur, bur buttercups, and desert paintbrush. Also look for the delicate blooms of the mariposa, or sego, lily, a beautiful flower in such an arid environment.

If you turn your eyes upward, you are likely to see red-tailed hawks floating on the thermals or northern harriers hunting in the winter. Great horned owls rest like sticks in the treetops and call as night falls. Golden eagles are not common, but a treat to spot sailing over the mesas. These hunters nest and raise their young at Hovenweep, as do scrub jays and ravens. Also look for Clark's nutcrackers and piñon jays. Chickadees, bushtits, and titmice all breed in the monument as well. Ash-throated flycatchers flit into the air to catch bugs at Hovenweep, only to swing back to their original perch to watch for more. Pause frequently and listen for the falling trill of the canyon wren, a delight for your ears.

Several species of reptiles can be found at Hovenweep, including midget faded rattlesnakes, which grow up to 30 inches long. They are not aggressive snakes, but it's still a good idea to steer clear of them. You may see gartersnakes and eastern racers as well. Collared, desert spiny, sagebrush, and long-nosed leopard lizards dart across rocks and into the shadows as visitors hike by. It is possible that chorus frogs and salamanders may be in some of the permanent spring areas, while spadefoot toads hop around the drier spots.

Many bats hunt for insects in the evening sky above the springs, including spotted bats and western pipistrelles. Look for desert cottontails and black-tailed jackrabbits as well as chipmunks and antelope squirrels. Pocket mice, deer mice, grasshopper mice, and woodrats are common, as are the coyotes, gray foxes, and kit foxes that feed on them. Badgers are uncommon in the monument, but have been seen. Bobcats and mountain lions are rare. Mule deer, the favorite food of mountain lions, however, are a familiar sight.

Jackrabbit   © Wendy Shattil/Bob Rozinski

Human History

Nomadic Paleo-Indians hunted on Cajon Mesa as many as 10,000 years ago, and evidence shows that people were planting crops in the area about 2,000 years ago. These people are known as the Basketmakers because of the woven containers they used for carrying all sorts of things, from grain to water. They even cooked food in their baskets.

Then, about 1,100 years ago, these early farmers learned to shape clay into pottery. The use of the baskets declined. They raised crops of corn, beans, and squash and built pithouses for shelter. As time passed, their culture developed and they began to cluster their homes into small villages and then into larger communities.

About 800 years ago, they built the structures of the Hovenweep area. The walls that have survived so many centuries are a testament to the skill of the stonemasons who erected them. It is estimated that as many as 2,500 people populated the Cajon Mesa at that time.

Near the end of the 1200s, the people of Hovenweep began to walk away from their villages, never to return. There is much debate about what caused them to do this, leaving pots, shoes, stores of grain, and other valuables—plus the elaborate towers they built just a few generations earlier. Even though they weathered prolonged drought in the past, they did leave during a particularly dry time, so this is one of the leading theories for their exodus. Others believe they overused the resources of the area or were victims of warfare or disease. Whatever the cause or causes, a huge mass of culturally similar people left the entire region surrounding Hovenweep by about 1300 and moved to northern New Mexico and Arizona.

In 1854, Mormons on a trip led by W. D. Huntington reported seeing the deserted stone towers at Hovenweep. In 1874, photographer William Henry Jackson visited the area. He used the Ute word, *Hovenweep,* which means "deserted valley" for the place. Representatives of the Smithsonian Institution recommended that Hovenweep be protected and in 1923 it was proclaimed a national monument.

Hovenweep Castle looms near the head of Little Ruin Canyon.

Restaurants and Picnic Areas

There are **no restaurants and no official picnic areas** at Hovenweep, but a few **tables** and a drinking water spigot are located near the headquarters.

When eating outdoors, please make sure to sit well away from any archaeological sites. The crumbs from your picnic will attract small rodents and insects, which like to burrow in the soft dirt. If they dig around the ruins, they can undermine the integrity of the fragile spots. It's best to snack in the shade of a tree with a nice view of the buildings, but not near the ruins themselves.

Lodging and Camping

There is **no lodging** available at Hovenweep National Monument.

Hovenweep Campground is located in scrubby piñon-juniper stands between two small canyons. It has 30 sites, most of which are designed for tent use. Five sites accommodate 35-foot RVs or car/trailer combinations, but the remainder of the campground will not accommodate rigs longer than 25 feet. Picnic tables, drinking water, and flush toilets are provided, as well as shelters from the intense sun. Trash cans and recycle bins are located in the campground. However, due to the remote location, trash pickup is quite expensive, so campers are asked to pack out their own trash if possible.

Camping in Hovenweep includes views of canyons and Sleeping Ute Mountain.

Nearby Towns

Cortez is about 45 miles east of Hovenweep. The Colorado Welcome Center for southwest Colorado is located in Cortez, and offers a full array of maps and brochures for nearby services and activities. The town boasts more than 160 acres in parks, all right off Main Street behind the Colorado Welcome Center. They include duck ponds, skateboard tracks, ball fields, and a swimming pool. The new $7.5 million recreation center has an indoor swimming pool with a water slide, gymnasium, racquetball courts, climbing wall, fitness area, and a hot tub as well as showers.

Several chain and independent hotels and motels offer family lodging, and some have their own swimming pools. There are many restaurants to choose from, as well. Southwest Memorial Hospital is located at 1311 North Mildred Road, in the southwest part of town, and it offers a Level IV trauma center as well as acute-care beds, surgery, orthopedics, and obstetrics.

The Cortez Cultural Center museum offers interpretive displays about the Ancestral Puebloans who lived in the area in the past and the Ute people who live there today. Open year-round, the Cortez Cultural Center has an art gallery displaying the work of local artists and a gift shop. Native American dances are held there during the summer. Visit www.mesaverdecountry.com or call 800-253-1616 for more information.

Special Considerations for Families

The official Park Service map shows the location of Hovenweep's headquarters and visitor center, but not the outliers. Rangers ask that folks stop by to get a detailed map and directions to the remote sites. They want to be sure that your vehicle can handle the rough roads and that you understand the sensitive, fragile nature of the ancient buildings before you visit them.

The programs at Hovenweep are extremely family friendly, and the staff seems eager to provide activities and information that are interesting to youngsters. But they are also concerned with the safety of your children. It is important to preserve the archaeological sites and fragile desert lands for future visitors as well. Rangers ask you to keep a close eye on kids around canyon edges, and to stay only on marked trails. Touching the rock art or leaning or climbing on the ancient structures can accelerate their deterioration, so teach your children to look, listen, and smell only. If you or your kids find any artifacts such as potsherds or arrowheads, please leave them exactly as you found them. You wouldn't want to mess up the valuable clues they provide to archaeologists.

When hiking, carry as much as one quart of drinking water for each person, and wear hats, long sleeves, sunblock, and lip balm for protection from the sun. Long pants are also a good idea, and sturdy footwear, such as hiking boots, is a must.

Watch carefully for rattlesnakes and scorpions and remember that this is mountain lion country. Hike in groups only, with the children between the adults. Ask your kids to walk—not run—on the trails.

What Makes Hovenweep National Monument Special

Hovenweep is kind of lonesome. While Rocky Mountain National Park entertains millions and Mesa Verde swarms with rangers shepherding tour groups and directing traffic, Hovenweep sits on its mesa top and watches cloud shadows on the sage. It snoozes in the desert sun and rouses itself when the occasional family ventures down one of its trails. Hovenweep is a heck of a drive from anywhere, but the remoteness keeps the crowds at bay. Here, you can get the feel of an Ancestral Puebloan neighborhood without a lot of distractions. Sometimes it seems the spirits of the ancient ones are whispering. You have to be in a quiet place to hear them well.

Sunset paints Sleeping Ute Mountain pink.

Bird's-Eye View: Bony Fingers

Near the southwest corner of the state, the La Plata Mountains shoot up to 12,500 feet above sea level. The Mancos River and its tributaries drain those high peaks. The snowmelt pours over the Colorado Plateau, carving out canyons and wide basins. Between those wide valleys, flat-topped mesas rise. These, in turn, are notched and carved by smaller streams until the tablelands resemble arthritic hands with gnarled and bony fingers above the valley floors. Mesa Verde is one such high area.

Within Mesa Verde as a whole, two of these long, thin plateaus have archaeological sites you can visit. They are Chapin Mesa, where many of the most famous sites are, and Wetherill Mesa, where Long House and Step House are. The ruin areas are clustered at the ends of the fingerlike tablelands.

Mesa Verde's turnoff is on US 160, between Durango and Cortez. From the entrance station, it is 4.5 miles along a two-lane road to the campground and Morefield Village. Another 10.5 winding miles will take you to the Far View Visitor center and Far View Terrace, which has a snack bar. Far View Lodge is also located in this area. After 12 more miles of scenic curves, you arrive at the Wetherill Mesa sites. The end of Chapin Mesa is almost 6 miles from Far View.

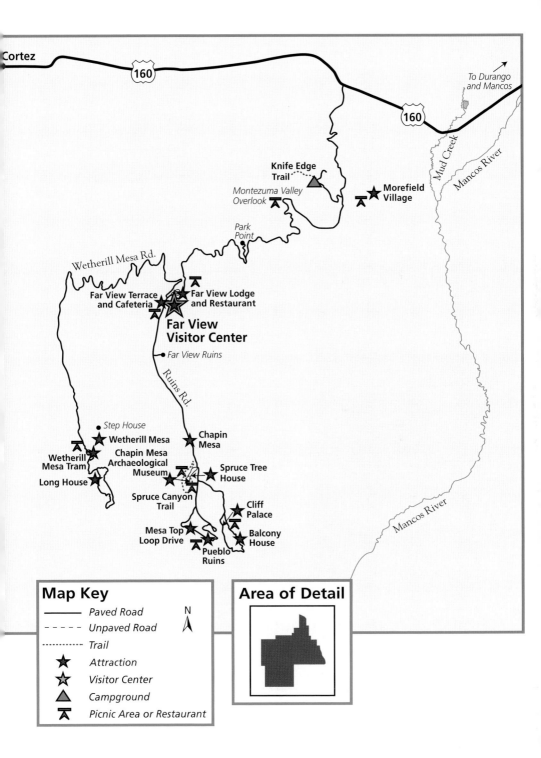

Cortez

160

To Durango and Mancos

160

Mud Creek

Mancos River

Knife Edge Trail

Montezuma Valley Overlook

Morefield Village

Park Point

Wetherill Mesa Rd.

Far View Terrace and Cafeteria

Far View Lodge and Restaurant

Far View Visitor Center

Far View Ruins

Ruins Rd.

Step House

Wetherill Mesa

Chapin Mesa

Chapin Mesa Archaeological Museum

Spruce Tree House

Wetherill Mesa Tram

Long House

Spruce Canyon Trail

Cliff Palace

Mesa Top Loop Drive

Balcony House

Pueblo Ruins

Mancos River

Map Key

— Paved Road

- - - - Unpaved Road

··········· Trail

★ Attraction

☆ Visitor Center

▲ Campground

⊼ Picnic Area or Restaurant

N

Area of Detail

Attractions

Far View Visitor Center

With a kiva's circular shape, the Far View Visitor Center is an architectural attraction in itself. Climb the ramp that sweeps around the outside of the building and a vast panorama of canyons, mesas, and spires unfolds before you. With interpretive displays and very friendly rangers to help you plan your trip, this is the obvious place to start. Plus, the visitor center is the only place to buy tickets for ranger-guided tours of the most popular archaeological sites. A line forms around the 8 a.m. opening time as people compete for limited spaces on the tours they want most. Rangers do a good job of controlling the crowd and answering questions at the same time.

Chapin Mesa Archaeological Museum

Newly renovated with a modern air-conditioning system, this museum houses a spectacular collection of Ancestral Puebloan artifacts. You can also see a 25-minute movie about Mesa Verde, which is shown every 30 minutes. Junior Rangers in the making must study the museum's dioramas, which do an excellent job of explaining the Ancestral Puebloans' lives and cultural evolution in the area.

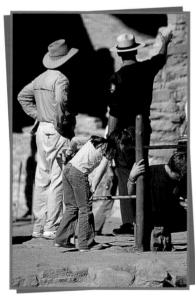

Spruce Tree House has the only kiva that visitors can enter.

Spruce Tree House

A trail from the back door of the museum leads into the shady canyon of Spruce Tree House. Rangers are on hand and booklets are available for a self-guided tour of this cliff dwelling. A spring provides moisture for comparatively lush vegetation—a relief after the glare of the desert above. However, those lush plants include healthy patches of poison ivy, so be sure to watch the kidlets accordingly.

Spruce Tree House has the only kiva in the park that is open for visitors to enter. While you are welcome to climb the ladder down into the kiva, the space should be respected as the religious structure that it is.

Mesa Top Loop Drive

A self-guided driving tour, the Mesa Top Loop Drive is a fantastic way to get a sense of Ancestral Puebloan cultural development. Many of the sites are not built into the cliff walls, but rather were discovered on the mesa's flat surface. And unlike some of the more famous cliff dwellings, these sites are left mostly unreconstructed. Roofs were built over the excavations to protect them from the elements, and interpretive signs and a booklet do a good job of explaining how archaeologists work and think. This is

OUR EXPERIENCE:
iN THE HoMES oF THE ANCiENTS

The morning wind blows hot, and we screw our eyelids down to narrow slits that still let in too much sunlight. The trail, paved in black tarmac, plunges over the canyon's edge. Our skin itches with sweat. We chat and laugh as we hike, holding our kids' hands lest they stray too close to the cliff. At switchbacks we pause and the ranger points out plants of interest. Shading our eyes, we gaze over the maze of canyons opening below us. Then, turning to hike on, my 6-year-old pipes up, "Hey! It's a ruin!" He's become adept at spotting stone blocks in neatly mortared rows.

The ranger steers us under an overhanging cliff's brow and stands silently as our group coalesces and settles itself. Slowly our eyes uncrinkle in the stone's cool, dark shadow. Rock walls, doorways, windows, and plazas materialize before us. The pueblo's stoniness absorbs the shuffling, sniffing, zipping, and clicking sounds of our tour, even as those sounds echo back to us. We grow quiet.

We have arrived at Long House, the second-largest cliff dwelling in Mesa Verde National Park. Perhaps because of its location at the end of a long, winding road, separate from most of the other major park attractions, only 15 percent of the park's visitors see it.

Ranger Gordon Nothum speaks of the buildings here, and the people who went about their business in the places where we now stand. He tells of the kiva's ceremonial role, and of the unusual acoustical properties of this rock alcove. He shows us seep springs and points out where ancient people carved circular holes in the rock floor just big enough for a ladle to collect water.

Ranger Nothum talks quietly, and even the young children on the tour play quietly in the sand at their parents' feet or sit on stones listening. Respect for the ancient people of the canyons and their efforts here infuse our group. An American kestrel falcon flies from the forest and lands on its nest in the cliff above. The ranger and several of the visitors smile at its presence.

The evening before, a Hopi woman—descended from the Mesa Verde people and a new ranger to boot—gave her first campfire talk. With a shaking voice that grew firmer as she warmed to her message, she wove the present and the past together, trying to help us grasp the significance of the ancient structures.

I'd asked her if it made her feel uncomfortable to have the tours, 60 people every 30 minutes in some sites, tromping through the cliff dwellings. She replied that yes, it made her very uncomfortable, because those people, the ancient ones, still live there in spirit. She admitted that every time she enters with a tour, she stops and says a prayer of thanks for allowing us to walk through their homes.

Now, sitting in Long House, I know what she means. And I do feel a little bit like a trespasser. Yet, I also sense that through their architecture and artifacts, and even in the very location of their endeavors, the cliff dwellings have much to teach us, if only we will settle ourselves long enough to listen.

Cliff Palace, the largest cliff structure at Mesa Verde, has become an icon for the park.

a good tour for families who are fascinated by what they see in the more popular sites and are hungry to learn more.

Cliff Palace

This most famous of cliff dwellings has become the icon for Mesa Verde. It is a good thing it is so big, because the park service starts a group of 60 people through every 30 minutes. In such a large group, it is hard to get a sense of the spiritual nature of the structure, much less have time for many questions. The discussion of the site offered by the ranger was very basic, which is understandable since for many visitors this is their first exposure to the Ancestral Puebloan people.

Wetherill Mesa Tram to the Long House Tour

Perhaps it is the 12-mile-long, narrow road that twists its way to Wetherill Mesa. Or maybe it is that so many sites are concentrated on Chapin Mesa that people figure it is more efficient to see some of those and call it good. Whatever the reason, 85 percent of Mesa Verde's visitors never make it out to Long House. But the sheer relief from the bustle and congestion of Chapin Mesa makes this tour worth the drive.

The steep, 0.75-mile round-trip tour of Long House involves climbing three ladders. However, the buildings arc around the canyon's top with a pleasing rhythm and the view from the central plaza captures visitors' thoughts. A seep near the alcove wall adds a bit of humidity to the desert air. Our ranger was obviously in love with the place, and very knowledgeable about his subject. "To me, it is one of the most special places in the park," he said.

Mesa Verde National Park at a Glance

Location: Southwest Colorado, between Durango and Cortez

Address: P.O. Box 8, Mesa Verde National Park, CO 81330-0008

Telephone: 970-529-4465; 877-264-4884 for lodge and bus tour reservations

Website: www.nps.gov/meve

Size: 52,122 acres

Elevation: From 6,000 feet above sea level in the lowest canyon bottoms to 8,571 feet above sea level at Park Point

Major Activities: Archaeology, scenic drives, photography, wildlife watching, hiking, picnicking, camping, and stargazing

Weather: Summer highs reach into the 90s, with cool nights; winter lows drop to below freezing and the park can see as much as 10 inches of snowfall.

Best Seasons: Spring, summer, and fall, when services such as gasoline, lodging, and food are available; full interpretive services, including the Far View Visitor Center, are only available from mid-May through early September

Hours: The Far View Visitor Center is open from 8 a.m. to 5 p.m. daily, mid-April through mid-October. The Chapin Mesa Archaeological Museum is open from 8 a.m. to 6:30 p.m. daily, mid-April through mid-October, and 8 a.m. to 5 p.m. daily the rest of the year.

Closures: The park and its Chapin Mesa Archaeological Museum are open daily year-round. The Far View Visitor Center is closed in the winter. The campground is closed from mid-October to late April.

Cost: Costs are $10 per private vehicle (for seven days) and $2.75 each for ranger-guided tours of Cliff Palace, Balcony House, and Long House. Rooms in the Far View Lodge are around $106 per night. ARAMARK bus tours run from $35.75 to $55.75. Camping is $20 per night for non-hookup sites and $25 per night for sites with hookups.

Facilities: The Far View area offers a visitor center with wheelchair-accessible restrooms that include diaper-changing stations, a bookstore, exhibits, and displays. The Far View Terrace cafeteria is just up the road. Gift shops are located at Morefield Village, in the Far View Lodge, and at the Far View Terrace. Park headquarters is located on Chapin Mesa near the archaeological museum. Ranger stations are located at Morefield Village, on Wetherill Mesa, and on Chapin Mesa. There is also a post office near the park headquarters. Shuttle bus tours can be purchased through the park concessionaire, ARAMARK. Sites on Chapin Mesa can only be reached by tram, once you make the drive out there. Toilets are available at Morefield Village, in the Morefield Campground, at the Far View complex, on Wetherill Mesa, at the Chapin Mesa complex, and at the Montezuma Valley Overlook. Showers, laundry, and a convenience store are available at Morefield Village. You can buy fuel at Morefield Village. The campground has an RV dump station.

Accessibility: Wheelchair-accessible restrooms are located in the Far View Visitor Center, at the park headquarters on Chapin Mesa, on Wetherill Mesa, and in the campground. This park has excellent descriptions of options for hearing-, sight-, and mobility-impaired visitors on its website.

Balcony House

With tall ladders to climb and an 18-inch-wide, 12-foot-long tunnel to crawl through, the Balcony House tour is great fun for kids. Parents enjoy it, too, but the exposure to heights means they have to be vigilant. It isn't recommended for acrophobes, but the views from the ladders are outstanding. The talk the rangers deliver while touring Balcony House is fairly basic, making this a good first tour and introduction to the culture of the people who built the cliff dwellings.

Morefield Village

As far as I can tell, Morefield Village hasn't changed since I first visited Mesa Verde as a small child. Tucked into a pretty valley between mesas, the complex has a parking lot the size of Wal-Mart's. This is surrounded on three sides by a gas station, a shower/laundromat building, and a gift shop/convenience store/snack bar building.

Directly behind the complex, but mostly hidden by low hills, stretches the park's campground. Stop in at the gas station to fuel up and to reserve a campsite or a bus tour run by ARAMARK. When we were there, the snack bar was closed except in the morning, when you could purchase a pancake breakfast to eat on their patio.

The convenience store is well-stocked and the gift shop is full of the polished rocks, beaded purses, and feathered plastic "Indian" drums kids love. The souvenirs at Morefield Village may not be as highbrow as the ones at the Far View Lodge, but neither are their prices. The laundromat is clean, spacious, and full of big tables for folding laundry. The showers are institutional, but clean and free of charge.

Cliff dwellings perch in the most impossible places at Mesa Verde.

Programs and Activities

Programs and activities at Mesa Verde are so abundant that it is a good idea to print the schedule of offerings from their website before you go.

Several of the cliff dwellings and other archaeological sites are serviced by **guided tours.** You have to buy tickets for most of the tours, but some are free, depending on the time of year. Purchase tickets at the Far View Visitor Center.

The park service offers a **tram ride** at the end of Wetherill Mesa, where you can take a guided ranger walk of Long House. The tram also passes many Ancestral Puebloan mesa-top sites. The park concessionaire, ARAMARK, offers some **bus tours.** Ranger guides describe such features as the Mesa Top Loop Drive, Cliff Palace, the Chapin Mesa Archaeological Museum, Spruce Tree House, and Balcony House.

Step House on Wetherill Mesa and the Far View Ruins, including Mummy Lake, are among the **self-guided tours** you can take. Nordenskiold Site Number 16 has a booklet about native plants and their uses, but the area burned in 2000 and so is exposed to unrelieved sunshine. The Mesa Top Loop roadway also has a booklet, which can be purchased at the museum.

Every half-hour a video plays in the **Chapin Mesa Archaeological Museum** auditorium and other exhibits help visitors understand the timeline of Ancestral Puebloan culture. The museum also houses a truly impressive collection of pre-Columbian artifacts.

Every year, the park service holds a **summer lecture series,** celebrating Native American culture. Check the website and at the museum desk for information, and look for the posters around the park and local towns. **Evening campfire talks** may be held at the Morefield Campground. Check with the rangers for information.

Multimedia programs are held occasionally by ARA-MARK in the auditorium at the Far View Lodge.

Native Americans dance during the summer Indian Arts and Culture Festival.

Natural History

Even without Ancestral Puebloan archaeology, Mesa Verde's scenery, geology, and wildlife make it worth a family vacation.

Geology: Perfect for Building

The mesa rears more than 1,200 feet above the valley floors around it. During the Dinosaur Age it was under a shallow sea. Thousands of feet of mud accumulated under the water and eventually became the material, Mancos shale, which forms the tall slopes of Mesa Verde. The entrance road climbs up through the Mancos shale, which is slippery and constantly producing landslides.

Back when dinosaurs were around, the Rocky Mountains began to gradually rise and the muddy sea retreated. When the seashore was over what is now Mesa Verde, the beach deposited a sandy layer that later hardened into sandstone. This layer is known as the Point Lookout sandstone.

Then swamps grew at the edge of the ancient sea. The swamp plants died and were covered by more sandy shoreline material. The swamps eventually became a layer of shale and coal, known as the Menefee formation. The Menefee is sandwiched between the Point Lookout sandstone, below, and a thick layer of Cliffhouse sandstone, above. This Lookout-Menefee-Cliffhouse sandwich is called the "Mesa Verde Group" of rocks.

Layers of tough sandstone protect slopes of Mancos shale to create Mesa Verde.

A HiKE FoR
LiTTLE LEGS

Mesa Verde focuses on preserving the sites and artifacts, which have a history of being looted. Because of this, hiking opportunities are limited. Still, several trails provide the opportunity to stretch your legs and take in spectacular panoramas. Starting from the western edge of the campground, the 2-mile, round-trip Knife Edge Trail traverses the northern edge of Mesa Verde, giving kids a sense of the scale of the landform that supports the national park. Yellow sandstone cliffs rise above the fairly level former road while gray Mancos shale slopes below it. Extensive views of the Montezuma Valley and points beyond stretch out to the north. Pick up the well-written booklet at the Far View Visitor Center to help kids understand plants and other natural features along the route.

Families who want to do a much shorter walk—with a fascinating and scenic endpoint—can visit Park Point, the highest elevation on the mesa. At the top, they can chat with the fire ranger who keeps an eye out for smoke from the fire tower located there.

Hiking at Mesa Verde includes the Spruce Canyon Trail, near park headquarters.

Without the Mesa Verde Group, Mesa Verde National Park would not be here today for two reasons. The first reason is that the Mesa Verde group forms a protective cap, which slows the slip-sliding erosion of the Mancos shale. Without the cap rock, Mesa Verde would have washed away long ago and be as flat as the sage plain at its feet. Mesa Verde's elevation also helped it catch windblown silt, ground from the mountains by Ice Age glaciers. The silt makes a thick layer of topsoil, great for growing beans.

The second reason the Mesa Verde Group of rocks is so important is that it is perfect for building cliff dwellings. Water from rain and snowmelt soaks down through the Cliffhouse sandstone on top of Mesa Verde. When it hits the Menefee shale and coal layer, it runs horizontally until it reaches a canyon wall, where it seeps out. As it does this, it erodes away the soft Menefee layer. Eventually, some of the heavy Cliffhouse sandstone above drops away, leaving a nice alcove in the rock face. The cliffs of Point Lookout sandstone made these alcoves easy to defend from attackers below, and the overhang above protects them from the weather.

Plants and Wildlife: Kick My Tent

Mesa Verde is chock-full of wildlife. The mesas are covered in piñon-juniper forests, which offer tremendous resources—not the least of which are piñon nuts and juniper berries, yummy food for animals. Humans, too, are fond of the piñon nuts. (You be the judge of juniper berries.) Mormon tea, serviceberry, yucca, and prickly pear cactus are also common on the tablelands. Open areas are populated with sagebrush, grasses, and wildflowers like the pretty, hardy mariposa lily; paintbrush; penstemon; lupine; and larkspur. Douglas fir trees and Gambel's oak can be found in the canyons. Creek bottoms have plants typical of desert riparian zones, including cottonwoods and single-leaf ash trees.

Turkey vulture © Wendy Shattil/Bob Rozinski

Be watchful of rattlesnakes in rocky areas and on the less-busy hiking trails. Other snakes found in the park include bullsnakes, six-lined racerunners, and yellow-bellied racers. Look for collared lizards doing little push-ups on the rock outcroppings.

The changing elevation of Mesa Verde creates habitat for a variety of birds. As air currents rise along the front prow of the mesa, hawks, vultures, and eagles are commonly seen riding the thermals. Peregrine falcons and golden eagles nest near the Knife Edge Trail. Cooper's and sharp-shinned hawks hunt smaller birds in the broken woodlands of the mesa tops. Steller's jays, scrub jays, and magpies are common, and nuthatches are sometimes seen in their upside-down hunt for bugs along tree trunks. Violet-green swallows soar and dip in the canyons, and lucky visitors may hear the clear, dribbling music of a canyon wren's call.

Visitors to the campground almost can't help but see mule deer. Remember that these animals are not tame and you should not feed them. One quiet afternoon, when I had retreated to my tent to make notes, I felt something kick the nylon wall of my shelter. I poked my head out to come face-to-face with a mule deer standing a few yards off. There were no other animals or people around, and it did not bolt at the sight of me. It just stood there and stared—I couldn't believe a deer would kick my tent!

Chipmunk © Wendy Shattil/Bob Rozinski

Rodents of all descriptions are common in the park. Look for chipmunks and prairie dogs. Although black bears are rarely seen, rangers will tell you to pack up your food when you are not actively cooking or eating. Chow left out overnight is more likely to be pilfered by deer mice. Their cousins living in the park include woodrats, voles, pocket mice, and antelope ground squirrels. Abert's squirrels, recognizable by their tufted ears, and noisy chickarees are often seen in the Spruce Tree House area. Beaver have even been sighted in the wetter river bottoms, although these areas are off limits to visitors. Bobcats, coyotes, and gray foxes hunt jackrabbits and cottontails. Elusive mountain lions haunt quieter, less-populated parts of Mesa Verde.

A special treat is to watch the evening sky, just after sunset. Watch carefully and you may see several varieties of bats doing their best to rid the air of insects.

Human History

As long as 10,000 years ago, Paleo-Indians hunted in the area of Mesa Verde. It wasn't until about 2,000 years ago that the first farming people, known as the Basketmakers, came into the area, but there is no evidence that they occupied Mesa Verde itself at that time.

The oldest sites in the park date from around the year AD 550. The Basketmakers developed the tablelands and were farming and hunting them. They originally built pithouses in canyon alcoves as well as on the mesa tops. Around the year 750, they started to use bows and arrows and also to build pithouses together in small towns, or pueblos. For the next 250 years or so, they seemed to be experimenting with different building styles and materials, eventually coming to erect their homes in groups around pithouses. Eventually, the pithouses took on more ceremonial purposes and became kivas.

By the year 1100, the culture was becoming highly developed. The Ancestral Puebloans, also known as the Anasazi, were excellent potters, and made beautiful pieces with

Another magical Mesa Verde sunset.

intricate patterns painted on them. They kept domestic dogs and turkeys, wove cloth from cotton, and traded for items that came from as far away as the Pacific Ocean. They grew squash, corn, and beans, and built check dams and water-storage systems to irrigate their crops. Their stonemasonry skills were advanced, too, and they began to build towers.

Then, around the year 1200, a large number of people began to build towns in the alcoves of the canyon walls again. The archaeological debate rages over what caused them to do this. The cliff dwellings are elaborate, would have taken significant labor to build, and housed many people. Yet, the people moved onward less than 100 years later, settling in northern New Mexico and Arizona. The Mesa Verde folks and their neighbors from all around the Four Corners region migrated to Arizona and New Mexico, where they became part of the Pueblo people who live there today.

The two major population shifts—first from the mesas to the cliff walls and then out of the region altogether—are the subject of intense research and conjecture among archaeologists and tourists alike.

In the mid-18th century, Spanish explorers traveled through the region, skirting the Mesa Verde area. In the mid-1800s, American explorers recorded climbing to a high point within Mesa Verde, calling it by name, but not mentioning any cliff dwellings. By the 1870s, white men were recording their findings of archaeological sites throughout the region, including the cliffhouses at Mesa Verde. Around the turn of the 20th century, enough public support existed for designating it a national park, and by 1906, President Theodore Roosevelt signed the bill. Within two years, Smithsonian Institution archaeologist J. W. Fewkes was excavating and developing the sites for visitors.

In 1976, 8,500 acres of the park were designated as a National Wilderness Area. Two years later, the United Nations Educational, Scientific, and Cultural Organization (UNESCO) listed Mesa Verde National Park as a World Heritage Site. Around a half-million people visit Mesa Verde every year.

Restaurants and Picnic Areas

The **Metate Room** in the Far View Lodge is a fine-dining restaurant and lounge, serving dinner only. Giant windows offer panoramic views of the distant canyons and mesas of the Colorado Plateau. Its nouveau-Mexican cuisine includes lots of sage-spiced, piñon-nut-encrusted dishes that are both creative and delicious.

A children's menu offers favorites such as chicken fingers, hamburgers, and pasta primavera. If an extended wait after ordering makes young diners wiggly, parents can take them for a walk to view the Southwestern art decorating the restaurant or out onto the terrace. We enjoyed watching deer browsing for their supper right below our tableside window.

The **Far View Terrace** cafeteria, nearby, serves up breakfast, lunch, and vast park vistas. **Snack bars** on Wetherill Mesa and near the museum offer a choice of sandwiches, fruit, sodas, and bottled water.

You also can eat your lunch outdoors at several **picnic grounds** throughout the park. The **Mancos Valley Overlook** is marked as a picnic area, but it offers only a covered stone bench and no picnic tables. Closest to the park entrance and campground, the overlook features a sweeping view to the north and east over the Mancos River and the San Juan Mountains. Just up the road, the **Montezuma Valley Overlook** has sunny picnic tables and a trail leads to a spectacular view of the canyon country to the west. On Chapin Mesa, the best picnic ground is near the **Spruce Canyon Trail**. Formerly the park's campground, it offers fire grates and restrooms with running water. The shade from its trees is lovely, and the cliff-side picnic sites have beautiful views. You'll find more tables near **Cliff Palace** and the **Pueblo Ruins** as well, but these tend to have less shade. The **Wetherill Mesa** parking area also has a few tables, and even though the trees burned to gnarly black sticks in a recent forest fire, the bare branches are thick enough to offer some shade.

Lodging and Camping

The **Far View Lodge** sits upon 8,160-foot-high Navajo Hill in the heart of the park. Private balconies open to panoramas that stretch more than 100 miles. (I had trouble getting the kids ready for bed—I couldn't take my eyes off our big picture window and the changing color patterns as the sun set over the canyons.) No televisions or telephones are in the rooms. Evening programs are held from time to time in the multimedia auditorium. The lodge is open from mid-April to mid-October. To make reservations, call toll-free: 877-246-4884.

Mesa Verde's campground has never filled up.

With 435 sites, one of the largest campgrounds in the entire National Park Service system is at Mesa Verde. **Morefield Campground** never fills up as evidenced by the various campsites grown over with grasses and wildflowers. The views are beautiful. Sites include picnic tables and fire grates, and 15 sites have RV hookups. Drinking water and flush toilets are available, as are shower and laundry facilities and a convenience store.

Nearby Towns

Cortez is 10 miles from the Mesa Verde entrance station. The Colorado Welcome Center for southwest Colorado is located in Cortez, and offers a full array of maps and brochures for nearby services and activities. The town boasts more than 160 acres in parks, all right off Main Street behind the Colorado Welcome Center. They include duck ponds, skateboard tracks, ball fields, and a swimming pool. The new $7.5 million recreation center has an indoor swimming pool with a water slide, gymnasium, racquetball courts, climbing wall, fitness area, and a hot tub as well as showers.

Several chain and independent hotels and motels offer family lodging, and some have their own swimming pools. There are many restaurants to choose from, as well. Southwest Memorial Hospital is located at 1311 North Mildred Road, in the southwest part of town, and it offers a Level IV trauma center as well as acute-care beds and surgical, orthopedic, and obstetric services.

The Cortez Cultural Center museum offers interpretive displays about the Ancestral Puebloans who lived in the area in the past and the Ute people who live there today. Open year-round, the Cortez Cultural Center has an art gallery displaying the work of local artists and a gift shop. Native American dances are held there during the summer. Visit www.mesaverdecountry.com or call 800-253-1616 for more information.

Eight miles east of Mesa Verde National Park's entrance, the town of **Mancos** lies between the Mancos River and Chicken Creek. With just over 1,000 people, the community offers motels, restaurants, shops, outfitters, the Dog Hotel boarding kennel, a public library, and a pioneer museum. Find more information at www.mancosvalley.com.

Thirty-six miles east of the Mesa Verde entrance gate on US 160 is **Durango.** This small city features 839 acres of parks and open space. Many of the 32 parks have picnic tables, playgrounds, and restrooms, and several spots—including Santa Rita Park, Rotary Park, and Schneider Park—offer fishing access. The hard-surfaced Animas River Bike Trail winds for 5 miles along the river through town, crossing five bridges in the process. Durango's Community Recreation Center has a swimming pool and numerous other facilities.

The historic downtown area along Main Avenue features boutiques, coffeehouses, and art galleries. The depot for the Durango & Silverton Narrow Gauge Railroad is downtown as well. Mercy Medical Center, at 375 East Park Avenue, is centrally located and has a Level III trauma center and 83 acute-care beds.

Lodging options include everything from new, chain hotels with complimentary breakfasts and indoor pools to the historic Strater Hotel on Main Avenue. The size of Durango and its tourist economy ensure several family-friendly restaurants with decent menus.

The Children's Museum of Durango is dedicated to providing educational and playful spaces where children of all ages can stimulate their imaginations and discover more about themselves and the world around them. Located on the second floor of the Durango Arts Center, it is closed on Mondays.

Check out the City of Durango website at www.durangogov.org, or visit the tourism and vacation website at www.durango.org. You can also call 800-525-8855 for information.

Special Considerations for Families

Although most of the attractions at Mesa Verde are along very well-maintained trails, it is still important to watch your kids around cliff edges. Also, some of the ladders for visiting the cliff dwellings are quite tall, and even though the kids love the idea of climbing them, falling is a risk.

Help your kids understand that the archaeological sites are rare antiquities, and they should be treated with reverence and care. Don't allow children to sit, lean on, or climb the walls of the cliff dwellings.

One of the best ways for your family to get a feel for Mesa Verde is to hit the trails, but the activity has some hazards. The bright Colorado sun can burn delicate skin, so hats, sunblock, and lip balm are essential—so is *lots* of water. We flavor our kids' with a touch of lemonade powder, so they are more likely to keep drinking. Watch for rattlesnakes on the trail and in the rocks.

Mesa Verde's elevation can make it hard to breathe for some visitors from lower elevations or with lung or heart problems. Drink lots of water to counteract altitude sickness, avoid alcohol, and take it easy the first few days. Emergency medical care is available at the Far View Visitor Center and at the park headquarters.

What Makes Mesa Verde National Park Special

Fantastic geology, abundant wildlife, unparalleled vistas, great camping, a grand old lodge, and world-class archaeology: Take your pick. For me, however, it was being haunted by the spirits of the ancient people who lived there. I was thrilled and humbled at the same time.

Mesa Verde's Far View Ruins are a great place for kids to explore.

E N T R Y

NATIONAL PARK SERVICE PASSPORT STAMP

Bird's-Eye View: Marsh Mounds

In the far southwestern corner of Colorado, the Rocky Mountains run down into the layer cake desert of the Colorado Plateau. Jagged peaks and ridges flatten out into the blocky jumble of canyon country.

Like a straying toddler, Sleeping Ute Mountain sticks up through the layered rock strata several miles west of the high ranges. Reaching more than 9,300 feet in elevation, it is a landmark for hundreds of miles around.

The Montezuma Valley runs at the foot of Sleeping Ute Mountain, separating it from Mesa Verde. Straight north is the rise of the McElmo Dome, upon which Hovenweep National Monument and Canyons of the Ancients National Monument rest. At sunset, the town of Cortez lies in the shadow of the mountain.

If you drew a line on a map between Mesa Verde and Hovenweep, passing just south of Cortez and across the shoulder of Sleeping Ute Mountain, it would pass over tiny Yucca House National Monument in the heart of the Montezuma Valley. It lies off US 160, near the headwaters of Navajo Wash.

Hidden beneath the dry surface here, groundwater flows between rock layers. At Yucca House, it rises to the surface in a series of small seeps and—of all things—a marsh emerges in the desert. Ancestral Puebloans might have yelled some variation of "Bingo!" as they tromped across the dry land, looking for a

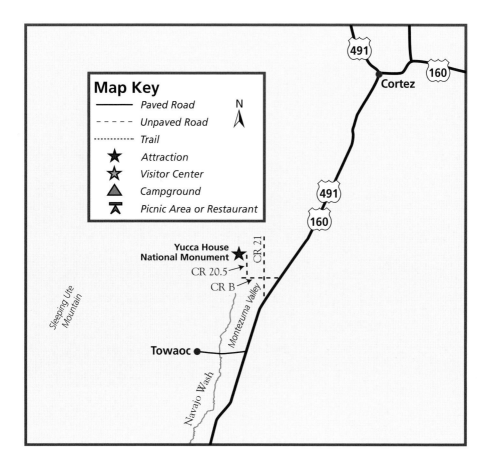

place to camp. Eventually, the area became a trading center. When Professor William Holmes first described Yucca House in 1877, it was the largest Ancestral Puebloan dwelling to be discovered at that time.

Today, like the volcanic forces that pushed up Sleeping Ute Mountain and the water that flows underground, Yucca House lies mostly beneath the surface. Only one wall remains standing and the rest of the settlement appears only as rocky mounds in the desert. The largest mound is known as Upper House while the wall is part of Lower House. To unearth the pueblo would inevitably cause some destruction, so until the benefits of the research outweigh the potential for damage, the site will remain unexcavated.

Yucca House's value to the American people is scientific and archaeological. The National Park Service does not encourage casual visitors to travel to this monument, although it is not prohibited, either.

The entrance to Yucca House National Monument is in a cow yard.

Reaching Yucca House

Yucca House lies about 8.5 miles south of Cortez, near County Road B and the private County Road 20.5, both of which are impassable in wet weather. The parking spot for Yucca House is next to a ranch house. To walk to the site, you will be crossing private land, so please leave all gates closed as you pass through to keep their livestock from escaping.

Attractions

The piles of rock and dirt that make up **Yucca House** and its marshy seep are all there is to see. The attraction lies in wondering what stories lie beneath the rubble, greasewood, and yucca plants.

Since the monument is undeveloped, kids may not learn much from Yucca House—except to understand that other archaeological sites in the Four Corners area once looked like this. It may be a good lesson in avoiding judgments based on surface observations alone.

OUR EXPERIENCE:
NEEDLE GRASS

The grid of farm roads leading to a ranch house's front yard made us wonder if we were heading to the right place. But there, on a fence surrounding a cow lot, was the sign for Yucca House National Monument. We parked behind the rancher's horse trailer and headed across the mud.

On the other side of the corral, a path dodged prickers and dry grass clumps to an elevated rocky area. It took us a minute to realize that the rocks were the exact size and shape of the rocks we'd seen in other Ancestral Puebloan ruins. A big hill of the rocks and dirt, supporting scrubby bushes, surrounded a bowl of lush grasses. Once I figured out that this was the pueblo, it occurred to me how big the buildings must have once been. People would have been able to see them for miles around.

Back at the car, we spent 20 minutes picking needle-like grass seeds from our socks and shoes, the quiet emptiness of Yucca House echoing in our minds.

Ancestral Puebloans wove yucca fibers into shoes and other necessities.

A HiKE FOR LiTTLE LEGS

There are no designated trails at Yucca House National Monument, but you are welcome to take a walk on the existing paths around the site.

Programs and Activities

The park service offers **no scheduled programs** or Junior Ranger Program at Yucca House National Monument.

Natural History

Geology: The Sleeping Ute

The Montezuma Valley skirts the northwest side of Mesa Verde and would stretch smoothly out into Utah, except that a giant, underground volcano, or laccolith, grew up in the middle of where the valley lies today. The molten rock of the laccolith elbowed its way between the rock layers, bending some of them up and some of them down. The result is Sleeping Ute Mountain, at whose base Yucca House lies.

Plants and Wildlife: A Spring in the Desert

Above Yucca House, rainwater and snowmelt soak into the ground and through the upper layers of rock. The water flows underground to emerge as a spring in the desert. This spring, which is surrounded by farm- and ranchland, is a wild oasis. The available surface water allows cattails and reeds to grow near it. In the surrounding dry areas, sagebrush, greasewood, cactus, and, of course, yucca thrive. Coyotes, bobcats, and foxes hunt cottontail rabbits, mice, and voles. Rattlesnakes are common and hunt the rodents as well. Mule deer come to drink and browse on the bushes and songbirds make their homes here. Hawks and crows soar in the clear Colorado skies overhead, looking for a meal below. Yucca House is also home to several rare "species of concern" that may be eligible for the Threatened and Endangered Species list.

Crow © Wendy Shattil/Bob Rozinski

Yucca House National Monument at a Glance

Location: Southwest Colorado, about 9 miles south of Cortez

Address: c/o Mesa Verde National Park, P.O. Box 8,
Mesa Verde National Park, CO 81330-0008

Telephone: 970-529-4465

Website: www.nps.gov/yuho

Size: 34 acres

Elevation: 5,880 feet above sea level

Major Activities: Archaeological site

Weather: Summer temperatures can be 100 degrees or higher; winter temperatures range from lows in the single digits to highs in the 50s; precipitation is rare, but it makes the roads slippery with mud and often impassable.

Best Seasons: September and October

Hours: There are no facilities with established hours.

Closures: The monument is open all year long as weather permits access.

Cost: Access to the monument is free.

Facilities: There are no facilities at Yucca House. The National Park Service doesn't recommend travel to this monument for the casual visitor.

Accessibility: The monument is not accessible according to ADA standards.

Only one wall remains standing at Yucca House.

Human History

Artifacts found at Yucca House indicate that the pueblo was active during the Pueblo III period, from about 900 to 700 years ago. Its location suggests that it may have been a center for trade in pre-Columbian times, and its layout links it to the Chaco Canyon–influenced pueblos rather than the Mesa Verde structures. The Navajo and Ute people who live in the area have known about the site for centuries. The first written documentation was in Professor Holmes' U.S. Geological Survey report in 1877.

Hoping for excavation, the original landowner, Henry Van Kleek, donated it to the federal government and it became a national monument in 1919. Lack of funding, access, and public interest prevented it from ever being excavated.

Restaurants and Picnic Areas

There are **no restaurants or picnic facilities** located within Yucca House National Monument.

Lodging and Camping

There is **no hotel lodging or camping** at Yucca House National Monument.

Red fox   © Wendy Shattil/Bob Rozinski

Nearby Towns

Cortez is about 9 miles northeast of Yucca House National Monument. The Colorado Welcome Center for southwest Colorado is located in Cortez, and offers a full array of maps and brochures for nearby services and activities. The town boasts more than 160 acres in parks, all right off Main Street behind the Colorado Welcome Center. They include duck ponds, skateboard tracks, ball fields, and a swimming pool. The new $7.5 million recreation center has an indoor swimming pool with a water slide, gymnasium, racquetball courts, climbing wall, fitness area, and a hot tub as well as showers.

Several chain and independent hotels and motels offer family lodging, and some have their own swimming pools. There are many restaurants to choose from, as well. Southwest Memorial Hospital is located at 1311 North Mildred Road, in the southwest part of town, and it offers a Level IV trauma center as well as acute-care beds, surgery, orthopedics, and obstetrics.

The Cortez Cultural Center museum offers interpretive displays about the Ancestral Puebloans who lived in the area in the past and the Ute people who live there today. Open year-round, the Cortez Cultural Center has an art gallery displaying the work of local artists and a gift shop. Native American dances are held there during the summer. Visit www.mesaverdecountry.com or call 800-253-1616 for more information.

Special Considerations for Families

Yucca House is an undeveloped and wild bump in the bush. Be wary of rattlesnakes in the rocks if you do visit. This is also a pristine, undisturbed archaeological site—it is imperative that you leave the rocks and soil of the site and any potsherds or other artifacts exactly as you find them.

What Makes Yucca House National Monument Special

This place is special for what it *isn't*. Because Yucca House was never dug up and put on display, hardly anyone ever goes there. There is some belief within the National Park Service that the value of Yucca House is in its archaeological and scientific potential rather than as a site for extensive visitation. It just may not be appropriate to draw large numbers of people to the monument.

As a result, Yucca House isn't a tourist attraction. It isn't a museum. It is just a bump in a sage plain where a bunch of people used to live a thousand years ago and now they're gone. They left their buildings, some of their stuff, and their pretty little wetland in the desert. And for now, the National Park Service has elected to let it all rest in peace.

Mountains

Long bands of mountains rise sharply up from the Great Plains and run through the heart of Colorado from north to south. Made from very old crystalline rocks, some rise higher than 14,000 feet above sea level. On either side, layers of sedimentary rock bend upwards, lining the ranges with hogbacks and ridges.

Some of America's great rivers were born in these mountains, and they have carved great valleys between the peaks. But icy glaciers, which gouged and scoured the rocks into sharp points and ridges, were the major sculptors of the scenery we enjoy today.

Rocky Mountain National Park, Florissant Fossil Beds National Monument, Black Canyon of the Gunnison National Park, Curecanti National Recreation Area, and Great Sand Dunes National Park and Preserve reflect varying aspects of this jagged, fierce stretch of ground. All are sights to behold, and all are well deserving of their place in America's chest of natural jewels.

Black Canyon of the Gunnison displays some of the oldest rocks in Colorado.

The dunes of Great Sand Dunes National Park are a stark contrast to the nearby Sangre de Cristo Mountains.
© John Fielder

E N T R Y

NATIONAL PARK SERVICE PASSPORT STAMP

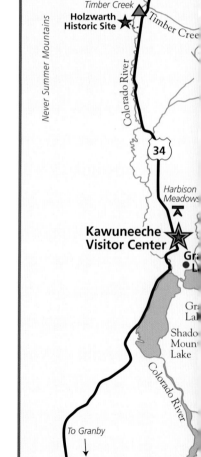

Specimen Mountain

Pou
L
Milner Pass

Never Summer Mountains

Timber Creek
Holzwarth Historic Site ★

Timber Cree

Colorado River

34

Harbison Meadows

Kawuneeche Visitor Center ★

Gr
L

Gra
La

Shado
Moun
Lake

Colorado River

To Granby

Bird's-Eye View: High Ground

As the sun rises over the edge of the Great Plains, its golden rays illuminate Rocky Mountain National Park's high peaks. About 30 miles south of the Wyoming border, the park lies smack in the middle of the state from east to west. It takes one-and-a-half or two hours to drive there from Denver on generally northwest-trending US 36.

This national park is shaped roughly like a rectangle, 20 miles wide and 26 or so miles from north to south. The Continental Divide, the high ground separating the Atlantic and Pacific Ocean drainages, runs through the park from north to south. Cutting across the park from west to east, Trail Ridge Road scales the divide. Like a squiggly jump rope, the road swings up into the sky between heavily visited areas in valleys on either end.

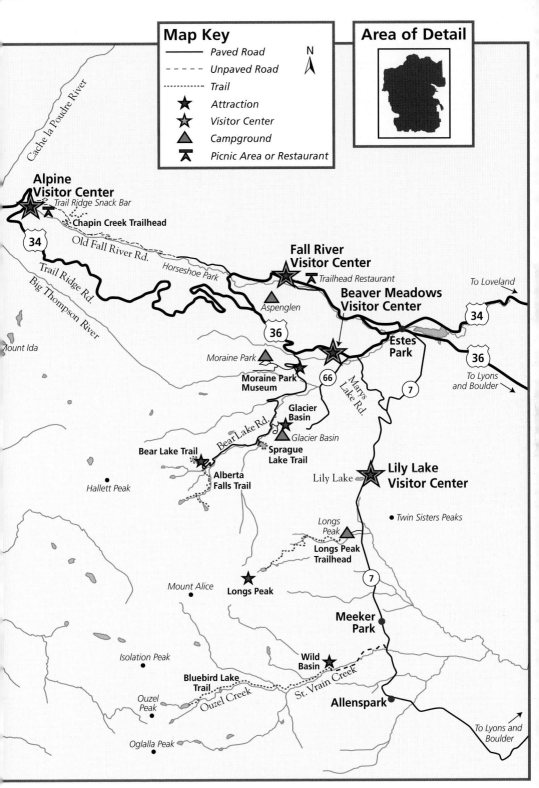

Map Key

— Paved Road

- - - - Unpaved Road

·········· Trail

★ Attraction

☆ Visitor Center

▲ Campground

⊼ Picnic Area or Restaurant

N

Area of Detail

Cache la Poudre River

Alpine Visitor Center

Trail Ridge Snack Bar

Chapin Creek Trailhead

34

Old Fall River Rd.

Horseshoe Park

Trail Ridge Rd.

Big Thompson River

Mount Ida

Fall River Visitor Center

Trailhead Restaurant

Beaver Meadows Visitor Center

To Loveland

Aspenglen

36

34

Estes Park

Moraine Park

36

Moraine Park Museum

66

To Lyons and Boulder

Marys Lake Rd.

7

Glacier Basin

Glacier Basin

Bear Lake Trail

Bear Lake Rd.

Sprague Lake Trail

Alberta Falls Trail

Lily Lake

Lily Lake Visitor Center

Hallett Peak

• Twin Sisters Peaks

Longs Peak

Longs Peak Trailhead

7

Mount Alice

Longs Peak

Meeker Park

Isolation Peak

Wild Basin

Bluebird Lake Trail

St. Vrain Creek

Ouzel Peak

Ouzel Creek

Allenspark

Oglalla Peak

To Lyons and Boulder

The Continental Divide forms the backbone of the Rocky Mountains in Colorado.

Highlands gather around giant peaks, which rear up in the center of the park. Thus, a long band of stony summits divides Rocky Mountain National Park into the east side and the west side. Tiny lakes sprinkle the mountainsides, and rough and tumble creeks splash between them. Eventually these creeks join, forming important Western rivers. They plunge through deep valleys, thousands of feet below the mountaintops.

The east side of the park sees the bulk of the three million annual visitors. A network of trails connects campgrounds, picnic areas, and scenic drives. South of Estes Park, Colorado State Route 7 (the Peak to Peak Highway) parallels the park boundary and offers hiking access to the Twin Sisters, Wild Basin, and Longs Peak.

On the west side, Trail Ridge Road drops down into the Kawuneeche Valley, where it runs along the baby Colorado River. The road provides access to a campground, picnic areas, historic sites, and hiking trails before it leaves the park near the town of Grand Lake.

Giant swaths of the park are designated as wilderness areas, and as such can only be accessed via foot trails (and much of the territory isn't even touched by those).

OUR EXPERiENCE:
FiERCE!

Chilly winds slide down jagged peaks and lay golden grasses low. We've pulled into a turnout with a picnic table to eat our lunch, but in spite of the bright sun, the kids are shivering. We grab our sandwiches and dive back into the car, but open the windows an inch to let in a bull elk's piercing bugle. In the heat of the rut, he herds his harem of females together down by the Big Thompson River. Multi-pointed antlers swing this way and that as he watches rogue bulls pacing nearby.

We spot two fuzzy coyotes trotting across Moraine Park. They seem unaware of each other, except that both disappear into the same shadowed pocket of forest. They appear in a clearing, harassed by magpies in black and white plumage. With no warning, one of the coyotes snaps at an offending bird, catches it, then leaves it dead on the ground. The coyote follows its companion into the underbrush.

A red-tailed hawk hangs in the wind, searching for mice and voles in the grasses below, continuing the life and death drama set against the fierce backdrop of the Continental Divide.

This is no carefully edited and soundtracked episode on Animal Planet network. When we venture from our car, we feel the wind and smell the dampness of the meadow and the musk of the elk. We look up and see mountains soaring to 13,000 and 14,000 feet above sea level. Our family is in the scene, our picnic just another small event in a magnificent theater. The set is indifferent to our trials and tribulations, and nature does not seem to care at all if we are there. It feels humbling and empowering at the same time, and the words of an old Quaker hymn echo in the back of my mind:

'Tis a gift to be simple
'tis a gift to be free
'tis a gift to come down
where you ought to be...

Elk   © Wendy Shattil/Bob Rozinski

Attractions

Beaver Meadows Visitor Center

Located just inside the park boundary on US 36, the Beaver Meadows Park Headquarters and Visitor Center is the only structure in the National Park Service to be designed by Frank Lloyd Wright. Built in 1966, it is now listed as a National Historic Landmark.

Inside, helpful staff and literature send families up the right path as they head into Rocky Mountain National Park. An exhibit showing a large topographical relief map of the area lets you get a feel for the lay of the land. Rangers behind the counter have maps and all kinds of flyers describing hiking trails, campgrounds, historic sites, wildlife viewing spots, life zones, scenic drives, and much more. A 20-minute film describes the park and a small bookstore offers reference brochures, pamphlets, and books. Restrooms are available, and the women's room has a diaper-changing station.

Fall River Visitor Center

New in 2000, the Fall River Visitor Center and adjacent facilities are a family-friendly partnership between private and public entities. The log frame buildings, located near the Fall River Entrance Station, house a large gift shop, a sit-down restaurant and restrooms. The visitor center has rangers to answer questions and help with trip planning. Interpretive exhibits about the park's history and wildlife help families who stop in to understand the park better. Kids love the Discovery Center with its dress-up section. There, they find clothing to try on from different periods in park history plus exhibits they can touch and smell. (Check out the trapping display—pee-uw!)

The Fall River Visitor Center houses the Discovery Center, a great stop for kids.

Rocky Mountain National Park at a Glance

Location: North-central Colorado, about two hours northwest of Denver

Address: 1000 US Highway 36, Estes Park, CO 80517-8397

Telephone: 970-586-1206; 800-365-2267 for campsite reservations

Website: www.nps.gov/romo

Size: 265,828 acres

Elevation: From 6,860 to 14,259 feet above sea level

Major Activities: Scenery viewing, wildlife watching, auto touring, hiking, camping, backpacking, photography, fishing, and mountain climbing

Weather: Summer highs up to 80 degrees, although 60s and 70s are more common; summer snow squalls are not uncommon nor are freezing nighttime temperatures; afternoon thunderstorms occur almost every day in the summer; winters are cold and windy with highs of 20 to 30 degrees and lows of 10 to 20 degrees.

Best Seasons: Summer and fall

Hours: The Beaver Meadows Visitor Center is open 8 a.m. to 9 p.m. in the summer and 8 a.m. to 4:30 p.m. the rest of the year. The Fall River Visitor Center is open 9 a.m. to 6 p.m. in the summer and 9 a.m. to 5 p.m. the rest of the year. The Kawuneeche Visitor Center is open 8 a.m. to 6 p.m. in the summer and 8 a.m. to 4:30 p.m. the rest of the year.

Closures: The Alpine Visitor Center is closed from snowfall in the fall (mid-October) until Memorial Day weekend. Holzwarth Historic Site is closed from Labor Day through late June. The Lily Lake Visitor Center is closed for the time being due to budget constraints.

Cost: The fees are $20 per passenger car (good for seven consecutive days) and $20 per night for camping ($14 per night when the water is turned off for the season).

Facilities: The Beaver Meadows Visitor Center, which is also the park headquarters, features a ranger station, restrooms, a diaper-changing station, and a bookstore. The Fall River Visitor Center has a ranger station, restrooms, a family restroom, a gift shop, a bookstore, and a full-service restaurant. The Alpine Visitor Center has restrooms, a ranger station, a gift shop, and a snack bar. The Kawuneeche Visitor Center has a ranger station, a bookstore, a gift shop, and restrooms with a diaper-changing station. Ranger stations can also be found at the Wild Basin Trailhead and the Longs Peak Trailhead. The visitor centers all have interpretive displays, and Moraine Park on the east side and Holzwarth Historic Site on the west side have museums. In the summer, free shuttle buses loop throughout the Bear Lake/Moraine Park areas. Dump stations are located at the Moraine Park, Glacier Basin, and Timber Creek campgrounds. Showers, laundromats, convenience stores, and gas are available in the gateway towns of Estes Park and Grand Lake.

Accessibility: The visitor centers and museums are at least marginally accessible to wheelchairs. The campgrounds at Glacier Basin and Moraine Park have wheelchair-accessible campsites. Sprague Lake has a backcountry campsite that will accommodate up to six wheelchairs. Five trails throughout the park are wheelchair accessible, with wide, relatively smooth pathways in particularly scenic spots. Wheelchairs can navigate the Bear Lake Trail, although it is steep and uneven in some places.

Alpine Visitor Center

Weather permitting, the Alpine Visitor Center is open from Memorial Day through mid-October (when the snow gets too deep). Perched at 11,796 feet above sea level on a steep, glacier-gouged mountainside, the visitor center overlooks the junction of the Old Fall River Road and the newer Trail Ridge Road, plus mountain ranges that stretch into Wyoming and all over Colorado. Families will appreciate the extensive gift shop and bookstore there as well as a large snack bar and vault toilets. Rangers lead interpretive talks and walks through the alpine landscape and answer visitors' questions about this unusual landscape.

Trail Ridge Road

Traversing 48 miles between the villages of Estes Park and Grand Lake, Trail Ridge Road is one of America's most famous alpine skyways. Its broad sweeping curves lift drivers through a series of life zones from montane and subalpine

Families take in the sweeping view just outside the Alpine Visitor Center.

forests to alpine tundra. Several of the turnouts allow families to pull over and enjoy vast panoramas. Along the way, picnic grounds, wildlife viewing spots, and hiking trails tempt folks to leave their cars and explore mountain wildlands and wonders. Steep drop-offs along the side of the road in some spots make even seasoned mountain drivers grip the wheel tightly and breathe a little faster.

Old Fall River Road

Old Fall River Road is the original auto route to Fall River Pass, which rises 11,796 feet above sea level. Built in 1921, this gravel track winds through several hairpin curves and steep sections to emerge above timberline in glacier-carved terrain. The road is so narrow that vehicles cannot pass each other safely, hence its one-way-uphill designation. Its curves are so tight that your car must be shorter than 25 feet to navigate them. With a speed limit of 15 miles per hour, the 14 miles feel like a nature hike as much as a drive. Still, it is worthwhile to get out of your car and put your boots to the ground at the Chapin Creek Trailhead. When you lift your eyes off the path, they will appreciate the view. Try to get to the Chapin Creek Trailhead before 9 a.m. as parking is extremely limited.

Bear Lake

Trail Ridge Road aside, the Bear Lake corridor is arguably the most visited part of Rocky Mountain National Park—and for good reason. Shuttle buses, ranger hikes, church groups, families, photographers, hikers, backpackers, mountain climbers, fishermen, and a couple of parking lots the size of Wal-Mart's still don't spoil the gorgeous, wild beauty of the place.

The scenic drive from the Beaver Meadows entrance passes through 10 miles of montane forests and open meadows. It crosses ancient glacial rubble piles and winds through thick, shady spruce-fir forests. You can drive the whole way and fight traffic and pray for a parking space, or you can catch the shuttle and skip the hassle.

From the parking lot/shuttle stop at the top, walk a few feet over a rise to where the trees part and chunky, cliffy peaks soar over the blue waters of Bear Lake. It's scenic enough to stop right there as many folks do—but they are missing the incredible hiking that starts at that point. Easy, moderate, and difficult trails lead to some of the best scenery that Colorado has to offer. Bear Lake, pretty as it is, is only the beginning. Rangers are often stationed at the parking lot to offer advice and ideas to fit your family's interests and abilities. Marked posts and a booklet take families on a self-guided nature hike around Bear Lake itself.

Sprague Lake

Wheelchair accessible also means stroller accessible, and at Sprague Lake, the 0.5-mile, level trail and the vista of soaring peaks make for one pretty family stroll. A level path leads from Glacier Basin Campground to the lake, or you can drive to the trailhead of the lake's loop. Along the circular route, kids can check out the transparent water, the fish that live in the lake, the marshes that border the pond, and the scenic, jagged, mountainous backdrop. A self-guided nature trail helps families understand and appreciate what they are seeing, and picnic tables offer a place to eat. A livery is there if your family wants to take a horseback ride.

Kids examine natural wonders from the boardwalk at Sprague Lake.

Moraine Park Museum

Big picture windows on the second floor of the historic log building that houses the museum frame a scene that looks like a living Bierstadt painting. When a summer snowstorm blows through or afternoon showers dampen spirits, the view is made all the more lovely by the warm, stout walls that provide escape from the elements. An excellent educational stop anytime, the Moraine Park Museum is a perfect port for families caught in a mountain storm.

Interactive exhibits help kids understand the geological and biological processes that created the view outside the windows and a small gift shop and bookstore sell guide-books and souvenirs. The museum also has restrooms. When the weather clears, a nature trail, just over 0.5 mile in length, winds through the montane forest behind the museum. Benches along the path offer a place to rest and take in the scenery.

Longs Peak

The highest point in Rocky Mountain National Park, Longs Peak is an icon for the park and for Colorado as well. About 10,000 people summit the 14,259-foot peak every year, and many more attempt it, but never make it all the way. The Keyhole Route is a nontechnical climb on nice days, but still extremely challenging. It has sections where climbers must traverse a narrow ledge exposed to a lethal drop. Passable in dry weather, it is dangerous when snowy, icy, or wet. In any weather, the 16-mile, round-trip with an elevation gain (and descent again) of 4,850 feet is a grunt even for very fit climbers. Check out the park service brochure on climbing Longs Peak and get advice from a ranger if you have such lofty aspirations.

Wild Basin

Place names in Wild Basin suggest that this area, tucked into the southeast corner of the park, is a great spot for bird watching. And it is true that Ouzel Creek is full of the chubby gray birds that have a habit of diving into waterfalls. But Pipit, Junco, Bluebird, Ouzel, and Finch Lakes offer much more than feathery wildlife viewing. Easy and moderate trails meander through forests and over brooks beneath the 13,176-foot crags of Copeland Mountain. Here streams and ponds are full of the native greenback cutthroat trout, which once teetered on the edge of disappearing from our world.

Great for family hiking any time of year, in the winter, cross-country skiers and snow-shoers soak in the frosty air and Wild Basin scenery as well.

Kawuneeche Visitor Center

Located at the west entrance of Rocky Mountain National Park, the Kawuneeche Visitor Center helps families orient themselves to the park and to plan their trip. A large relief map provides an overview of the mountains and valleys in the park, while exhibits help explain the geology and wildlife of the area. Cultural displays show how people have interacted with the landscape here over the years. Visitors settle into comfy auditorium seats for two excellent orientation films. One of the films, titled "Colorado Secrets of the Source," is 50 minutes long and shows daily at 1:15 p.m.

Trail Ridge Road offers an unparalleled view of Longs Peak.

Its outstanding wildlife photography, including footage of kingfishers and dippers diving into and "flying" underwater, captivates and thrills viewers. The slow-motion sequence of a mountain lion chasing a hare through the snow had my kids on the edge of their seats. Rangers and volunteers at the information desk help you find answers and plan your visit. In the auditorium, ranger talks are held on Saturday evenings during the summer. Accessible restrooms, drinking water, and a small bookshop are also available.

Holzwarth Historic Site

A historic guest ranch, the Holzwarth Historic Site gives visitors a feel for life in the Kawuneeche Valley at the turn of the 20th century. Walk the level, stroller-friendly, 0.5-mile trail from the parking lot to the old log buildings and ranch implements. Short, volunteer-run orientation tours are held throughout the summer. A historic taxidermy shop on the premises shows kids how they make those deer heads that stick out from the top of fancy lodge walls. Pick up a brochure at the Kawuneeche Visitor Center and read the interpretive signs at the site. On the way back to the car, stop on the bridge that crosses the Colorado River, still a small creek at this point. It offers a unique perspective of this deep glacier-dug trough in the earth's crust that is the Kawuneeche Valley.

Programs and Activities

Ranger walks and talks abound in Rocky Mountain National Park. Pick up the park newspaper, the *High Country Headlines*, to check out schedules. A handy chart outlines ranger walk length, difficulty, topics, location, and times. Saturday evening talks, called lyceum presentations, are also outlined.

Evening campfire talks at Glacier Basin, Moraine Park, and Timber Creek Campground amphitheaters are conducted from Memorial Day weekend through the end of Labor Day weekend. Lasting from 45 minutes to an hour, start times and days of the week vary. Check the park newspaper for details.

Rocky Mountain Field Seminars, sponsored by the nonprofit Rocky Mountain Nature Association, use the park as a classroom and are conducted by experts on the subjects. Ask at the visitor centers for a free catalog or check out their website at www.rmna.org.

Teachers can visit www.heartoftherockies.net to learn about lesson plans, trip planning, and other educational opportunities in Rocky Mountain National Park. The website lists materials and contact information for a park educational coordinator.

Natural History

Geology: Soap

Way, *way* back when the earth was still pretty young, the continents looked nothing like they do today. About 1.7 billion years ago, a small piece of continental material called a craton was rafting around on the earth's crust in a process known as continental drift. The rocks that are now in Rocky Mountain National Park were formed on the edge of this craton when some islands bumped into it and began to grind under it. That set off volcanoes, which puffed material all over the surrounding area. The volcanic and sea sediments were pushed together and heated up so much that they turned into metamorphic rock.

About 1.4 billion years ago, another slow collision caused subsurface crust to melt and squeeze up into cracks on the new little continent's underside, forming granite intrusions.

Through the years this ancient rock floated nearly halfway around the globe, crunching with continents that rammed into one another and broke apart again. More than once collisions caused the ground to wrinkle up into mountains, only to be eroded nearly flat again by wind, water, and gravity.

Much more recently, about 72 million years ago, an intense period of mountain building began again, and the high ground of Rocky Mountain National Park rose up. Thick layers of sedimentary rock eroded away, to be deposited at the base of the mountains and out onto the plains. And the crust compressed the mountains until the old rock that once lay at the edge of the craton slid up along faults "like a wedge of soap squeezed between your hands," according to geologists Halka Chronic and

A HiKE FoR LiTTLE LEGS

More than 360 miles of trail wind through Rocky Mountain National Park, and the brochure they hand you at the entrance stations lists only a few. Check the park newspaper for a more complete listing or ask a ranger for suggestions. One of our favorites for trekking with the kids is the easy 0.9-mile Alberta Falls hike in the rugged Glacier Gorge area.

The lovely Beaver Meadows Ranger Walk is just one of many programs that are offered in Rocky Mountain National Park.

Felicie Williams. What once lay in the basement of the continent now juts 14,000 feet above sea level.

Just when the "soap" was slipping up between the "hands" of the continent, about 25 million years ago, volcanoes began to erupt in and near Rocky Mountain National Park as well. As you drive over Trail Ridge Road west of the Alpine Visitor Center, look for a large mountain northwest of the road, across the Poudre River valley. That's Specimen Mountain, a 12,489-foot high volcano. If you are observant, you'll see that its color differs from the granite and schist of the surrounding peaks. When it was active, it was likely much taller, but erosion and glaciers have taken their toll. Look for bands of light-colored volcanic ash in roadcuts near the Continental Divide. The Never Summer Mountains, guarding the west side of the Kawuneeche Valley, are volcanic as well.

The soaring heights of Rocky Mountain National Park affect the weather. Moist winds travel across the land until they bump into the slopes, where the air rises and slows down. With cooler temperatures and stalled winds, moisture drops out as rain or snow.

This extra water and the steepness of the terrain create rushing streams and rivers. The energy of the falling water digs out narrow, V-shaped valleys and deposits large alluvial fans at the edge of the mountains.

From time to time, the climate cooled, compounding this effect. Glaciers grew and then cut away at the mountains. Some geologists believe that the process, though hidden from our eyes, is still continuing today.

Starting twenty or thirty thousand years ago, during the most recent Ice Age, wind-driven snow built up on the east side of the peaks. When year after year more snow accumulated than melted, it turned to ice under its own weight. In some places, the snow and ice filled entire valleys to the brim, with only the highest peaks poking out of the ice caps surrounding them.

Eventually, some of the ice began to slowly groan its way down the mountainsides. As it flowed, it dragged giant boulders and tiny grains of dirt with it. These scraped against the ground, leaving long striations in the rocks and digging huge U-shaped valleys. The glaciers extended from the highest elevations down to about 8,000 feet above sea level, where they melted into rushing rivers of water. At their bottom-most reaches, along their sides, and sometimes down the middle when two glaciers came together, they piled up giant, long hills of debris. When a toddler pushes a plastic bulldozer through the dirt, he will pile up lines of sand in the same way.

The baby Colorado River flows through the Kawuneeche Valley.

The piles of debris are called moraines and can easily be seen around Moraine Park. The Moraine Park Museum sits on the flanks of 8,906-foot-tall Eagle Cliff Mountain, a moraine left at the base of a huge glacier. The steep, heavily forested slope to the south of Moraine Park is the South Lateral Moraine. When viewed from the sunroom of the museum, the size of the moraine helps children and their parents understand the magnitude of the ice rivers that once flowed through the area.

The high country on Trail Ridge Road, around Bear Lake, and along the Continental Divide toward Longs Peak provides textbook examples of several glacial features. Look for cirques, giant bowl-shaped depressions near the summits. Arêtes, the jagged, narrow ridges between cirques, often lead to a steep-sided pinnacle, or horn, where three or more cirques come together. Hanging valleys are troughs carved by small glaciers that were tributaries to larger ones; you can see the bottoms of hanging valleys emerging high up on large glacial valley walls. Numerous glacial tarns, or lakes, dot cirques along the east side of the high peaks. Forest Canyon and the Kawuneeche Valley are plunging, forest-filled gaps in the mountainous terrain. Their depths were dug in relatively straight lines not by the rivers that flow through them, but by colossal glaciers. The masses of ice could plow a direct path, instead of winding around as liquid water does.

Some evidence exists that deep ice, now covered by rocks, continues to flow downhill, carving away at the bedrock beneath it. One such possible rock glacier is the boulder field of Longs Peak.

Plants and Wildlife: Elderly Krummholz

These tough, old rocks—cracked and fractured by continental crashes, shoved high into the atmosphere, quarried by ice, and scoured by wind and water—make great places to settle down for all kinds of wild plants and animals. But as with any real-estate decision, it's a trick for wildlife to find just the right location. The extreme elevation changes of Rocky Mountain National Park create an array of choices. Plus, the bare rocks along the Continental Divide act as an effective barrier, and life differs significantly between the east and the west sides.

This far north on the earth, the prevailing winds come from the west. When they run into the high peaks of the Continental Divide, the air piles up like water being held behind a dam. As the pressure builds, air begins to spill over the mountains, rushing down the eastern slope in great gusts. The Estes Park side of Rocky Mountain National Park is much windier than the Kawuneeche side.

Because of this, moisture, mostly in the form of snow, tends to drop out in the relatively calm air on the western slopes. The Kawuneeche Valley receives as much as 10 inches more moisture each year than does the Estes Valley. Consequently, the forests reflect this difference with an absence of ponderosa pines and other, drier plants, such as prickly pear cactus that grow on the eastern side of the divide. The winters are colder on the Kawuneeche side, and moose and river otters inhabit the wetter areas in this region as well. The mountains are much more glaciated on the east, and temperatures tend to be warmer there.

Montane Life Zone

On any given day, the weather is likely to be warmer deep in the valleys of Rocky Mountain National Park than it is on the mountaintops. Here, in the montane neighborhood, between 5,600 and 9,500 feet above sea level, Douglas fir and lodgepole pine trees dominate along with aspen trees in more recently disturbed areas and ponderosa pines on the drier, southern slopes. The forests are interspersed with junipers. Kinnikinnick and antelope bitterbrush provide food for deer to browse upon, while wax currants are yummy for black bears. Oregon grapes grow in the shade of taller trees and offer berries, too. Big sagebrush grows on sunnier, drier slopes, along with grasses beneath the ponderosas. Grasses and sedges also fill open areas, such as the bottom of the Kawuneeche Valley and Moraine and Horseshoe Parks. Look for mountain muhly, spike fescue, needle-and-thread grass, and blue grama grass. Prickly pear and mountain ball cactus grow on south-facing slopes on the east side of the park, and the latter have pretty pink flowers with a rose fragrance—but don't sniff too closely!

Penstemon are common in the montane life zone.

Wildflowers in the montane zone bloom in the summer and put on a pretty show for visitors. Drier exposures have bright yellow sulphur flowers, plus whiskbroom parsley and gumweed clusters, and the tall, pale stalks of the miner's candle reaching for the sun. Penstemon varieties with their stems of blue and sometimes pink blossoms scatter across the slopes, as do varieties of daisy and wild geraniums. Look for delicate sego lilies in the meadows and try to spot the Colorado State Flower, the blue columbine, in moist areas on north-facing slopes.

Visitors are likely to see swallowtail butterflies as well as bumblebees dancing among the flowers. Pine beetles are not particularly visible, but they are busy munching away under the bark of some of the lodgepole and ponderosa pine trees. Marshy and streamside areas, especially in treeless Moraine Park and Horseshoe Park, are home to many aquatic and semiaquatic insects such as mosquitoes, stoneflies, mayflies, and caddis flies. These, in turn, are tasty treats for the park's few amphibians, including tiger salamanders, boreal toads, and chorus frogs.

Some amphibians in Rocky Mountain National Park are in trouble. In spite of the acreage set aside, and the relative infrequency of human visitation to much of the park, populations of boreal toads have seen serious declines. And although they have been searching high and low, scientists have lost track of the northern leopard frogs, a species that seems to have disappeared altogether from the park.

Aquatic insects serve as groceries for the fish found in the park's waters. Colorado cutthroat trout swim in the streams of the Kawuneeche Valley, while greenback cutthroat trout inhabit the east side. Rainbow, brown, and brook trout offer competition to the native cutthroat species. However, biologists have been able to remove these

Hummingbird © Wendy Shattil/Bob Rozinski

non-native species from streams that have a natural barrier, such as a waterfall, which creates an effective separation from downstream populations. In many creek sections, only the native cutthroat species swim around. In fact, Rocky Mountain National Park is a source of pure greenback cutthroat strains for reintroduction into other Colorado streams.

As the fish swim below, mallards commonly paddle around on the ponds' surfaces. Wilson's snipes and killdeer inhabit the lakeshores and wetlands. Watch for great horned owls in wooded riparian areas as well as northern flickers and tree swallows. Steller's jays, magpies, and mountain chickadees scold and twitter from the branches overhead, while broad-tailed hummingbirds perform their acrobatic displays throughout the summer. Pygmy and white-breasted nuthatches search tree trunks and branches for insects. Look for green-tailed towhees in grassier areas and mountain bluebirds in the aspen stands.

Some of the most obvious mammals in the park are the little chipmunks and the similar-looking golden-mantled ground squirrels that skitter around the campgrounds and scenic overlooks. As cute as they are, resist feeding them or any other animals. Food from people is bad for wild animals.

If you walk across a meadow, especially in moister areas along the streams, stop to brush aside the grass stalks and look for vole runs. Meadow voles look like little brown mice, without the big ears, and they cut miniature highways in the grass, close to the ground. That way, the leaning stalks hide them from predators as they run around foraging in the fields. Their cousins, the muskrats, also like moist meadowlands, and if you see them, they are likely to be swimming in a pond. Look for their side-to-side motion as they move through the water and build dens that look like smaller versions of a beaver's lodge. Porcupines, common in Rocky Mountain National Park, are also quite good swimmers—surprise!—but they prefer to spend their time in trees. So do Abert's squirrels, with their tufted ears. They are common in the montane forests of the east side of the park, but don't live on the west side.

The Kawuneeche Valley, west of the Continental Divide, is home to a population of moose, who until recently weren't found on the Estes Park side. However, their numbers seem to be increasing, and there may even be a permanent small group in the northeast quadrant of the park. Visitors are very likely to see moose in the flat meadows area between the Grand Lake entrance station and the Harbison Meadows Picnic Area. About once a year, visitors will send rangers a photo of a moose with twin calves. I hope the photographers use very long lenses to take the pictures—moose are notoriously cranky and wild. A mother protecting her babes from a perceived threat won't hesitate to stomp the threat into mush. If a moose looks at you, you are too close!

Bighorn sheep also range widely, coming down into the Kawuneeche Valley from the Never Summer Mountains and into the montane zone of Horseshoe Park during the summer months. In both places, mineral licks attract them. Researchers debate whether the licks provide the sheep with important nutrients, such as calcium for lactating ewes, or if they just taste good, since the rams slurp the ground there, too. Bighorns are some of the wildest of the park's animals, and can be extremely sensitive to even the remote presence of humans. Please respect closed areas.

Mountain lions will occasionally hunt for bighorn sheep, but are more likely to go after mule deer and elk. These ungulates are very common throughout the park at all elevations, depending on the season. Coyotes may take a sick or injured elk, and are predators of bighorn sheep as well. However, they are more likely to hunt rabbits, hares, woodrats, and other rodents. Other predators include long-tailed weasels, badgers, and bobcats, all of which prefer mice, squirrels, or bunnies for dinner.

Sometimes hunters, but more often scroungers, black bears roam through the montane and subalpine forests in Rocky Mountain National Park. As omnivores, they eat herbs, berries, roots, flowers, insects and their larvae, fish, small mammals, and birds. They seem to relish people food as well, which can endanger their health for a variety of reasons. This is bear country, so please pack your food and toiletries away in the car at night or when you are away from camp or cabin.

Endangered river otters were introduced to the Kawuneeche Valley in the 1980s. Sightings of these graceful animals are rare. They migrate up and down the Colorado River, in and out of the park, looking for the best swimming and fishing opportunities. Recent counts seem to show that their numbers are declining, but whether that is due to drought and lower water levels or other factors is still the subject of study.

Subalpine Life Zone

From around 9,000 feet above sea level to timberline, the trees of the subalpine life zone dominate. Here, where the winters are colder and the snowpack is heavier, Engelmann spruce, subalpine fir, and some limber pine trees cover the slopes, while lodgepole pines fill in disturbed areas. At this elevation, potentilla shrubs and wild roses bloom in sun or dappled shade, while myrtle blueberries grow commonly in the shade of spruce trees. Look also for wax currants and elderberries.

Cousins of the elderberry, twinflowers are only slightly woody, growing in a mat along the ground, with sets of two pink or white flowers sticking up. Nearby, lupines send up spikes of blue flowers on hillsides and in meadows. Different arnica varieties may be found from dry forests to wet meadows, along with the lovely and quite common blue Colorado columbines. In wet meadows, you'll find deep pink spikes of flowers that, when examined closely, look like tiny elephant heads, known as elephantella. They may be joined by the pretty, purple-fringed gentians. In the cool shade of deep forest pockets, look for the inside-out pink blossoms of the pipsissewa. Here, where the soil is very moist, you may be lucky enough to find an endangered orchid, the fairy slipper. Spectacular displays of subalpine wildflowers peak in July.

As you hike along the mountain rivulets in the subalpine zone, watch for water ouzels and belted kingfishers diving into the stream for their lunch. Red-naped sapsuckers, red-breasted nuthatches, and brown creepers rest on tree branches and trunks, while gray jays, also known as camp robbers, look for opportunities to steal hikers' snacks. Watch

Porcupine © Wendy Shattil/Bob Rozinski

also for mountain chickadees, ruby-crowned kinglets, and yellow-rumped warblers. Clark's nutcrackers will venture all the way up to the very edges of timberline, and are sometimes seen in the krummholz there.

Most of the mammals found in the lower, montane zone also wander through the subalpine ecosystem. Additionally, watch for pine martens, weasel-like animals hunting in the trees, and one of their favorite foods, the chickaree, or pine squirrel, scolding passersby. Furry, yellow-bellied marmots waddle along the ground, while cottontails and hares turn into statues in the underbrush, only to hop away suddenly when you get too close.

Alpine Tundra Life Zone

About one-third of Rocky Mountain National Park lies at altitudes higher than 11,000 or 11,500 feet above sea level, where trees stop growing. As you gain elevation, the forests become shorter and sparser. Eventually, there is more open ground than trees, and what trees there are grow not up, but sideways. They do this to escape the extreme winter winds by huddling beneath the snowpack in winter. As they grow, the branches that come close to the ground put down roots. Known as krummholz, some of these plants become quite elderly, as much as 1,000 years old!

Above the krummholz, the only shrubs are willows, hunkering in drainages. Between the rocks, however, a community grows, filled with plants as pretty, tough, and fragile as china teacups.

Among a variety of grasses, cushion plants bloom in low masses near the ground. Their short stature and rounded shapes allow them to shed the cold wind. Many of them have a purplish cast to their leaves, imparted by chemicals called anthocyanins. These chemicals, which give red cabbage its purple color, darken the foliage of alpine plants, allowing them to absorb just a little more heat from the sun. With the added energy, the flowers can move their life processes along a bit more quickly, and hopefully complete a blooming-pollinating-seeding sequence in the very short growing season at this altitude.

In addition to being crafty, the alpine tundra flowers delight with their delicate shapes and bright colors. Some of the most common are the bistorts as well as the alpine forget-me-nots. Look for the yellow blossoms of the alpine avens, whose foliage turns deep red in autumn, and pink-blooming moss campion. Marsh marigolds and snow buttercups do well in the frigid waters melting from snowbanks or soaking the ground in boggy areas.

Pika © Wendy Shattil/Bob Rozinski

Look for white-tailed ptarmigans running year-round among the rocks and krummholz above treeline, changing their plumage to match the season. Horned larks, with their distinctive black mustaches, nest in the tundra during the summer and flock to the lower grasslands in the wintertime. Birders may see American pipits on the tundra, but these little brown birds nesting among the cushion plants usually are not noticed by most people.

Many of the mammals that prowl the lower elevations venture into the tundra in the warmer months. These include chipmunks, ground squirrels, marmots, coyotes, red foxes, weasels, bobcats, elk, and bighorn sheep, among others. Above timberline, it is especially easy to spot the work of pocket gophers, which dig up the soil, leaving long mounds of dirt behind as they plow across the landscape. Cute little pikas live their lives in alpine scree fields. They zip around all summer, clipping grasses and stashing them under the rocks. The grass dries like hay, providing food all winter beneath the snowpack. If you go on an alpine hike, listen for their distinctive "Eee!" calls. If you practice, you can make the sound, too, and sometimes they will talk back to you.

Human History

Tundra plants are tough enough to withstand intense ultraviolet radiation and extreme cold, but they just can't handle it when a lot of people step on them. And they take a long time to recover when a trail is worn through. In fact, the hint of an old Ute trail is still visible off of Trail Ridge Road, long after it was abandoned.

Clovis points, the earliest stone projectile points used by Paleo-Indian people, suggest that people have been hunting in the park for as many as 12,000 years. A half-dozen of the projectiles have been found on the surface in the mountain passes. Dating of the points shows that people ventured into the high country on the heels of retreating glaciers at the end of the Ice Age.

Early people left abundant evidence of their hunts. Mt. Albion projectile points and stony remnants of game drives 6,000 to 7,000 years old suggest that people retreated to the mountains during periods of drought on the plains. The Flattop Mountain game drive site has low rock walls and stone hunting blinds. The walls were used to herd or funnel the animals together, while people drove them from behind. At the end of the walls, hunters hiding downwind behind the blinds would ambush the animals, killing several at one time.

In spite of the ingenious methods for capturing game, the ancient people left no evidence that they wintered in the high country. For that matter, very few animals spend the cold months at high altitude, or even in the Kawuneeche Valley. It is likely that the people followed the game to Middle Park.

The Ute (or a linguistically related people) used the resources in what is now Rocky Mountain National Park since those archaic times. More recently, Apache ceramics from around AD 1500 appeared in the area, and the Arapaho people arrived around 1800. Several place names in the park bear Arapaho names, including the Kawuneeche Valley, the Tonahutu Creek and Valley, and Onahu Creek and Trail. In the Arapaho's language, *Tonahutu* means "big meadows" and *Onahu* means "one who warms himself by a fire" and refers to a horse with that habit. The Upper Beaver Meadows area bears the remains of a battle between the Apache and the Arapaho that lasted for three or four days in about 1838.

Although the highest peak in Rocky Mountain National Park bears his name, Stephen Long and his 1820 expedition never ventured closer than about where Denver is now. From there, he turned south and three members of his expedition climbed Pikes Peak. (Zebulon Pike never climbed the mountain named after him, either.)

Although mountain men hunted, trapped, and traded in the area, the first recorded European-American settlers came in 1859. Joel Estes and Milton, his son, ventured into the valley of the Big Thompson River below Lumpy Ridge that year, bringing the rest of the family back the next summer to settle. William Byers, of the *Rocky Mountain News*, was the first to refer to the place as Estes Park.

The Estes family found ranching there to be too hard, and sold their claim. Their cabin was used to shelter guests, foreshadowing the industry that was to become the main livelihood for most of the valley's residents.

The breathtaking scenery around Nymph Lake leaves nothing to be desired.

The scenery attracted adventurous tourists and hoteliers to cater to their needs. By 1874, a stage line ran from Longmont to Estes Park. In 1909, Stanley Steamer inventor F. O. Stanley built the Stanley Hotel, and promoted auto touring in the Fall River area.

The second half of the 19th century saw several gold and silver strikes throughout the Colorado Rockies. The mineral wealth sent waves of prospectors into the mountains looking to strike it rich. Miners built as many as 40 mines on the east side of the park and 10 on the west side. Lulu City and Gaskill sprung up to support the miners, but busted quickly enough when the mines did not strike enough color to pay.

Towns and ranches on the west side of the park found income in tourism after mining's bust. Visitors ventured into the valley to hunt, fish, and recreate at dude ranches in the area.

Even as tourism increased and was encouraged, residents of the valley began to see the need to protect the natural landscape from growth. In the early 20th century, the Estes Park Protective and Improvement Association was established. In 1909, Enos Mills, a local lodge owner and guide, proposed national park status for the area. He wrote, spoke, and lobbied in favor of a huge national park that would cover more than 1,000 square miles. In 1915, President Woodrow Wilson did sign the bill designating Rocky Mountain National Park, although it encompassed only 358 square miles at the time.

Since then, the park has added acreage, and in 1976 it received status as a Biosphere Reserve from the United Nations. Trail Ridge Road was designated an All-American Road and National Scenic Byway in 1996, and status as a Globally Important Bird Area was conferred upon the park in 2000.

Restaurants and Picnic Areas

The **Trailhead Restaurant,** located next to the Fall River Visitor Center, offers sit-down dining for breakfast, lunch, and dinner. Large windows look out at the forest-covered valley of Fall River, while the décor inside features heavy log beams and snowshoe lamp sconces. Carved wooden bears, plush cuddly moose, and antler lamps from the gift shop encroach on the dining room. Outside, tables embedded with colorful tiles featuring hummingbirds, moose, and cabins offer fresh-air dining on nice days. Quiet guitar and nature-sounds music plays in the background. The menu offers American fare, with game meat selections including bison meatloaf and a savory elk stew served in a sourdough bread bowl.

The **Trail Ridge Snack Bar,** adjacent to the Alpine Visitor Center on Trail Ridge Road, hangs over a steep glacial cirque. Views from the giant picture windows bring the bare, jagged mountains above timberline into the building. A long line forms during lunch-time in the summer, as folks order chili dogs, nachos, vegetable beef soup, barbecue pork sandwiches, and smoothies. One young visitor pronounced his macaroni and cheese to be "Great!" Plan to eat early or eat late if you want to get a table.

On the official park map, 17 icons indicate locations of designated **picnic areas** within Rocky Mountain National Park. Many, but not all, have fire pits or grills and vault toilets associated with them. Additionally, picnic tables sit just off the roadways here and there throughout the park. Some of the best meals, however, are spread on the surface of a glacier-scoured boulder or downed log, while hiking to yet another heart-stopping viewpoint.

Families can hike to Cub Lake right from the Moraine Park Campground.

Lodging and Camping

No hotel lodging is available within the boundaries of Rocky Mountain National Park. However, camping is huge here. Five established campgrounds host 590 sites altogether, in addition to 267 backcountry sites for backpackers.

Aspenglen, with 54 campsites, has tent pads, picnic tables, fire grates, vault toilets, and drinking water. Reservations are not accepted, and this first-come, first-serve campground fills up on weekends in summer and fall. Located just inside the Fall River entrance, ponderosa giants shade this campground. Rocky outcrops offer active munchkins hours of scrambling fun.

Moraine Park is the largest of Rocky Mountain National Park's campgrounds, with 247 sites. Although it is huge, the wide spacing and placement of the sites provides enough privacy and natural areas for campers. Views of Longs Peak improve the experience even more. When glaciers plowed through here long ago,

Rocky Mountain National Park's campgrounds offer a place to pitch your tent in the shadow of the Great Divide.

they pushed aside titanic piles of rubble, making great outdoor climbing gyms for campground kids. Drinking water is turned on in the summertime only. Flush or vault toilets, picnic tables, and fire grates are available to all campers. Reservations are accepted and recommended during the summer.

Glacier Basin campground sits at 8,600 feet above sea level and on the edge of a meadow that stretches below the rugged Continental Divide. The 150 sites accommodate both tents and RVs, but only tents are allowed in the 15 group-camping sites adjacent to the main campground. Every site has a picnic table and fire grate, and drinking water and flush toilets sit at convenient spots throughout the campground. Glacier Basin Campground is closed from mid-September through late spring.

Folks attempting to summit the park's highest point often use **Longs Peak Campground** at the base of the famous mountain. Its 26 sites are open only to tents, but picnic tables, drinking water (turned off in the winter), and vault toilets are provided.

Tucked in the depths of the Kawuneeche Valley, the **Timber Creek Campground** is surrounded by thick forests on the edge of ponds near the Colorado River. The peaks of the Never Summer Range rear up to the west, while the summits within Rocky Mountain National Park rear over the campsites from the east. The 98 sites have picnic tables, fire grates, and toilet facilities. Drinking water and a dump station are available, and you can buy firewood there in the summer. Water is turned off in the colder months, although the campground remains open.

Nearby Towns

Rocky Mountain National Park's eastern gateway community, **Estes Park,** runs right up against the federal boundary in some spots. The main business district lies less than 3 miles from the Beaver Meadows Visitor Center. With a year-round population of about 5,600 people, the town swells during the high season between Memorial Day and Labor Day.

With family activities ranging from horseback riding and miniature golf to a giant slide and aerial gondola rides, this is a city dedicated to entertaining tourists. Numerous restaurants offer anything from burgers and fries to fancy dining, although the atmosphere in most places is very casual. In fact, folks frequently eat as they stroll past the plentiful souvenir shops and T-shirt emporiums. The smell of caramel corn and saltwater taffy float along with the summer crowds. For a break from the commercial hustle, head out to Stanley Park, southwest of Lake Estes. There, you'll find ball fields, picnic shelters, a skate park, play areas, and a place to let your dog run and meet other pooches. Boarding kennels offer a hotel for your best friend if you plan to hike on any of the trails in the national park.

Estes Park has the capacity to shelter thousands of people in its lodges, cabins, rental condominiums, and hotels. Even so, on busy weekends it can be hard to find a room. Contact the local chamber of commerce for guidance and be sure to reserve a pillow ahead of time.

Clouds blow over Moraine Park on a chilly day.

The Estes Park Medical Center, located at the base of Prospect Mountain at 555 Prospect Avenue, has 24-hour emergency services and a family medical clinic. Two large grocery stores offer a place to stock up on necessities. For information about Estes Park and services available in the community, contact the Estes Park Convention and Visitors Bureau at 800-433-7837 or online at www.estesparkcvb.com, or the Estes Park Chamber of Commerce at 800-378-3708 or online at www.estesparkresort.com.

On the western side of Rocky Mountain National Park, the town of **Grand Lake** and its namesake tarn lie tucked in a notch in the park's boundary. The city limits run up against Rocky Mountain National Park, and the town is a little over 1 mile from the entrance station. Although its population is just shy of 450 people, Grand Lake offers a surprising variety of restaurants and lodging options. Here, as in Estes Park, expect a casual atmosphere. A small grocery/convenience store stocks essential foodstuffs and a few camping supplies. Lodging tends to be rustic,

The Never Summer Range of mountains is volcanic in origin.

with cabins and lodge rooms for rent. The town is built right up to the shores of Grand Lake, Colorado's largest natural lake. A huge glacier carved the Kawuneeche Valley to the north of Grand Lake, and the rubble pile it left when it retreated forms the lake's dam. Fishing and boating are popular summertime activities. To get more information, contact the chamber of commerce at 800-531-1019 or www.grandlakechamber.com.

Special Considerations for Families

Sunburn

The high elevations in Rocky Mountain National Park create problems families must prepare for. The thin air doesn't filter the sun's rays very well, so sunburn comes quickly and severely to those who aren't protected. Apply thick layers of heavy-duty sunblock often throughout the day and wear wide-brimmed hats. Sunglasses make eyes much more comfortable when checking out the scenery, especially if that scenery includes water, snow, or large expanses of exposed rocks.

Shortness of Breath

The thin air also delivers less oxygen to the body, so your lungs compensate by breathing more rapidly and more deeply. People often feel out of breath, even when simply walking across a parking lot. It takes a few days—up to three weeks—for your body to adjust to the altitude, and in the meantime you or your kids might experience such symptoms as shortness of breath, headaches, nausea, and fatigue. Listen to those symptoms and take it easy. Plan only short, easy walks for the first few days.

Dehydration

Dehydration often makes altitude sickness worse, and the high, dry air sucks the moisture right out of your body. Adults can drink a quart or more of water while hiking, and it still may not be enough. Encourage water drinking by adding a bit of flavored drink powder to water bottles. Adults should avoid consuming caffeine and alcohol, which can can cause symptoms to intensify.

Car Sickness

The high altitude plus the winding roads can bring on a nasty case of car sickness. At this writing, we have yet to drive over Trail Ridge Road without having a kid throw up at some point on the trip. You might want to act like an airline and keep a "sick sack" handy.

Cold

It's cold in Rocky Mountain National Park! You can find snow there 365 days a year. Even during high summer, on the warmest days, it is often sweater weather. Summer snow squalls are not unusual, and the wind above treeline is at least chilly. No matter when you visit, bring warm hats, mittens, and coats for the kids. If you are camping out, be prepared with good sleeping bags, long underwear, and fluffy socks.

Wildlife

Humans can't seem to resist the big eyes and twitchy little noses of woodland creatures, and they often feed them. It is a cruel thing to do. People food is bad for these wild animals, and frequently makes them quite sick. In addition, the extra calories allow more chipmunks to survive the summer than normally would, and the animals don't learn normal food gathering behaviors. This causes many to starve in the winter when visitors aren't there.

What Makes Rocky Mountain National Park Special

"I never felt so awestruck or insignificant!" said Cindi Hopwood of Augusta, Kansas, after traveling the Fall River Road. The sight of all those behemoth mountains, shoving and jostling each other to stretch the highest into the sky, can be almost overwhelming. It makes you feel kind of puny and grand at the same time. The experience never gets old—walking to a viewpoint or on a trail, gazing out over the vista, and letting the enormity and the beauty soak in.

NATIONAL PARK SERVICE PASSPORT STAMP

Bird's-Eye View: Ancient Details

About 20 miles southeast of Colorado's exact geographic center, and tucked beneath the western ramparts of Pikes Peak, lie the broad, grassy meadows and rolling forests of Florissant Fossil Beds. Not quite 6,000 acres in size, the area is mostly square.

Two roads divide the monument. County Road 1, also known as the Cripple Creek–Florissant Road, runs through its middle from north to south. County Road 42 (Lower Twin Rock Road) enters from the east and runs into the Cripple Creek–Florissant Road near the southern third of the monument. All of the hiking trails, as well as the picnic areas and the visitor center, are north or northeast of the intersection.

The landscape of the monument is relatively gentle, with low hills of mixed forests, meadowlands, and rock outcrops. North of the visitor center is a historic homestead with several log buildings and wagons. To the east, outside the monument, Pikes Peak stretches to 14,110 feet above sea level, about 5,000 feet higher than the fossil beds. Views of the massif dominate the eastern skyline. But the main attractions are the ancient animal and plant remains, uncovered with their tiniest details still intact. These beds are some of the richest fossil deposits in the world.

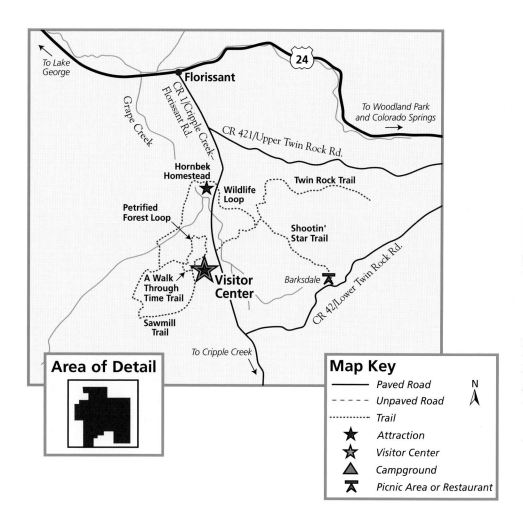

Area of Detail

Map Key

		N
———	Paved Road	⋏
- - - - -	Unpaved Road	
··········	Trail	
★	Attraction	
☆	Visitor Center	
▲	Campground	
⊼	Picnic Area or Restaurant	

Map labels:
To Lake George
Florissant
24
To Woodland Park and Colorado Springs
Grape Creek
CR 1/Cripple Creek–Florissant Rd.
CR 421/Upper Twin Rock Rd.
Hornbek Homestead
Wildlife Loop
Twin Rock Trail
Petrified Forest Loop
Shootin' Star Trail
A Walk Through Time Trail
Visitor Center
Barksdale
CR 42/Lower Twin Rock Rd.
Sawmill Trail
To Cripple Creek

Attractions

Visitor Center

Offering information for visitors and a museum devoted to the fossil history of the area, the visitor center is a necessary first stop. Housed in a historic farmhouse, this is where you will find rangers to answer your questions and help you plan your visit. Wall displays and a collection of fossils help kids understand what life was like here 35 million years ago—and what happens when you live 18 miles from a lively volcano. A bookstore sells maps, posters, postcards, books, and other items. The building also has restrooms.

A Walk Through Time Trail

Parts of this 0.5-mile loop trail are badly eroded and uneven, yet it is still a good choice for young hikers. The path leads behind the visitor center, past huge petrified sequoia stumps, and through a montane forest. For those wanting a self-guided tour, booklets available in the visitor center explain features along the route.

Hornbek Homestead

In the late 1870s, Adeline Hornbek and her family homesteaded this beautiful mountain valley. Eventually they developed a prosperous ranch, rich with livestock, including large herds of horses and cattle. Families can view the Hornbek home and root cellar, plus some outbuildings and ranch equipment while learning about life here in the 19th century. Twice a year, once in the summer and once in December, the homestead hosts an open house with interpreters in period costume teaching visitors about the historic site. Pick up a self-guided tour brochure at the visitor center to help interpret the homestead if you walk around it when the buildings are closed. Or check the schedule in the summer to see if a ranger will be leading a tour there.

Adeline Hornbek's homestead is an important piece of Colorado history.

OUR EXPERIENCE: COLORADO SEQUOIAS?

Were our whole family to hold hands and stretch out, we would not be able to reach even halfway around one of these giant trees. Their massive trunks rear up from the ground like silent monuments to virgin forests.

And monuments are all they are. When they grew, Colorado was a much warmer and more humid place. Their species, *Sequoia affinis*, is now extinct. All that remain are colossal stones, shaped and textured exactly like the trees that once thrived in those very spots.

Wasps, birds, ferns, palm leaves, butterflies, spiders, even a marsupial—all were neighbors of the giant sequoias, and all turned to stone after being smothered by ash from a nearby volcanic eruption. Today, those stones emerge into the sunlight amid the scenery of Florissant Fossil Beds National Monument, one of the best fossil sites in the world.

Stumps are all that is left of giant sequoia trees that once grew in Colorado.

Sawmill Trail

One of the loveliest trails through Florissant Fossil Beds National Monument, this 2.2-mile loop starts at the visitor center. It leads past intermittent streams and through montane forests full of birds, only to emerge in wildflower-decorated meadows. As it tops wavy hills, visitors are greeted with surprise views of Pikes Peak. A single-track dirt path, the park service designates it a moderate hike.

Petrified Forest Loop

Walk with your kids on this 1.4-mile loop, which is partially stroller and wheelchair accessible, across meadows that were once an ancient lakebed. Numbered stops correspond to points of interest along the trail. A matching booklet helps families understand how volcanoes killed thousands of birds, butterflies, spiders, mammals, fish, trees, and herbs. The path then wanders past their remains and the booklet explains how they turned into fossils. Be sure to stop and ponder Big Stump. It is all that is left of a gigantic sequoia tree that once lived with its buddies along the lakeshore until the volcano got them all.

Programs and Activities

Ranger walks are offered daily during the summer months. They usually last about one hour and follow the Petrified Forest Trail. See the schedule in the visitor center for details.

Ranger talks are held in the amphitheater during the summer and cover the natural history and other topics of interest about Florissant Fossil Beds. They last about 20 minutes and are held hourly. Check in the visitor center for times.

Junior Ranger booklets are available at the visitor center. Activities for kids ages 5 and up include word searches, mazes, word jumbles, and picture drawing to help kids understand nature's processes within the monument.

Teacher resources, which correspond to Colorado curriculum guidelines, are available online for local schoolteachers who are interested in taking their classes to the monument for field trips. Check the monument website for more details.

Florissant Fossil Beds is full of grassy meadows.

Florissant Fossil Beds National Monument at a Glance

Location: Central Colorado, 35 miles west of Colorado Springs

Address: P.O. Box 185, Florissant, CO 80816-0185

Telephone: 719-748-3253

Website: www.nps.gov/flfo

Size: 5,998 acres

Elevation: From 8,200 to 8,920 feet above sea level

Major Activities: Fossils, hiking, historic pioneer homestead, picnicking, and bird-watching

Weather: Summer highs average 78 degrees and lows average 41; afternoon thunderstorms with lightning are common; winter temperatures average in the high 30s by day, dropping into the single digits at night.

Best Seasons: Summer and early fall

Hours: The visitor center is open from 9 a.m. to 5 p.m. year-round.

Closures: The monument is closed Thanksgiving, Christmas, and New Year's Days.

Cost: Fees are $3 per adult (good for seven days) with no fee for children 15 and younger. An annual pass is $15.

Facilities: The monument's visitor center is open year-round, and offers a good introduction to the fossils. Interpretive displays and preserved fossil specimens in the museum help visitors understand the processes that formed the unusual pieces. The monument's only ranger station is in the visitor center. Also located there is a fine gift shop and bookstore, with a good selection of books on Colorado's natural history. Restrooms at the visitor center do not have diaper-changing stations. The Barksdale Picnic Area is equipped with vault toilets.

Accessibility: The visitor center and its restrooms are mostly wheelchair accessible.

On the ranger walks, rangers explain how volcanic debris covered the forests and lakes.

A HiKE FoR
LiTTLE LEGS

A handful of trails wander through Florissant Fossil Beds National Monument. Check the website for descriptions or ask a ranger for suggestions. Labeled as moderate for the area, the Shootin' Star Trail starts at the pleasant Barksdale Picnic Area, crosses a chatty little creek, and heads through meadows and forests. Families can venture as far as they like before turning back, or hike the entire 2.2-mile length (one way) to the visitor center.

A fossilized sequoia stump shelters plants along the Petrified Forest Loop Trail. It looks like a regular tree stump, but it is huge and is made of solid rock.

Natural History

Geology: Ashy Slop

Thirty-five million years ago, when this part of the world was much warmer and wetter, a local volcano began to erupt. Ash and pumice blew from deep inside the earth. It mixed with rain and perhaps snowmelt, creating giant mudflows, called lahars, that ran across a mountain valley and inundated a sequoia forest. The volcanic debris also dammed the stream flow in the valley, making a lake. Shaped like a slice of moon, the lake eventually reached 12 miles long. At its widest, it was 2 miles across.

Life thrived along the shores and in the waters of the lake. As plants and animals died, they fell into the lake or were carried there by wind and water, settling to the bottom. When the volcanoes erupted again, the wind spread ash over the lake. This, too, settled on the lake bottom, covering plant and animal bodies, preserving them. Layer upon layer of clay, ash, and dead bodies built up this way and eventually hardened into a rock called shale. Although the plant and animal bodies decayed to a point, some of their original carbon was left, creating very detailed fossils.

When the eruptions sent ash falls and mudflows into the forests at the edge of the lake, smaller trees and brush were covered or knocked down, but the giant sequoia trees were tall enough and strong enough to withstand the onslaught. A silica-rich ashy slop buried the bottom of their trunks and eventually hardened into a volcanic mudstone.

Through the years, more sediment was deposited on top of the mud and ash, and all that weight hardened the soft layers into shale. Ground water seeped through the shale and mudstone, picking up silica and then depositing silica minerals in the cells of the dead plants and animals, turning their bodies into fossils. Silica from the ash surrounding the fallen trees and sequoia trunks seeped into the wood, cell by cell, turning the trees to stone.

At the Hornbek Homestead, interpreters in period costumes help kids learn about pioneer life.

Eventually the land under the old lakebed began to rise as the Rocky Mountains formed. When the ground lifted, layers of sediment eroded away and the shale and petrified wood came to the surface. Now, paleontologists search ancient stream deposits to find bones and teeth from mammals that once lived in the valley. Looking for leaf and insect fossils, the scientists split layers of shale to find the secrets hidden within.

Plants and Wildlife: Tassels

Today, as in times past, this valley is rich with wild-life. The montane ecosystem is dominated by the large ponderosa pine trees you see growing mostly on the south-facing slopes. If you snuggle up to one and breathe deep with your nose close to its sun-warmed bark, you are likely to smell a butterscotch or vanilla scent.

Other trees commonly found in the monument include Douglas fir and various spruce trees. Stands of aspen finger their way through the evergreen forests, adding a pale green contrast that turns spectacularly gold in the fall.

Bluebird
© Wendy Shattil/Bob Rozinski

The grassy meadows wave in the breeze with drifts of wildflowers, including blue flax (which open in the mornings), all kinds of asters, several varieties of penstemon, and paintbrush. In shady pockets, you may be lucky enough to find a pretty columbine blooming. We were lucky enough to visit on the last weekend in July, when the wildflowers were at their peak, bursting across the fields with brilliant color.

Florissant Fossil Beds National Monument treats bird-watchers with a large variety of mountain songsters. Look for the resident pine siskins flitting through the forest branches, and listen for the noisy call of the chipping sparrow. Dark-eyed juncos are also common. Brilliantly colored western tanagers breed in the forests, as do yellow-rumped warblers and hermit thrushes. Keep your eyes open for the gorgeous blue flash of both mountain and western bluebirds. Brown creepers and white-breasted and pygmy nuthatches all forage for bugs hiding in tree bark.

Gray and Steller's jays are likely to scold and hop greedily around any picnic, while their cousins, the crows and ravens, caw from the branches high overhead. Beautiful black-and-white magpies are often seen bouncing around in the meadows, looking for food. Various flycatchers, such as western wood pewees and olive-sided flycatchers, commonly breed in the monument. Look also for flickers and Williamson's sapsuckers.

Abert's squirrel © Wendy Shattil/Bob Rozinski

American kestrels, a type of falcon, hunt in the meadows while red-tailed hawks, turkey vultures, and golden eagles soar on the thermals above. Closer to the ground, look for several different kinds of squirrels, including chipmunks, golden-mantled ground squirrels, and the golden brown Richardson's ground squirrel. Abert's squirrels are often seen in the trees and can be identified by the tassels on the tops of their ears. Although they can be gray or reddish, in Florissant Fossil Beds

National Monument the squirrels are almost always black. If you hike through aspen forests, you are likely to see sign of porcupines, and you might spy one sleeping in the top of a tree. Beaver and muskrats have been known to swim in the streams in the monument and build their lodges here as well.

Cottontail rabbits are common around the visitor center, and jackrabbits have been sighted in the meadows. Both are considered a yummy dinner for the coyotes that often sing in or near the monument after dark. Red foxes roam the fields and forests in the area, too. Mountain lions have been seen, so keep your eyes open and hike in groups, with adults both in front of and behind the children. Occasionally, a black bear has been known to wander through the area.

Human History

Archaeologists have explored only about three dozen sites in Florissant Fossil Beds National Monument. Discoveries of projectile points, scrapers, knives, manos for grinding seeds, and hearths suggest the area has seen at least seasonal use for 8,000 years or more. Evidence points to late Paleo-Indians hunting now-extinct giant animals, transitioning to smaller game with the declining number of megafauna. They seemed to prefer camping in places with views of the surrounding countryside.

Historically, the central mountains of Colorado were Ute territory. There is some evidence that Arapaho, Jicarilla Apache, Comanche, and Kiowa people visited the area, as well. The Utes were organized in small groups that moved frequently, following game. Twenty-six ponderosa pine trees within the monument bear scars created when Utes peeled the bark for food, medicine, and other purposes. These trees are protected by the National Historic Preservation Act.

By the middle of the 1800s, the area was visited by mountain men, searching for furs. Gold prospectors and homesteaders soon followed. The first to stake a claim on what is now the national monument was the Reverend David P. Long. Arriving in 1873, he built a home and a school in the area he called the "petrified forest."

A year later, Arthur C. Peal, a geologist with the Hayden Expedition, wrote poetically of the scientific significance of the site. By 1883, a commercial quarry was established, selling fossils and pieces of the petrified forests. Through the years, commercial operations came and went, but the fossils themselves just went. Reports suggest that people removed entire petrified trees that had been lying horizontally with branches still attached. Whole stone tree trunks were taken far afield. Our family was surprised to find one on display in Disneyland in California.

A tree dubbed the Big Stump, however, stayed put, always defying efforts at removal and sometimes taking prisoners. A rusty saw blade still sticks out of a gap cut in this geological treasure. In 1920, owners of the second commercial quarry at the fossil beds built a pavilion and ticket booth. Today, it is used as the monument's visitor center and park service personnel refer to it as an old farmhouse.

In 1915, the National Park Service was aware that the fossil beds needed protection, but it wasn't until the 1960s that Congress took up the issue. For nearly a decade, action stalled—in fact, in 1969, developers were ready to bulldoze the area to build a housing development. Estella Leopold, daughter of the famous conservationist Aldo Leopold, Beatrice Willard, and others formed a citizens' group called The Defenders of Florissant. The group obtained a restraining order to stop construction. Finally, on August 20, 1969, shortly before the restraining order was set to expire, President Richard Nixon officially signed Florissant Fossil Beds National Monument into existence, protecting it for future generations.

Florissant Fossil Beds incorporated the Hornbek Homestead into the monument boundary in 1973. Under the Homestead Act of 1862, single mothers as heads of their households could claim land for homesteading. In 1878, Adeline Hornbek took the

Florissant's wildflowers, like this blue flax, rank among the most beautiful in the state.

opportunity to settle in the Florissant Valley. When she arrived, she had enough money to build a relatively large log house on her homestead. She and her family prospered, growing vegetables, cutting hay, and raising cattle. Today, visitors can tour Adeline Hornbek's homestead; pick up a pamphlet at the visitor center.

Restaurants and Picnic Areas

There are **no restaurants** within the monument. However, two **picnic areas** offer lunch spots with gorgeous views. Near the **visitor center** you'll find several tables with a vault toilet nearby. Drinking water and flush toilets are available at the visitor center. The **Barksdale Picnic Area** has tables and a vault toilet. Both of the picnic areas have charcoal grills.

Lodging and Camping

Florissant Fossil Beds National Monument is a day-use area only. **No hotel lodging or camping** is available inside the monument. However, several Forest Service campgrounds in the area have beautiful sites, and nearby Mueller State Park offers electrical hookups. Reservations are generally required to ensure a space. Florissant, Woodland Park, and Colorado Springs have a wide variety of hotels to choose from.

Nearby Towns

Tiny **Florissant,** less than 1 mile from the monument's northern boundary, is not much more than a crossroads with a convenience store, gas station, and restaurant.

Lake George, just 5 miles from the monument's north entrance, doesn't have any hotels or motels, but you can rent a cute little cabin with a kitchen for the night or a space for your RV at the Lake George Cabins and RV Park.

Woodland Park, with about 6,500 people, offers more: two grocery stores plus several gas stations, restaurants, and hotels. The Langstaff-Brown Urgent Care clinic on US 24, is open 9 a.m. to 9 p.m. daily, and provides comprehensive health-care services. Memorial Park, close to the center of town, has a playground, tennis courts, a pond, and picnic tables. The town is 15 miles east of Florissant Fossil Beds. Contact the Woodland Park Chamber of Commerce at www.woodlandparkchamber.com or 800-551-7886.

Special Considerations for Families

Located so close to Colorado Springs, Florissant Fossil Beds National Monument is an easy day trip from Denver. Temperatures can be cool, even during the summer, so it is a good idea to bring jackets and raingear. At over 8,200 feet, the sunlight can be intense. Put a hat, sunglasses, and sunblock on everyone in the family and bring lots of water to drink.

Note that, as with all sites in the national park system, it is illegal to remove anything from Florissant Fossil Beds National Monument. However, this area has a history of being severely exploited. With images of entire stone trees that once lay across the meadows tucked in your head, be especially careful about removing—or even moving—natural objects. Take care to avoid activities (such as trying to hold hands and reach all the way around a fossil redwood) that might damage them. You do not want to be what 19th-century paleontologist Samuel Scudder called a "vandal tourist"!

What Makes Florissant Fossil Beds National Monument Special

The London Museum of Natural History, the Smithsonian Institution, the Peabody Museum of Natural History at Yale University, the Museum of Comparative Zoology at Harvard University, the National Museums of Scotland, the Field Museum of Natural History, the Carnegie Museum of Natural History, the Denver Museum of Nature & Science, and several other esteemed institutions all house little pieces of Florissant Fossil Beds. More than 1,700 different species of plants and animals were caught in Florissant's ancient volcanic eruptions, and scientific publications have been talking about them for over 130 years.

But nothing beats being here. Kids feel a special excitement when they get to scuff their feet in cooled volcano emissions. The creatures caught in the catastrophe, frozen forever in the tiniest detail, catch the imagination of young explorers. And the trunks of extinct sequoias leave children in awe at their size and the power of the forces that killed them. These fossils leave families pondering the evidence of the humid, warm-temperate world that once existed on ground that now supports a dry montane life zone.

All in all, the fossils of Florissant are a puzzle—one that will keep your kids occupied all day long.

E N T R Y

NATIONAL PARK SERVICE PASSPORT STAMP

Bird's-Eye View: Hidden Heights

As the pointed Rockies slope down to the canyonlands of western Colorado, the Gunnison River digs a jagged trench deep into ancient bedrock. This is the Black Canyon of the Gunnison, so named for its dark metamorphic rocks and the shadows in its depths. It lies just off US 50, west of Gunnison and northeast of Montrose.

The park, split by the chasm, is divided into two parts, the North Rim and the South Rim. US 50 loops around the south side of the park, while CO 92 loops around to the north. To reach the North Rim area, you can leave US 50 at either the Blue Mesa Dam or at Delta, drive toward Crawford, and then branch off into the park from there. The North Rim Road is only partially paved and closed in winter. The turnoff to reach the South Rim is about 8 miles east of Montrose. Turn north on CO 347 and climb up toward the park through sagebrush-covered gray and yellow hills.

Views of the Uncompahgre Plateau lie to the west, and the West Elk Mountains rise up to the east of the park. To the south is the sweeping San Juan range. Small hills terrace down to the rim of Black Canyon, which drops 2,700 feet at its deepest point. At the Chasm View Overlook, kids love to wave to visitors on the other side, across only 1,100 feet of ravine that drops 1,800 feet between the two points. The spot isn't recommended for anyone with a fear of heights.

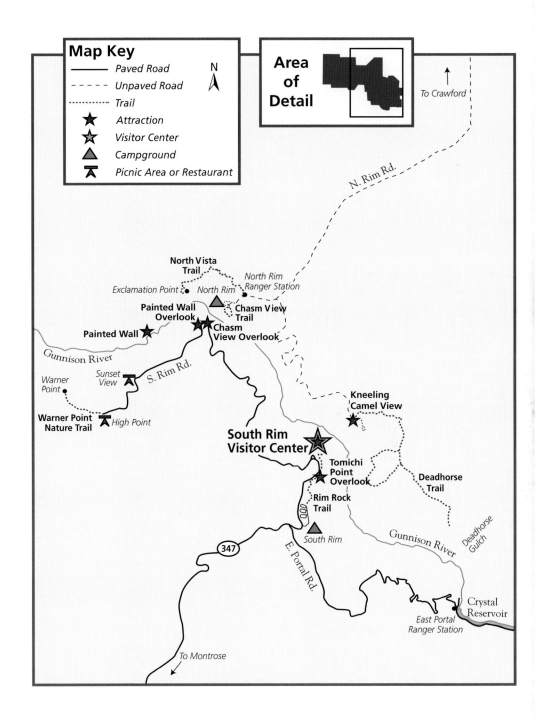

Map Key

—— Paved Road

- - - - Unpaved Road

· · · · · · Trail

★ Attraction

☆ Visitor Center

▲ Campground

⊼ Picnic Area or Restaurant

N

Area of Detail

To Crawford

N. Rim Rd.

North Vista Trail

Exclamation Point

North Rim

North Rim Ranger Station

Painted Wall Overlook

Chasm View Trail

Painted Wall

Chasm View Overlook

Gunnison River

Sunset View

S. Rim Rd.

Warner Point

Warner Point Nature Trail

High Point

Kneeling Camel View

South Rim Visitor Center

Tomichi Point Overlook

Deadhorse Trail

Rim Rock Trail

347

E. Portal Rd.

South Rim

Gunnison River

Deadhorse Gulch

Crystal Reservoir

East Portal Ranger Station

To Montrose

OUR EXPERIENCE:
THRILL WALKING

Freed from the stuffy confines of our tightly packed car, my 6-year-old and I ran down cement steps past the interpretive signs at Tomichi Point and stepped onto a trail. We passed through scrubby Gambel's oak trees and a fresh breeze filled our lungs. Then, to the right of the path, the ground dropped away to sheer nothingness, sucking the air right out of us. Describing the Black Canyon of the Gunnison as "breathtaking" is an understatement.

If we had tripped and fallen off the trail, we would have rolled to a stop before coming to the edge of the 1,000-foot cliff—but the idea was still terrifying enough to make us really watch our steps. Yet, with our feet firmly on the trail, the layered, convoluted view was thrillingly beautiful.

It's hard to take your eyes off Black Canyon of the Gunnison.

Opposite: Black Canyon of the Gunnison
© John Fielder

South Rim Attractions

South Rim Visitor Center

Perched on the canyon's edge, this building has great interpretive displays about the geology of the area and the wildlife that inhabits the canyon. A video describes the processes that formed the chasm and tells the story of human relationship to it. The visitor center also has a good-size bookstore with lots of kids' books, maps, and posters.

Outside, the porch offers a vista of the canyon with the Gunnison Point Trail and Overlook in the foreground. It's a good thing they sell extra film inside.

South Rim Road

The South Rim Road is pretty but not terribly scenic, as it winds through scrubby, rolling hills near the canyon. It does, however, feature plenty of turnouts. From these, short trails lead out to the brink of the precipice, where established overlooks offer guardrails and interpretive signs. At each overlook, the startling drop commands all your attention for a minute as the image of falling through all that space messes with your mind. Once you shake off that image, you can enjoy the information about the geology and biology the plaques have to offer. The jagged walls with the often-snowy mountains rising behind them create a beautiful panorama as well.

At Chasm View, the canyon is far deeper than it is wide.

Chasm View and Painted Wall Overlooks

These two overlooks, sitting right next to each other on the South Rim Road, are two of the most spectacular viewpoints in the park. The railing at Chasm View Overlook is a bit more substantial than that of Painted Wall Overlook, and the orientation allows you to see up part of the length of the canyon. Painted Wall, opposite the Painted Wall Overlook, is the tallest sheer cliff face in Colorado, rising 2,250 feet above the river. Long ago, light-colored igneous rock squeezed up into spaces in the dark metamorphic rock and hardened there, causing a striking pattern to appear that inspired the name.

Warner Point Nature Trail

Starting at the High Point Picnic Area, families can hike guidepost to guidepost, learning about the plants and animals along the edge of Black Canyon.

Black Canyon of the Gunnison National Park at a Glance

Location: On the western edge of the Rockies, between Gunnison and Montrose

Address: 102 Elk Creek, Gunnison, CO 81230

Telephone: 970-249-1914, ext. 423

Website: www.nps.gov/blca

Size: 32,950 acres

Elevation: From 5,500 to 9,040 feet above sea level

Major Activities: Sightseeing, photography, rock climbing, hiking, wildlife watching, and camping

Weather: Summer highs vary between 60 and 100 degrees, depending on where you are in the park (rim or canyon bottom); winter highs range from 20 to 40 degrees; brief afternoon thunderstorms are common in the summer.

Best Seasons: Summer and fall

Hours: The visitor center is open from 8 a.m. to 6 p.m. in the summer, and 8:30 a.m. to 4 p.m. the rest of the year. The roads through the park are always open.

Closures: The visitor center is closed Thanksgiving, Christmas, and New Year's Days. The North Rim Ranger Station and the East Portal Road are closed all winter. In the winter, the North Rim Road is closed and the South Rim Road is open only to the visitor center.

Cost: Entrance fees are $8 per car (good for seven days) and camping is $10 to $15 per day.

Facilities: The visitor center offers two different video presentations and exhibits describing canyon geology and life zones. Vault toilets are located at the visitor center, in both campgrounds, and at the High Point and Sunset View Picnic Areas. On the North Rim, the Kneeling Camel View turnaround area and the ranger station have vault toilets. We could find no diaper-changing stations at Black Canyon. Ranger stations are located on the North Rim, near the campground, and at the South Rim Visitor Center.

Accessibility: The visitor center and toilet facilities on the South Rim are all wheelchair accessible. The South Rim Campground has accessible campsites. Some of the overlooks are accessible there, as are the High Point and Sunset View Picnic Areas. On the North Rim, the restroom and one of the overlooks are wheelchair accessible.

"This is a great trail for families, especially for those who have younger kids," said Jennifer Mandel, Interpretive Park Ranger at Black Canyon of the Gunnison. "It is fairly well shaded and recommended even at midday." Designated as a moderate hike in the park's literature, the path is "undulating, with several sets of stairs—about eight steps each—and they are wide enough to walk side by side," she continued. "At the end, you have a 180-degree view, north into the canyon and south over the valley and beyond to the San Juans. It's just gorgeous."

Be sure to pick up a brochure at the visitor center first, as they may run out at the trailhead. This trail offers excellent bird-watching early in the morning, and it is not as exposed to the abyss as some of the other backcountry trails. Rangers still advise that you hold your children's hands at the overlook at the end of the trail, though. The hike to the Warner Point overlook and back is 1.5 miles long.

North Rim Attractions

North Rim Road

The gravel North Rim Road winds back and forth between tributary gulches, with pull-outs and views of the south side of the park. Unlike its counterpart across the gap, this road curves perilously close to oblivion. Drive with care, especially if the road is wet or snowy, as it could be slick. Be sure to stop at each and every pullout—they all offer awesome peeks at the canyon, each with a different but worthwhile perspective. If you can peel your eyes away from the plunging cliffs, interpretive signs offer fascinating explanations of the natural features that surround you.

North Vista Trail to Exclamation Point

A 3-mile round-trip, this undulating trail leads through scrubby forests and fairyland wildflower patches out to a highpoint over a bend in the river. All along the way, hikers are treated to glimpses of the chasm yawning off to the south. Signs will direct visitors to overlooks, but the cliff-top view spots have nothing to keep you from falling 2,000 feet into the river. No railings, no fences, nothing. On the North Vista Trail,

The North Vista Trail undulates along the North Rim.

like other backcountry trails in this park, either you have the good sense to stay away from the edge or you don't.

We picnicked at Exclamation Point, and were a little nervous during the entire meal. As parents, we were like cats at a mouse hole, keeping an eye on our kids, ages 7 and 4 at the time. The boys were nervous, too. Our older son picked a spot well back from the edge to sit and eat his sandwich, and our younger one joined him, saying, "I'm too young to go over there." We ended up spending over an hour at the overlook, scrambling through the woods, climbing rocks, and admiring the view from a distance.

Chasm View Trail

This short loop trail from the campground leads to a view of the canyon at its narrowest point. A similar overlook perches right across the way. You could admire the outfits worn by South Rim tourists if you wanted to, but an 1,800-foot-deep crack separates you, making it a bit awkward.

Although some parts of the trail are exposed to steep drops into empty space, the main overlook areas are well-fortified with chain link and concrete for visitor safety. The vista, especially of Painted Wall, is outstanding and it changes throughout the day with the light. This overlook merits frequent visits.

Deadhorse Trail

A 6.5-mile round-trip mostly along an old service road, the Deadhorse Trail is exposed to direct sun as it rolls through oak brush and open meadows. About 1.2 miles from the trailhead, a spur loops out to two informal viewpoints. With no railings to protect you from falling, the spectacle is both awesome and anxiety provoking. The Tomichi Point viewpoint is directly across the canyon.

After the spur loop rejoins the main trail, the hike continues on for about 1 mile to a barbed-wire stock fence, which climbs a small rise to overlook the river and Deadhorse Gulch, a large side drainage. From the end of the trail, you can see the East Portal area of Curecanti National Recreation Area and round mesa tops rising in the distance.

Programs and Activities

Campfire talks are held at the South Rim Campground amphitheater. They start at 9 p.m. and last about an hour. In the past, they have been held on Friday, Saturday, and Monday nights; check at the visitor center for an updated schedule.

Overlook ranger talks are held throughout the summer months at the various viewpoints along the canyon's South Rim. The visitor center has schedules that include times and topics.

Special programs with guest speakers are held from time to time during the summer. They are usually held in the evening and have included star talks with an astronomer, a bird talk with slides from an avian expert, and stories of scaling the canyon walls from Colorado climbing pioneers. Check online, in the *Montrose Press*, and at the visitor center for more information.

A HiKE FoR LiTTLE LEGS

Leaving from the campground, Rim Rock Trail meanders for 0.5 mile along the edge of the canyon to the Tomichi Point overlook. A pamphlet describes the geology of the area, helping kids understand what happened in the earth beneath their feet to cause this phenomenon. The scenery here is terrific. Leashed pets are allowed on this trail. Parents of younger kids will want to hold their hands or tuck them in a backpack baby carrier.

The Black Canyon's **Junior Ranger Program** includes a workbook with several activities that are appropriate for a variety of age groups. From coloring and dot-to-dot pictures to crosswords and role playing, they help kids and their parents understand the forces at work in Black Canyon of the Gunnison. When kids have completed their assigned activities, they can return to the South Rim Visitor Center or the ranger station on the North Rim, where a ranger will ask them about their work and award them a Junior Ranger badge for the park.

The park offers lesson plans and pre- and post-visit activities for their **educational outreach programs.** The pre-K through 12th grade Curriculum Enhancement Series adheres to National Teachers of Mathematics, National Science Teachers Association, and Colorado

Nature trails throughout the park help kids appreciate the rugged environment.

Content standards. Teachers can download the lesson plans from the Black Canyon website and call ahead to reserve a time for a field trip. Teachers can participate in continuing education classes, and the park has Elderhostel offerings as well.

Natural History

Geology: Mud Between Your Toes

Painted Wall shows the best example of metamorphic and igneous rocks your kids are likely to see in their entire lives. Made mostly of Precambrian gneiss, it is some of the oldest rock in Colorado. Geologists believe that, once upon a time, these rocks were mud, sand, and stuff from volcanoes, all buried by dirt. As time went on, and more and more

Northern flicker
© Wendy Shattil/Bob Rozinski

layers of rocks piled on top of the mud and sand and stuff, the mess turned into stones and even melted. They got mashed, leaned on, and bent all out of shape. When they hardened again they formed crystals, turning into gneiss. Magma—or super-hot liquid rock—squeezed into cracks in the gneiss like mud squishes up between your toes when you step in it. This magma cooled and hardened, too.

Then, about 65 million years ago, the whole area was pushed up very slowly. The top rocks were washed away by streams and rivers, and the gneiss, near the bottom of the pile, was exposed. Then, after the Gunnison River cut down through it, people could see all those gorgeous stripes and wiggly lines.

Because gneiss is very hard, when the river sliced through it, the sides didn't crumble and slide into big piles as sand would have. Instead, it stayed standing in pretty straight walls. That's why the Black Canyon of the Gunnison is so narrow, compared to its depth.

Plants and Wildlife: Deep–Knee Bends

Water-loving plants find homes in the bottom of the canyon near the Gunnison. Cottonwood trees, willows, river birches, chokecherry, and box elders grow here. Poison ivy up to 5 feet tall grows along the river in places. The trees create homes for insects that feed fish, including rainbow and German brown trout. Dipper birds, which dive into the stream and do quick deep–knee bends on water-splashed rocks, also feed on the insects. Other birds seen in the canyon bottom include yellow warblers and great horned owls. Beaver and mule deer also have been spotted along the Gunnison.

The steep canyon walls themselves are home to a few special creatures. The north-facing wall gets less direct sunlight, so it is damper than the south-facing wall. Because it has more water to freeze and thaw several times during the winter, the north-facing walls have more broken rock and soil than their counterparts across the gap. As a result, they are less steep and have more plants. The shade also allows snow to stay longer into the

Skunks © Wendy Shattil/Bob Rozinski

spring, watering trees such as the occasional stands of aspen and Douglas fir. Wildflowers and grasses also grow on the canyon walls, especially on the north-facing side.

Violet-green swallows and white-throated swifts swoop after bugs, and peregrine falcons hunt the smaller birds in the gorge. If you walk quietly and listen carefully, you may be lucky enough to hear the tumbling notes of the canyon wren's song, a sheer delight. Every once in a while, someone spots bighorn sheep scrambling around on the canyon sides.

The gentle hills and mesas of the canyon rim areas are mottled with stands of piñon and juniper trees, interspersed with scrub oak, sagebrush and serviceberry bushes. Wildflowers such as lupine also grow here. Mule deer are common, as are chipmunks, ground squirrels, rabbits, marmots, skunks, and bullsnakes. Once in a while, elk are spotted. Look for Steller's jays, flickers, mountain chickadees, western tanagers, and hairy woodpeckers. Cooper's hawks also feed on the smaller birds. Maybe you will be lucky enough to spot the bright blue flash of a rare mountain bluebird. Occasionally, a black bear wanders through the area, so keep your food, cooking gear, and toiletries packed away in the car.

Human History

Long before white people arrived, the area around the Black Canyon of the Gunnison was traveled and used by Tabeguache Utes. There is no evidence that the Utes ever visited the river bottoms, although signs of their activity on the rim areas have been found. Captain John W. Gunnison explored the area in 1853. He thought the canyon to be impenetrable.

At the turn of the 20th century, farmers in the Uncompahgre Valley were eyeing the Gunnison River for irrigation. Looking for a way to divert some of the flow out of the canyon, they sent a party floating down the river in 1900. After only a few weeks, the men climbed out of the canyon, averting what they felt would be a disaster if they continued on by water.

A year later and better prepared for the trip, William Torrence and Abraham Lincoln Fellows floated the Gunnison through the canyon on rubber mattresses. They found locations for building a tunnel to divert the water, and by 1909 the project was complete.

In the late 1920s and early 1930s, Reverend Mark Warner, among many other citizens in the Montrose area, worked hard for the area to be added to the National Park System. In 1933, they were successful, and Black Canyon of the Gunnison National Monument was created. In 1999, Congress designated it a national park. The area within the gorge itself is a national wilderness area. The land immediately downstream of the park was designated as the Gunnison Gorge National Conservation Area, and is administered by the Bureau of Land Management.

Restaurants and Picnic Areas

There are **no restaurant facilities** at Black Canyon of the Gunnison National Park.

The **High Point** and **Sunset View Picnic Areas** are west of the visitor center along the South Rim Road. Both have vault toilets and are wheelchair accessible.

Lodging and Camping

There is **no lodging** available at Black Canyon of the Gunnison National Park.

The **South Rim Campground,** at 8,320 feet above sea level, is a cluster of 88 sites tucked into scraggly, dense Gambel's oak forest. Loop A is open year-round while Loops B and C are closed in winter. Picnic tables, fire grills, and vault toilets are provided. Water is trucked in from Montrose and available from mid-May to mid-October. Electrical hookups are available in Loop B. Rigs longer than 35 feet are not recommended.

The much smaller **North Rim Campground** has only 13 sites. It fills up every weekend in May and early June with rock climbers coming to explore the vertical world and their own limits on the walls of Black Canyon. They are mostly a quiet, respectful crowd. Picnic tables and fire grills nestle in the shade of twisty juniper trees here. Drinking water is available in the campground from mid-May to mid-October. The maximum rig length is 35 feet.

Lupine are among the many wildflowers that bloom in the park.

Nearby Towns

Montrose is just 15 miles southwest of Black Canyon of the Gunnison National Park. It is a flat, spread-out agricultural community with some great amenities for families. The pretty Baldridge Community Park has a big, modern playground with huge shade trees and restrooms nearby, an in-line skate park, ball fields, a small lake with an island and gazebo, bike and walking trails, and a Frisbee golf course. The Aquatic Center features a large indoor pool and an outdoor pool with a big waterslide (open in the summer).

The town also has several restaurants. At The Backwoods Inn, they let our kids split a burger, but still loaded up each plate with fries and the fixings. It was plenty of food for our little ones and they only charged us for one kid's meal. Several chain hotels, many with their own swimming pools, are scattered through the town, especially on US 50. The Cedar Creek RV Park has a dump station. Montrose Memorial Hospital is located at 800 South Third Street. The new, 91,000-square-foot addition was completed in July of 2005.

The Montrose County Historical Museum, on the corner of Main and Rio Grande, is open mid-May through September, and is housed in a cool old depot building. Contact the Montrose Visitors and Convention Bureau at 800-873-0244 for more information.

Tiny **Crawford** is 15 miles northeast of the park, just north of Crawford Reservoir and Crawford State Park. The town features cute, renovated Victorian architecture and a few false fronts. The municipal park has a nice, big playground; hungry travelers can stop in at the Branding Iron restaurant; and a roadside kiosk offers information on the West Elk Historic and Scenic Byway. A trading post in town was not open when we passed through and the one gas station had burned down. We had to drive about 12 miles or so to Hotchkiss for groceries and gas.

Special Considerations for Families

Colorado mom Sue Hessler commented on her visit to the park with a 3-year-old, "We went to Black Canyon of the Gunnison, and boy, was that nerve-wracking! All those drop-offs. Brian isn't a wild kid, but he's not old enough to know the consequences of running up to the edge. It was pretty there, but I had to watch him so closely." It is hard to appreciate the view when you have to be hypervigilant of your children. But at Black Canyon, *you have to be* hypervigilant of your children.

Also, the canyon walls are a mecca for technical rock climbers. Several climbing routes snake up the walls right below viewpoints. Folks may be roped up and climbing a hundred feet below you, and because the walls are so steep and even overhanging in some spots, you might not even know the climbers are there. If you kick or roll rocks over the edge or throw rocks (even tiny ones) down into the canyon, you risk hitting a climber or his partner on belay, endangering their lives. Signs are everywhere, admonishing you not to throw rocks, and the park service is very serious about enforcing the rule. As tempting as it is for them, *do not allow your children to throw rocks into the canyon.*

What Makes Black Canyon of the Gunnison National Park Special

When I asked Supervisory Park Ranger and Interpretive Specialist Paul Zaenger what his favorite thing about Black Canyon of the Gunnison is, he responded, "Just one?" Clearly in love with the place, he enjoys going out in the evenings with his daughter for picnics—early mornings are another favorite time—to sit and watch the colors in the canyon. "Just sitting and listening and watching. There is a mental clearing that we don't get to do enough when we are so busy with things. It's good to just sit and be with a cool place."

The Gunnison Point Trail leads to an overlook just below the South Rim Visitor Center.

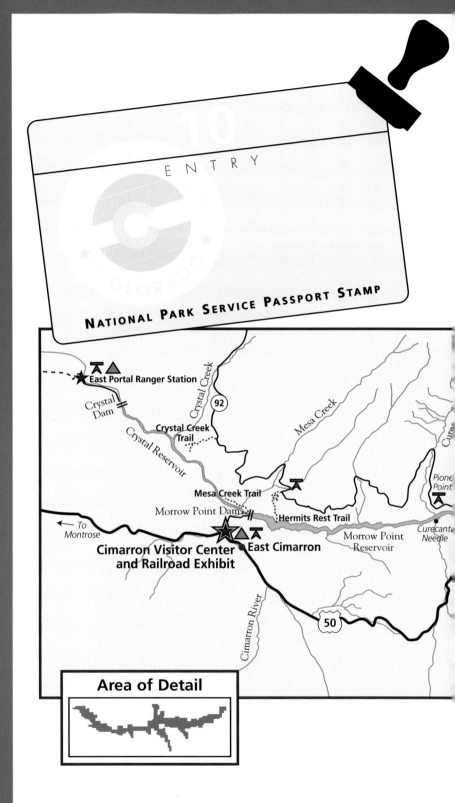

Curecanti National Recreation Area

ENTRY

NATIONAL PARK SERVICE PASSPORT STAMP

East Portal Ranger Station

Crystal Creek

92

Crystal Dam

Mesa Creek

Crystal Creek Trail

Crystal Reservoir

Pione Point

Mesa Creek Trail

Morrow Point Dam

Hermits Rest Trail

← To Montrose

Curecant Needle

Morrow Point Reservoir

Cimarron Visitor Center and Railroad Exhibit

East Cimarron

Cimarron River

50

Area of Detail

Bird's-Eye View: Three Reservoirs

About 200 miles southwest of Denver, on the western edge of the Rocky Mountains along US 50, the Curecanti National Recreation Area follows the path of the Gunnison River. Along that path, three dams hold back three reservoirs, each with their own topography and personality. At the eastern end, the largest reservoir, Blue Mesa, is also the largest body of water in Colorado. Long, thin Morrow Point Reservoir lies just downstream of the Blue Mesa Dam. At the western end, Crystal Reservoir fills a slice of space between the deepening walls of Black Canyon.

Cliffs and steep rock faces squeeze Crystal and Morrow Point Reservoirs for most of their length, while Blue Mesa Reservoir is able to spread into large basins, above. Where creeks enter these basins, the reservoir waters reach into side canyons with long, spidery arms. With more than a million visitors per year, Curecanti is one of Colorado's most popular playgrounds.

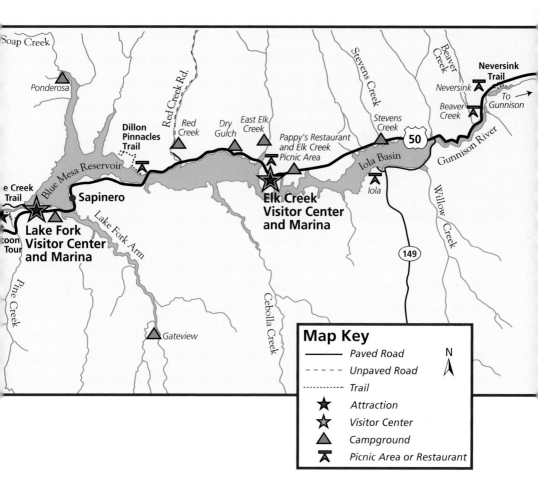

Eroded volcanic material forms dramatic cliffs near the Soap Creek arm of Blue Mesa Reservoir.

Attractions

Fishing

More visitors come to Curecanti to fish than for any other activity. More than three million fish are stocked into its three reservoirs each year. Species include kokanee salmon, rainbow trout, German trout, brook trout, and lake trout (mackinaw). Curecanti holds the Colorado records for rainbow trout, lake trout, and kokanee, the largest catch being a 46-pound, 12-ounce lake trout. According to the park service, fishing in the rivers, in the streams, and from the shores of the reservoirs can be very productive. The big lake trout like to hang out in the cold, deep underwater canyons of Blue Mesa Reservoir, so you must fish for them from a boat. Visitors can use their own gear or take a guided fishing tour from either the Elk Creek or Lake Fork Marina. A valid Colorado fishing license is required for all anglers over age 16. Buy a fishing license at the marina or a sporting goods store in nearby Gunnison. Check at the marina stores for limits and fishing and weather conditions.

Boating

Blue Mesa Reservoir is open to powerboats and sailboats during the ice-free months. The various watery arms that snake up into side canyons, plus campsites that are accessible only by boat, make this lake fun to explore. Water skiers also brave the reservoir's cold splashes in July and August, and several areas are ideal for windsurfing. Windy afternoon thunderstorms on the lake can make boating a challenge, but the views from the water are wide open and freeing.

Morrow Point Reservoir seems tailor-made for a canoe or sea kayak adventure. It can be accessed from the Pine Creek Trail. Here, boaters must carry their boat and gear down 232 steps leading into the canyon. A 1-mile foot trail rambles along the water's edge from the bottom of the stairs. However, you can put your boat in the water below the stairs a few hundred feet, depending on the water level. When water is being released

OUR EXPERiENCE:
FooLed Me

For years I have been whizzing through Curecanti in my car, bored stiff by the blur of sagebrush and flat water. I was snobby about those silly boaters out there, and how much better my three-day weekend had been in the spectacular high peaks or slickrock canyons. I am ashamed to admit it, but I only planned to spend time in Curecanti because I was researching this book. It seemed odd to me that it is the second-most visited national park unit in Colorado.

With my little spiral notebook tucked in the palm of my left hand and my camera bag open at my feet, for the first time I really looked at Curecanti as we drove west from Gunnison over Memorial Day weekend. I opened the car window to smell and feel it.

The Neversink Picnic Area and trailhead startled me. We were in Curecanti already, and here were cottonwood sentinels, towering over a lush bosque and the babbling Gunnison River. Next loomed a cliffy mini-canyon I'd never noticed before. As we headed toward our campsite, pockets of forest revealed themselves in the curves and dips of the landscape. I saw the remnants of volcanic-eruption competitions on the mesas. Why hadn't I ever noticed how tall those things are?

Volcanic palisades near Blue Mesa Reservoir

Over the next few days, the mesas and basins, pinnacles and cliffs, aspen forests, and open water sucked our family in and we somehow became a part of the country. We shivered at night as the cold West Elk air seeped into our campsite. We scrunched our faces against the icy gray spray of Blue Mesa Reservoir when an afternoon thunderstorm tossed our boat in 3-foot swells. We ran for the shelter of Cebolla Arm and explored its curves past ghost forests of bare ponderosa trunks sticking up from the water. We thrilled at the cry of a golden eagle carrying fresh kill to its aerie, high over our heads on the cliffs of skinny Black Canyon.

In Curecanti, our family discovered beauty, adventure, and a solitude we never imagined was there. So much for first impressions.

from Blue Mesa Reservoir, the upper 0.5 mile of the Morrow Point Reservoir flows very swiftly. Boaters must be prepared to battle at least 0.5 mile of current back upstream at the end of the trip. Then, they have to haul their gear up those 232 steps out of the canyon. However, the reservoir stretches nearly 12 miles, and a day or two of watching craggy cliffs reflected in the mirror of Morrow Point Reservoir make the hike and hauling a small price to pay.

More visitors come to Curecanti to fish than for any other activity.

Boating Crystal Reservoir can be more like running a river than floating on a lake. The put-in is a 0.25-mile hike from the car at the confluence of the Cimarron River with the Gunnison. The water level fluctuates, and often the water flows over rocks and around obstacles, creating small rapids requiring river-running skills. But this skinny reservoir is deep in the Black Canyon itself, although it is still a part of Curecanti National Recreation Area and not in the neighboring national park. It has an adventurous feel, imparted by the rugged cliffs soaring all around, and you can imagine how the pioneer river runners must have felt. Remember, though, that you have to make your way back upstream to take out at the same place you put your boat in the water. A water release from the reservoir above makes the trip difficult, and a small motor could come in very handy.

Elk Creek Marina

Boaters can find mooring, fuel, and service, provided by the recreation area's concessionaire, at the Elk Creek Marina. A huge boat ramp there attests to the amount of traffic this area receives in the summer. A convenience store full of fishing and boating gear, a restaurant, a 160-site campground, and National Park Service visitor center make this the hub of Curecanti. Boat rental and guided fishing tours can also be arranged here.

Lake Fork Marina

The park concessionaire provides mooring, fuel, and service along with a convenience store selling food, drinks, bait, and fishing tackle. The 90 sites in the nearby campground offer spots to bed down for the night.

Cimarron Canyon Railroad Exhibit

Just off US 50, where the Cimarron River breaks through the ramparts of Black Canyon to join the Gunnison, the Cimarron Canyon Railroad Exhibit hunkers beneath the cliffs. The Denver and Rio Grande Railroad used this break in the canyon's rock face to escape from an expensive and punishing riverside path. A railroad town grew up at the spot, which eventually became known for its hospitality to sightseeing tourists and

Curecanti National Recreation Area at a Glance

Location: West-central Colorado, between Gunnison and Black Canyon of the Gunnison National Park

Address: 102 Elk Creek, Gunnison, CO 81230

Telephone: 970-641-2337 and 877-444-6777 (for reservations)

Website: www.nps.gov/cure and www.reserveusa.com (for camping reservations)

Size: 41,972 acres

Elevation: From 7,500 to 9,000 feet above sea level

Major Activities: Fishing, boating, camping, wildlife watching, picnicking, hiking

Weather: Summer high temperatures vary between 60 and 100 degrees, depending on where you are in the recreation area (rim, canyon bottom, sagesteppe); winter highs range from 20 to 40 degrees; brief afternoon thunderstorms are common in the summer and strong winds can blow off of the reservoirs.

Best Seasons: Summer

Hours: The Elk Creek Visitor Center is open from 8 a.m. to 6 p.m. in the summer, and 8 a.m. to 4 p.m. the rest of the year. The Cimarron and Lake Fork Visitor Centers are open for limited hours during the summer months only.

Closures: Elk Creek Visitor Center is open year-round except for winter federal holidays; the other two visitor centers are generally closed from September through mid-May.

Cost: There are no entrance fees, but boat permits are $4 for two days or $10 for two weeks. Ranger-led Morrow Point boat tours are $12 per adult, $6 for kids 2 to 12, and free for children younger than 2. Most individual campsites are $10 per night, unless they have electrical hookups.

Facilities: The Elk Creek Visitor Center is the main contact point for boating permits, interpretive tour tickets, and trip planning. It offers exhibits on the recreation area and its points of interest, a well-stocked bookstore, and fully accessible restrooms (but no diaper-changing stations). The Cimarron Visitor Center has a railroad museum with both indoor and outdoor displays. During the summer, a park concessionaire runs showers, a convenience store oriented to boating and fishing, and Pappy's Restaurant at the Elk Creek Marina. The Lake Fork marina offers showers and another convenience store as well. Boaters can buy fuel for their powerboats at the marinas during the summer. Gas for automobiles is not available in Curecanti. The major campgrounds at Elk Creek and Lake Fork have dump stations that operate during the warm-weather months. A ranger station is located at the Elk Creek Visitor Center and at East Portal.

Accessibility: The visitor centers at Cimarron, Lake Fork, and Elk Creek are completely accessible. Stevens Creek has wheelchair accessible campsites and bathrooms. The Hermits Rest and Dillon Pinnacles overlooks are also wheelchair accessible.

later as a stock-loading station. The old railroad bed through Black Canyon is now mostly underwater, and the hotel, roundhouse, and other structures are gone. The National Park Service saved an old trestle and a short little train, which originally ran through the canyon. The area boasts a picnic area, campground, and visitor center as well.

East Portal

Accessible only by driving into neighboring Black Canyon of the Gunnison National Park and then creeping down the tortuously steep East Portal Road, the East Portal area is a secluded oasis in the stony chasm. With a ranger station, picnic area, and a campground, this stretch of river bottom is the starting place of the 6-mile-long Gunnison Tunnel. A National Civil Engineering Landmark, the tunnel diverts water from the river, through solid bedrock and out to agriculture in the Uncompahgre Valley.

Programs and Activities

Rangers hold **evening campfire programs** on weekends during the summer months at the Elk Creek Campground. Times vary, based on sunset, so check at the visitor center for a schedule and topics.

A 90-minute **interpretive pontoon boat tour,** given by rangers, launches on the Morrow Point Reservoir from the Pine Creek Trail the during the summer months. Talks include discussions of canyon geology, Curecanti's human history, and the development of the water project with its massive dams, power generation, and water-storage capabilities. The tour offers great wildlife viewing, especially bird-watching. A schedule and tickets are available at the Elk Creek Visitor Center.

Kids who want to participate in the **Junior Ranger Program** can pick up booklets at the Elk Creek Visitor Center. Activities include a safe-boating word match, a sensory walk journaling page, and mapping games. Check in at the Elk Creek Visitor Center to show the ranger your completed booklet and get a badge. A nice perk for younger visitors to the recreation area is that kids 4 and under (too young for the Junior Ranger Program) can get a coloring sheet and a Junior Ranger Buddy sticker.

Award-winning **educational outreach programs** are available at Curecanti. Tailored for various ages from preschool through university-level students, the programs use primary National Park Service themes and are linked to Colorado Educational Content standards. Check the website for a list of presentations for each grade level. When you click on a topic, you'll find a complete outline of the lesson, including materials needed for the program, and pre- and post-field-trip activities. The site is a schoolteacher's dream.

A HiKE FoR
LiTTLE LEGS

Since the reservoirs of Curecanti lie in the bottoms of canyons, the hiking trails in the recreation area are fairly short and often steep. Best bets for families include the Neversink Trail at the east end off the recreation area. It winds for 0.8 mile through a cottonwood bosque in the wide, flat floodplain of the Gunnison River. A booklet available in the Elk Creek Visitor Center about the Neversink area has excellent descriptions of the natural features of the area and is well worth reading. Near the western end of the recreation area, the Mesa Creek Trail near Cimarron follows a moderately easy path. Dotted with occasional picnic tables, it then crosses over a bridge and into the ruggedly pretty canyon along Crystal Reservoir. Trails from Colorado State Route 92 down the north side of Black Canyon to the Morrow Point Reservoir are steep in places, but offer spectacular views. Ask rangers at the visitor center for their hiking suggestions, given the ages and interests of your kids.

The Pine Creek Trail begins with 232 steps down into the canyon.

Natural History

Geology: Cleaning Up

Way back in the early Tertiary period, mountains were being pushed up all over the place in what is now central Colorado. The very crust of the earth was being shoved and crumpled together, and the deepest, oldest rocks, the Precambrian ones, wrinkled right along with all the layers lying on top of them. A big ridge of this old, Precambrian rock rose up underground right where Curecanti and Black Canyon of the Gunnison are now.

The river slowly erodes the hard Precambrian rock in this narrow, steep-walled canyon.

A period of relative peace and quiet followed. Then, some 40 million years ago, the land near what is now Curecanti began to erupt. The West Elk Mountains to the north and the San Juan Mountains to the south spewed hot ash and lava all over the place. The Gunnison River, innocently running down out of the high peaks of the Rockies, ran back and forth between the two volcanic areas. But since the volcanic activity lasted for 30 million years, it was hard to keep up with the mess. Eventually, pyroclastic materials of varying toughness blanketed the land.

Finally, things calmed down and the volcanoes fell asleep. The river and its tributaries started cleaning up, scrubbing down through the rocks made out of volcanic ash, cinders, and other fragments. You can see evidence of this in the area's plunging cliffs, such as the Dillon Pinnacles. These form when a capping layer of tough volcanic tuff protects softer materials (volcanic breccia) from erosion.

Yet, the Gunnison River continued to run, scouring away through the sedimentary rock layers under the volcanic ones. You can see them in the greenish-gray mesa slopes of Mancos shale north and south of Morrow Point and Crystal Reservoirs and in the sandstone cliffs beneath the Dillon Pinnacles at the picnic area there.

After a while, the river hit the tough old ridge of Precambrian basement rocks. But because it dug a course through the softer layers above, now the river is stuck. It spends its time grinding away at the rate of the width of a human hair every year.

This rock is so solid that it stays straight when it is cut, like a round of cheddar cheese with a thin wedge sliced out. The space stays pretty much in the same shape after you remove the sliver of cheese. That wouldn't happen with a stack of crackers. Their edges would fall apart, the crumbs filling the bottom of the space. Likewise, volcanic and sedimentary rocks to the east have canyons that aren't nearly as neat and narrow.

So in Curecanti, you can see right where the river runs into the old rock. East of there, the reservoir is wide, filling shallow basins with sloping hills and mesas all around. Then, right at Blue Mesa Dam, the canyon gets very narrow, with straight walls, like the spot where the cheese was sliced. Morrow Point and Crystal Reservoirs flow through skinny little spaces between increasingly high cliffs where the Gunnison River's path digs through the ridge of solid, old rock.

Plants and Wildlife: Zoning Issues

As you travel through Curecanti, you'll see that the different kinds of rocks and soils on the ground support different plants. These plants, in turn, make great homes and grocery stores for an assortment of animals. Add variability of moisture and sunlight, depending on the angle of the slope, and Curecanti has all kinds of neighborhoods.

The most obvious neighborhood, or life zone, around here is the semiarid shrub land. These wide-open stretches of treeless slopes and mesas go on for miles along Blue Mesa Reservoir. Dominated by big sagebrush and rabbitbrush, the area is too dry to support trees. In this life zone, sometimes called the sagesteppe, kids will also notice grasses such as blue grama, the Colorado State Grass, and squirrel-tail grass blowing in the breeze. A variety of wildflowers treat the eye with blooms depending on the season and the amount of recent precipitation. Look for Indian paintbrush, globe mallow, several different kinds of asters and fleabanes, larkspur, penstemon, and one of my favorites, the lovely sego lily. Prickly pear cactus thrive here as well.

You'd think that drainage zones, with their juniper trees, scrub oak and serviceberry bushes, and wild roses would provide a bit of relief from the monotony of the shrub land, but if you are whizzing by in a car, it is hard to appreciate them. When you hike through the area or bring your boat onto shore for a walk, you will find these neighborhoods in mostly low-flowing or dry streambeds and little gullies. Even though there is no moisture running on the surface, the depressions collect enough water when it does rain or snow for the plants to live. In some places, the moist areas spread out to create grassier meadows. In early summer, they can be decorated with gorgeous purple blossoms of wild iris. Look here for wild geraniums and lupine as well. The forbs, grasses, and insects of these drainage areas make attractive brood-rearing spots for the extremely rare Gunnison sage grouse, who like to bring their babies there in the spring.

When you stroll through riparian zones, on the other hand, you walk in a luxuriant neighborhood, indeed. Here, along the flowing Gunnison River or its tributaries, tall narrow-leaf cottonwood trees dominate. Their deep roots stabilize the riverbanks,

Boaters float beneath jagged Dillon Pinnacles.

creating a more secure foothold for willows and box elder. Insects feed on the plants and drop into the river to feed the fish lurking beneath the banks.

Blue Mesa Reservoir's Soap Creek arm reaches north to the foot of the 13,000-foot West Elk Mountains. Because of the higher elevations, more precipitation is collected in the soils, and big conifer trees move in, bringing a whole new dimension to the neighborhood. Here, you'll find groves of Douglas fir, spruce, and especially ponderosa pine trees. (Ponderosa bark, warmed by the sun, smells delicious—walk up and take a big whiff!)

The Douglas fir trees here have a nifty friendship with organisms in the forest floor. Sometimes a fungus attacks the trees' roots—kind of like athlete's foot—which is a bummer. But it turns out that there is another fungus in the soil that can protect the Douglas fir roots. So the tree lets the helpful fungus mooch food from its roots since it protects the roots from the dangerous fungus. Not only that, but together, the helpful fungus and the Douglas fir roots make a soil that holds water—a handy thing during dry periods.

Surrounding the lower reservoirs, steep canyon walls host their own unique communities. And those neighborhoods are very different, depending on whether they are on the north side or the south side of the canyon. On the south side, the canyon face receives little sun, especially in the winter months. When snow falls there, it hangs out longer. When it melts, the moisture stays in the soil. As the temperature drops at night, that moisture freezes, and the ice pushes apart the rocks, breaking them up. This process tears down the canyon wall on the south side, making it less steep and creating more places for plants to get a foothold. There you will find mountain mahogany, Douglas fir, serviceberry, dogwood, currants, raspberries, and wildflowers such as the flashy shooting star.

Across the water, the north wall of the canyon gets a lot more sunlight. This steams more water off the rocks so those rocks are much less likely to be broken down by frost heave. As a result, the north wall stands straight and tall, with only pockets of plant life clinging to ledges here and there. Look for hanging gardens of wildflowers, occasional juniper stands, and claret cup cactus blooming in early June.

Curecanti's landscape variety lends itself to great potential for spotting a wide array of wild animals. On the semiarid scrublands, prairie dogs are a keystone species, providing resources for other animals such as deer and grasshopper mice, foxes, coyotes, hawks, and eagles. Families can watch a prairie dog colony in action from the deck of the Elk Creek Visitor Center in Curecanti. Plateau and sage lizards dart about in the sagebrush shadows while mountain cottontail rabbits dash and huddle under the cover of the plants or a handy railing. While you might spot a garter snake sliding through the grasses, it's unlikely that you'll encounter a rattler. Rattlesnakes aren't recorded as inhabitants of Curecanti. During the winter, elk and bighorn sheep visit the recreation area, the latter usually hanging out on the steep mesa slopes.

A huge variety of birds sweep through the skies over Curecanti's sagebrush steppes. Golden eagles are fairly common here and breed within the boundaries of Curecanti. Rough-legged hawks and American kestrels join them. The extremely rare Gunnison sage grouse have gathering places to mate, or breeding leks, in the sagebrush fields of Curecanti and surrounding areas. Sandhill cranes are commonly spotted, and may breed in the recreation area as well. Look for the Colorado State Bird, the lark bunting, in the grasslands and shrubs, as well as savannah and vesper sparrows. The green-tailed towhees are abundant during the summer months and breed here. Virginia's warblers are common as are Say's phoebe and dusky flycatchers. Watch for the striking blue flash of mountain

Prairie dogs   © Wendy Shattil/Bob Rozinski

bluebirds, abundant in the recreation area. In the evening, listen for the solitary call of the nighthawk as it swoops and hunts in the dusk.

Evidence suggests that the drainage zones support a wide variety of life due to the water availability there. These little gullies often experience moisture in pulses, when the streambeds fill with water during a rainstorm or with spring snowmelt. Because they sometimes hold a bunch of water, yet are mostly pretty dry, they may have more species than in the surrounding sagebrush steppes or riparian zones. Animals from both life zones visit drainages. And who is home depends on whether the water is seasonal or permanent, according to Mike Ausema, biologist and park ranger. He mentions mule deer and suggests that if the trees or shrubs provide enough cover, black bears may be snuffling about as well.

Along the bigger streams and rivers, in the lush riparian zones, animal life thrives. Beaver can be found along—you guessed it—Beaver Creek, as well as along the Gunnison River east of Blue Mesa Reservoir and the other tributary creeks. Look for evidence of their work along the clear waters that drain the West Elk Mountains, such as Curecanti Creek and Crystal Creek. Mule deer and black bear frequent the shady Pine Creek Trail along the Morrow Point Reservoir as well as the depths of the canyon down through the East Portal area. Moisture in warmer, lower elevation riparian areas makes a wide variety of insects feel at home, including caddisflies, stoneflies, and mosquitoes. These in turn feed aquatic animals, which include chorus frogs, tiger salamanders, and fish swimming below the surface.

Stalking those fish, great blue herons are fairly common along the stream and reservoir banks. These dignified birds can stand over 5 feet tall! Other common shorebirds include killdeer and snipes, which are abundant from early spring through the middle of fall and breed in Curecanti. Look also for sandpipers, American avocets, and Wilson's phalaropes. You may also see green-winged, blue-winged, and cinnamon teals

Black bear   © Wendy Shattil/Bob Rozinski

during the spring and fall months. Mergansers and mallards are quite common throughout the year. From May through October, yellow warblers and Wilson's warblers are abundant in the riparian forests.

The higher-altitude forests of Curecanti, with conifer and mixed conifer-aspen groves, have their own list of residents. Here mule deer are common and elk pass through as well. Black bears have been sighted in the area and smaller mammals are common. Look for chipmunks and golden-mantled ground squirrels. We heard coyotes the night we camped there. Sharp-shinned and Cooper's hawks swoop through the broken forest canopy, searching for smaller birds to eat, while red-tailed hawks soar in the sky above the grass and scrublands as well as the forests. Great horned owls are fairly common and tiny broad-tailed hummingbirds are abundant. Look for woodpeckers such as flickers and the pretty downy woodpecker, all black and white with a red spot on the back of his head. Flycatchers and western wood pewees are also common.

The narrow canyons of the lower two reservoirs host a special citizenry. Bighorn sheep are especially adept at navigating the steep, rocky walls. If you hike along the Pine Creek Trail, look across the water at the opposite cliff wall. You will spot colonies of little mud nests attached to the bottom of rocky overhangs. These are the homes of cliff swallows, which swoop out over the water to catch insects attracted by the water. They are joined by violet-green swallows and white-throated swifts. In the lush growth on the south side of the canyon near Pine Creek, we spotted an impossibly colorful western tanager. With its bright yellow, red, and black body parts, it looked as if it belonged in the tropics rather than Colorado. Just then our ears were treated to the poetry of the canyon wren's call. This one was a chatty little bird, and continued to sing for nearly half an hour. If you take the Morrow Point Boat Tour, the naturalist on board can point out golden eagles and turkey vultures soaring above the abyss. And although peregrine falcons are so rare they are endangered, several nest in the canyons of Curecanti. Watch for cute, chubby water ouzels, or dippers, doing deep–knee bends on the rocks in the middle of the flowing water. They will suddenly dive into the rapids and "fly" underwater to catch insects. Next thing you know, they pop right back onto their rock again as if nothing happened.

The deep, cold waters of the reservoirs contain their own biological communities. Microscopic plants and animals thrive in the still waters, and the plankton is yummy to kokanee salmon, the most commonly caught fish in the recreation area. In the deep, cold underwater canyons of Blue Mesa Reservoir, mackinaw (lake trout) can grow up to 30 pounds. Insect-feeding rainbow trout and brown trout swim below the surface.

Meanwhile, the flowing waters of the Gunnison and its tributary streams are a hangout for brook trout, as well as brown and rainbow trout. They feed on the insects that thrive in riparian areas above.

Human History

In the valley now filled by Blue Mesa Reservoir, archaeologists have found evidence of several structures, hearths, and other features created by humans as long as 12,000 years ago, during Paleo-Indian times. Other sites in Curecanti date to the more recent archaic age, when people stopped depending on huge mammals such as mammoths and ancient bison, which had become extinct. Archaic people were more likely to fish or hunt smaller game and grind plant materials.

Eventually, Ute people lived in the Curecanti area, migrating between the mountains and the Uncompahgre Valley. One prehistoric Ute site overlooks Morrow Point Reservoir and may be more than 600 years old. Their lifeway seems to be consistent with the earlier archaic hunter-gatherers that made a living in the area, although evidence suggests that they migrated into the area from the Great Basin area of Utah.

After the Spanish began to colonize Mexico, establishing outposts in New Mexico, they ventured north to become the first Europeans in western Colorado with expeditions in 1765 and 1776. Afterward, they continued to trade with the Utes, as did fur trappers and mountain men. By the mid-1800s, the Mexicans had established a commercial trail, known as the Old Spanish Trail, between Santa Fe and Los Angeles. One branch of this business road passed along the Gunnison River through what is now Curecanti, skirting the depths of Black Canyon.

In 1853, Captain John W. Gunnison entered the area while searching for a railroad route to the Pacific. Although he met an untimely end, the explorer added considerably to the knowledge about the region and the river he followed bears his name today.

In 1881, the Denver and Rio Grande Railroad reached the town of Gunnison. In addition to a north-running spur to serve the mineral wealth of Crested Butte, the railroad continued on west in pursuit of a route to Salt Lake City. Kezar, Cebolla, and Soap Creek, tiny railway stations with saloons and not much else, popped up along the route. These spots are now submerged beneath Blue Mesa Reservoir, while the relocated town of Sapinero perches on a slope overlooking what was once the confluence of Lake Fork and the Gunnison River. Workers laid track to the head of Black Canyon, where the rock walls became very steep and hard. The railroad decided to press on along the river, right through the canyon rather than try to scale or go around the mesas on the south side of the gorge. Fifteen miles and more than $2 million later, the railroad reached the tiny stop of Cimarron. There the Cimarron River created a break in the canyon wall and a way for the railroad to continue out of the canyon. You can see part of the original old trestle, locomotive, and cars in the canyon just north of the town of Cimarron. In 1949, the last train passed over the route and it became a public road. Eventually, Morrow Point Reservoir submerged most of the route through the canyon.

As the 20th century approached, the farmers of the Uncompahgre Valley needed more water for their crops. The Gunnison River surged a short distance away, but the stony confines of Black Canyon trapped its water. A tunnel out of the canyon and through the mesa was proposed. One nearly disastrous trip to survey the canyon was followed by a successful run in 1901. Most of the construction money came from the federal government as one of the first projects of the Bureau of Reclamation, which finished the 6-mile Gunnison Tunnel in 1909. It is now a National Civil Engineering Landmark. The east portal of the tunnel, while in the boundary of Curecanti National Recreation Area, can only be reached by driving into Black Canyon of the Gunnison National Park. There, take the East Portal Road (with its steep 16 percent grade) to the bottom of Black Canyon.

The Bureau of Reclamation came back to the Gunnison River in the early 1960s, with the construction of the Wayne N. Aspinall Storage Unit. This unit is part of the Upper Colorado River Storage Project, a network of water-holding reservoirs including Navajo Lake, Flaming Gorge Reservoir, and Lake Powell. The Wayne N. Aspinall Storage Unit includes the three reservoirs in Curecanti. The bureau finished Blue Mesa Dam in 1965, designing it mostly for water storage. Morrow Point Dam was completed in 1967 with the primary purpose of producing electricity. In 1976, Crystal Dam was finished; it helps stabilize water flow through Black Canyon of the Gunnison National Park.

Curecanti National Recreation Area was established on February 11, 1965, under a cooperative agreement between the Bureau of Reclamation and the National Park Service.

Restaurants and Picnic Areas

There is one restaurant within the recreation area. Located at the Elk Creek Marina, **Pappy's Restaurant** dishes up fish, hamburgers, and French fries in a casual setting. There is no children's menu, however, so parents of young diners must pay full price for their kids' meals. Quality and portion sizes were only so-so when we visited.

As many as 19 marked **picnic areas** sprinkle the shores of the Curecanti reservoirs. All have picnic tables and toilets, but only **Elk Creek** and **Iola** have drinking water. Since most of the recreation area lies in treeless sagebrush country,

Ponderosa Campground has many sites that overlook rugged vistas.

picnic grounds are generally exposed to sun and wind. Elk Creek does have shelters over the tables and a hilltop location overlooking Blue Mesa Reservoir. The **Beaver Creek Picnic Area,** near the east end of the recreation area, lies along a splashy little stream with big cottonwood trees all around.

The picnic areas on the north side of the recreation area, along Colorado State Route 92, are a view junkie's delight. **Pioneer Point's** picnic tables are tucked beneath the branches of short aspen and juniper trees. A few feet away, a trail leads to two overlooks. One leans over sheer cliffs to afford glimpses of the Morrow Point Reservoir at the base of the Curecanti Needle. This jagged pinnacle of rock was an icon for the scenic railroad that passed beneath it in the 19th and 20th centuries. The other overlook allows visitors to gaze down into the Curecanti Creek Canyon, where whitewater rushes to meet the green waters of the Morrow Point Reservoir.

A large roof covers picnic tables at **Hermits Rest Picnic Area.** Two fire grates and a vault outhouse complete the picnic facilities. Look up over a nearby log fence, however, and you'll see the real attraction of the place. Just beyond the railing, the ground drops suddenly several hundred feet into the green waters of the Morrow Point Reservoir. Beyond that, the rocks rise abruptly again until the hills across the way are level with where you are standing. Behind them, the great massifs of the San Juans heave up, cleaving the blue sky with their snowy summits. It's quite a sight.

More of a trailhead, the **Crystal Creek Trail** offers a picnic table, a vault toilet, and a trash can. Those who venture the 2.5 miles of the gently undulating Crystal Creek Trail will find two overlooks. One is a spur peering back at the cones of the West Elk Mountains.

The other viewpoint is on the lip of the canyon overlooking Curecanti's most rugged reservoir, Crystal. In the distance, the peaks of the Uncompahgre Wilderness within the San Juan range rear up huge and rugged.

Lodging and Camping

No hotel lodging is available inside Curecanti National Recreation Area.

Camping, however, is a different story. At Curecanti, there is something for everyone. With at least 16 **developed campgrounds** to choose from, plus **dispersed camping** along the shores of Blue Mesa and Morrow Point Reservoirs, sleeping out is a major focus of this recreation area.

All sites in developed campgrounds have picnic tables, fire rings, and access to toilets. Drinking water is turned on in all developed campgrounds during the warm months. Only **Elk Creek** has water available in the winter, and that is located at the Elk Creek Picnic Area. At Elk Creek and **Lake Fork Campgrounds,** the toilets flush, but all the rest have vault toilets. Trees are completely absent from the largest campgrounds, some of which resemble RV parking lots more than anything. Dump stations are available at Elk Creek, Lake Fork, and **Cimarron Campgrounds,** and campers can find a shower at Elk Creek and Lake Fork. Elk Creek has some sites with electrical hookups. Reservations are required for **Stevens Creek,** Elk Creek loops A and D, Lake Fork's upper loop (sites 31 through 87), and group campgrounds **East Elk Creek** and **Red Creek.**

Several campgrounds can only be accessed by boat or backpacking in. These feature picnic tables, fire grates, and vault toilets, but campers must pack out everything they bring into the backcountry, including trash. These campgrounds have two sites each, and reservations are not accepted.

Additionally, dispersed camping is allowed in specific, nondeveloped sites along the shores of Blue Mesa Reservoir and Morrow Point Reservoir. Check with the rangers at the Elk Creek Ranger Station before heading to one of those.

A few **commercial campgrounds** lie just outside the Curecanti National Recreation Area boundary along US 50 between Gunnison and Sapinero. One such campground, **Blue Mesa Recreational Ranch,** is open May through October, with 324 RV sites and cabins for rent. Call 970-641-0492 for information.

Nearby Towns

Gunnison, a town of 5,300 people, lies on US 50, just over 4 miles from the eastern tip of Curecanti National Recreation Area. Its American Legion Memorial Park has a great playground and the city built a whitewater play park in the Gunnison River, west of town. The Gunnison Pioneer Museum is open in the summer and has an antique locomotive to climb on, in addition to old buildings and memorabilia from the town's early days. A few fast-food restaurants and chain hotels line the highway, while local motels, bed-and-breakfasts, and restaurants offer variety. Dining options include pizza, Mexican food, barbecue, and upscale seafood and wild game establishments. The Gunnison Valley

Hospital, 711 North Taylor, has 24-hour emergency services. Gunnison has two large grocery stores and a large discount store as well. Contact the Gunnison Chamber of Commerce at 970-641-1501 for more information.

Giant ponderosa pine trees grow at higher elevations in Curecanti.

Special Considerations for Families

Curecanti is about as family friendly a national park as Colorado has to offer. The different personalities of its three reservoirs offer a wide range of fun and adventure. The educational and Junior Ranger programs are top notch, and the ranger-guided Morrow Point Boat Tour is ideal for kids.

The recreation area is huge, though, and often you are a long way from towns with any services. Much of it is exposed to wind and sun, and all that water adds its own element of risk. The standard high-altitude, outdoor precautions apply. Pay attention to the weather, be prepared for contingencies and emergencies, and carry essential gear (see page 220). Overall, Curecanti National Recreation Area is a wonderful place for families to experience Colorado's outdoors.

What Makes Curecanti National Recreation Area Special

Although we visited at one of the busiest times of year, we frequently found ourselves in spots in Curecanti that felt downright lonely. Even on the sunny Saturday of Memorial Day weekend, when there were way more boats on the water than usual, we never felt crowded. Blue Mesa Reservoir is so big, and the surrounding countryside is so vast and wide open, that visitors can always find space.

The sheer amount of space is a big part of Curecanti's personality. Because treeless sagebrush steppes are its main feature, you become immersed in the elbow room, taking deep breaths, and focusing your eyes on the distant horizon. All that space in front of your face makes space in your mind. The unimpeded wind blows away the clutter.

Then, when a jagged cliff, snowy blue peaks, a pine and aspen forest, or a hard-rock slot canyon come into focus, they startle your eyes and make you smile. Curecanti is the quintessential, even mythical, Western landscape. We need the way it changes us.

ENTRY

NATIONAL PARK SERVICE PASSPORT STAMP

Bird's-Eye View: Surprise!

A great rift cleaves the earth's crust in North America. It stretches up from Mexico into central Colorado, forming valleys in the Rocky Mountains reaching as far north as Leadville. The largest of Colorado's valleys, the San Luis Valley spreads over the southern third of the state between the Sangre de Cristo Mountains on the east and the San Juan range to the west.

Averaging less than 8 inches of precipitation per year, the San Luis Valley is a true desert, but irrigation allows it to bear the fruits of agriculture. Its broad, flat plain supports fields and farms within the encircling arms of high peaks.

On the eastern side of the valley, the saw edge of the Sangre de Cristos climbs to 14,000 feet above sea level. Snowy peaks arch over conifer forests and glittering alpine lakes. Freshwater streams come laughing down out of this high country only to bump into a surprisingly vast pile of sand, the Great Sand Dunes. Covering 30 square miles, the dunes reach more than 700 feet high in places. This pile, in turn, stops the streams in their tracks, loads them up with more tiny grains than they can hold, and sets them on a path around the dunes' edges. On the other side, the streams can carry the sand no farther. They drop the sand, then flow out across the plain of the San Luis Valley. North, east, and south of the dunes, the streams flow through the sand sheet, a grassy, shrubby flat inhabited by desert plants and animals. Meanwhile, some of the stream's water hits the deck when it first runs into the dunes. It dives below the surface and seeps out later into what is called the sabkha area, southeast of the dunes. Here the water surfaces in pools and wetlands, supporting a variety of wildlife.

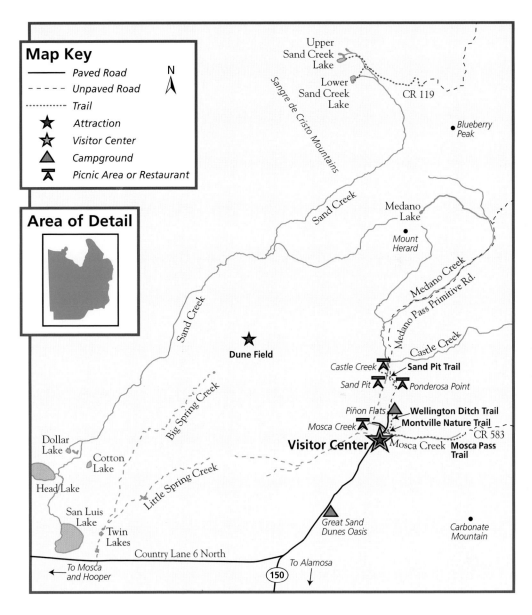

Map Key

— Paved Road
- - - - Unpaved Road
.... Trail
★ Attraction
☆ Visitor Center
▲ Campground
⊼ Picnic Area or Restaurant

N

Area of Detail

Upper Sand Creek Lake
Lower Sand Creek Lake
CR 119
Sangre de Cristo Mountains
Blueberry Peak
Sand Creek
Medano Lake
Mount Herard
Medano Creek
Medano Pass Primitive Rd.
Sand Creek
Castle Creek
Dune Field
Castle Creek
Sand Pit Trail
Sand Pit
Ponderosa Point
Big Spring Creek
Piñon Flats
Wellington Ditch Trail
Mosca Creek
Montville Nature Trail
CR 583
Dollar Lake
Cotton Lake
Visitor Center
Mosca Creek
Mosca Pass Trail
Head Lake
Little Spring Creek
San Luis Lake
Twin Lakes
Great Sand Dunes Oasis
Carbonate Mountain
Country Lane 6 North
To Mosca and Hooper
To Alamosa
150

The national park itself encompasses the main dune field plus parts of the sand sheet and sabkha regions to the north, east, and south of the dunes. The visitor center and campground sit just above the southeastern curve of the dune field within the national park. The Great Sand Dunes National Preserve curves around the eastern side of the national park, extending to the crest of the Sangre de Cristo Mountains.

Most of the park and the entire preserve are designated as national wilderness areas, where no motorized vehicles are allowed (except for the paved roads to the dunes parking area and campground, and the Medano Pass four-wheel-drive road).

Attractions

Dune Field

Before our first trip to the Sand Dunes, I told my then 2-year-old that we would be going to a place with a sandbox bigger than our whole neighborhood, piled higher than tall buildings. He looked at me, puzzled, not sure that he could believe me. When we got there, he immediately understood.

The heaps of sand rise into the heavens, and slope gently down to greet visitors. They are as inviting to climb upon as a sleeping lioness is to her cubs. And they are just as slippery and easy to fall off of. A favorite visitor activity is to hike to the top of the highest dunes. Early in the morning you can see the pilgrims winding their way up the ridges to stand as silhouetted specks against the sky. Others bring cardboard, snowboards, and skis for sliding down the steep, leeward slopes of sand. Always, folks who venture very far have shoes or boots on. The sand is fairly dark and surface temperatures can reach 140 degrees.

Hiking on the dunes feels ethereal, otherworldly. Their steepness creates a burn in your thighs, the unending wind sucks the water out of you, and the blowing grit scours your skin. The dunes' vastness and height swallows you, and their curves make you want to lie down on their grainy skin. How can you resist a sandbox like that?

The Sand Pit Trail leads to a quiet section of Medano Creek.

Medano Creek

Snowmelt from on high runs into Medano Creek, which skirts the dune field's eastern edge. As it spreads out over the sands at the base of the grainy slopes, the stream makes a perfect spot for sandcastles and engineering projects. Cottonwood trees arch over the water here and there, creating lovely spots for a picnic or to cool your toes after a burning climb up the dunes.

During the spring runoff, especially in years with heavy snowfall, the creek swells, carving into the foot of the sand pile. This is the best time and place in North America to see a

Opposite: The trail from the campground to the dune field travels through the sand sheet life zone.

Medano Creek is the perfect place to cool your toes.

rare hydrologic phenomenon called surge flow. The flowing water creates ripples, like tiny, wet dunes on the sandy streambed. These build as the water flows over them, depositing sand. Eventually, they form little dams, holding back more and more water as the grains pile up beneath the stream's surface. When the sand can no longer withstand the weight of the water it is holding back, the little dam breaks all at once, sending a flood of water downstream. These tiny sand waves, technically known as a bore, can be an inch high or a foot deep and full of whitewater. Add a floating toy plus a thick layer of sunblock, and the spring runoff can keep your teenager out of trouble all day. A pail and scoop are more than enough equipment for younger folks.

By the middle of summer, Medano Creek dwindles to barely a trickle, and by fall it usually disappears beneath the sand. In drought years, it may never run along the face of the dunes at all.

Visitor Center

The New Mexican Territorial architecture of the Great Sand Dunes Visitor Center fits well in the scrubby landscape of the San Luis Valley. Inside, a large lobby greets visitors. Interpretive displays introduce families to the dunes along with the plants and animals that live in the area. You can view a 15-minute video as well. A large, thoroughly stocked bookstore offers a variety of titles on the human and natural history of the area in addition to posters, postcards, and gift items. Although there are no diaper-changing stations in the men's or women's restrooms, there is a family restroom for parents and their small children. A large porch with benches offers a gathering place, and several times a day during the summer rangers conduct porch talks under the portal.

Mosca Pass Trail

This 7-mile round-trip is a popular venture into the high country of the Great Sand Dunes National Preserve. Following splashy Mosca Creek, the trail climbs to a low pass that was a historical avenue across the Sangre de Cristo mountain range. The pass

OUR EXPERIENCE:
CHILD'S PLAY

The sand must have gotten in my eyes, but I don't remember it. All I remember is the brown swirling all around. Millions of particles, suspended in water, rolling over and over me, filling my nose and ears, scrubbing the skin on my back and elbows and feet. The sound —the tick of all those grains hitting my head—blended together into a hiss that allowed no other sound through.

When it faded, when the surge of water eased down the streambed, I sat up, grinning and shaking water from my hair, looking around to see where the wave had deposited my companions. My bathing suit seemed padded—the water had carried sand between the lining and the outer fabric, and left it there, like a brightly colored sandbag. This situation amused me only for a second. Another wave was building, and I threw myself down in the main channel and waited for it to overtake me.

Medano Creek is Colorado's premier sand-sculpturing site.

As crazy kids, in our early teens, Medano Creek's pulsating flow was just part of a day's fun at the Great Sand Dunes. The thing is, every time I have visited since, I've searched the rivulet at the foot of the dunes for those waves. I've never seen the water level so high or the waves as big as they were that spring. If I did, I know I'd throw decorum to the wind and dive in again.

In truth, I don't need those big waves. The soaring peaks, the stream, and those undulating and sifting mountains of sand yell, "Come play!" and I can no more resist than I can will myself to stop breathing.

The Great Sand Dunes National Park and Preserve turns many a staid adult into a child again. Just plan on it—you'll get sand in your ears.

Pilgrims make their way up the dune field.

also plays a role in channeling the winds that drop their load of sand on the dunes. Along the way, hikers can view the dunes and surrounding countryside from an ever-broadening perspective.

Montville Nature Trail

This peaceful, 0.5-mile trail offers families a break from the harsh exposure of the dunes. The loop trail starts from the same trailhead as the Mosca Pass Trail. Winding through the lush vegetation along Mosca Creek, the points of interest and accompanying pamphlet reveal the remnants of a frontier town from the late 1800s. Pick up the booklet at the visitor center.

Programs and Activities

Campfire programs are held nightly in the amphitheater from Memorial Day through Labor Day. Check at the visitor center for topics and a schedule.

Ranger walks are scheduled throughout the summer. Check at the visitor center for times.

The Great Sand Dunes **Junior Ranger Program** offers kids from 3 to 12 years old a great opportunity to learn about and interact with the natural resources and people of this national park and preserve. Activities vary according to age group, and include safety checklists, Dunes Bingo, explorations, and art activities. Children who complete their booklet and take the Junior Ranger pledge earn a badge.

Educational programs include lesson plans, field trip plans, and other teaching aids, which are available on the website for teachers of grades K through 12.

Great Sand Dunes National Park and Preserve at a Glance

Location: South-central Colorado, about 30 miles northeast of Alamosa in the San Luis Valley

Address: 11500 Highway 150, Mosca, CO 81146-9798

Telephone: 719-378-6399

Website: www.nps.gov/grsa

Size: 149,500 acres

Elevation: From 8,500 to 13,500 feet above sea level

Major Activities: Playing on the dunes and in Medano Creek, camping, hiking, photography, horseback riding, and backpacking

Weather: Summer daytime highs average 70 to 80 degrees, and lows can drop to 40; winter daytime temperatures are moderate, with lows dropping below 0 some nights.

Best Seasons: Early summer through fall

Hours: The visitor center is open from 9 a.m. to 6 p.m., from Memorial Day to Labor Day, and 9 a.m. to 4:30 p.m. in the winter (November through February). In the spring and fall, the schedule is variable, with the center generally open from 9 a.m. to 5 p.m.

Closures: The park is closed Christmas, New Year's, Martin Luther King, and Presidents' Days.

Cost: Fees are $3 per person (good for seven days), $15 for an annual pass, and $12 per night for camping.

Facilities: The visitor center has a bookstore, exhibits, a 15-minute video, and restrooms, including a family restroom. A ranger station is located in the visitor center as well. Outdoor showers for rinsing the sand off (not for bathing) are located near the dunes parking area. Tire air is available in the amphitheater parking lot.

Accessibility: The visitor center and its restrooms are wheelchair accessible, as are the amphitheater and the bathrooms in the campground. The dunes parking lot also has a wheelchair-accessible restroom, and the picnic area there is generally navigable by wheel-chairs as well. Two of the campground's sites are accessible as is one backcountry campsite. The visitor center has a wheelchair with fat, air-filled tires that you can check out to take out on the dunes.

A HiKE FOR
LiTTLE LEGS

Drive your car up the sandy track of the Medano Pass Primitive Road to the Point of No Return parking area. Hop out and embark on the Sand Pit Trail, an undulating hike through a section of country where two life zones—the sand sheet and the montane forest—intertwine like the fingers of folded hands. At the end of the 0.5-mile path, the track dips down to Medano Creek, which almost always runs year-round here. The park map shows a picnic area here. Steep dunes rise right out of the creek and make a mad scramble up onto the dune field. The endless waves of sand seem like a landscape from another planet. The slide back into the stream brings giggles bubbling to the surface.

Several other hiking trails start at the visitor center and campground areas and skirt the dunes. The main dune complex is free of trails, yet it provides some of the most entertaining and strenuous hiking in the area. If you do choose to hike on the dunes, prepare carefully.

The Great Sand Dunes is a groovy spot for hip Colorado kids.

The sand can reach temperatures of 140 degrees, so shoes and socks are a necessity as are drinking water, a hat, sunblock, and sunglasses.

Within the national park, a few trails run through the piñon-juniper forest at the base of the Sangre de Cristos. The Wellington Ditch Trail starts in the campground and has great views of the dunes while offering a break from the relentless sun. It leads to the Montville Nature Trail, east of the visitor center. Other trails lead up into the preserve or along the northeastern curve of the dune field. Families with high-clearance, four-wheel-drive vehicles and good experience driving them over rough terrain can access the trail in the northern part of the preserve to the Upper and Lower Sand Creek Lakes.

Check the official visitors' guide, the *Breezes*, for a chart and descriptions of the various hikes, and check with a ranger for suggestions of trails that will fit your family's abilities and interests.

Natural History

Geology: A Good Rift Valley

Colossal forces causing the earth's crust to heave and buckle also make it stretch in some places. In one of those spots, all that crunching and stretching created a crack in the earth's crust that slowly widened into a rift. On either side of the rift, deep faults split the ground right down to the mantle, and the bit of land that happens to be between the faults dropped unevenly as much as 9,000 feet—and it hasn't stopped. Even today, it is sliding downward along the faults. It so happens that Great Sand Dunes National Park and Preserve sits right on that bit of ground, known as the San Luis Valley.

From the edge of the Sangre de Cristo Mountains, right behind the Sand Dunes, to the foothills of the San Juan range across the valley, the flat surface of the San Luis Valley sprawls about 45 miles. Its elevation, a fairly consistent 7,500 feet above sea level, is deceiving. Below the surface lie layers and layers of lava, volcanic ash, clay, sand, and gravel, sometimes more than 2 miles deep. These sedimentary layers have filled in the uneven spots in the rift, and in places the bedrock lies more than 5,000 feet below sea level—13,000 feet below the current valley floor.

Geologists figure the deep faults lying on the western edge of the valley provided a way for molten rocks from the earth's interior to push their way up. The volcanic San Juan Mountains lie right over the faults. The peaks are made in part from lava rocks containing lots of magnesium and iron, just like the earth's mantle. When the Ice Age came, glaciers and their robust rivers ground away at the old San Juan volcanoes, washing their material out into the rift of the San Luis Valley.

In this part of the world, the wind almost always blows from the southwest. And the San Luis Valley, lying in the rain shadow of the San Juans, is incredibly dry—a true desert. This allows the prevailing westerlies to pick up the volcanic material, now ground into sand, and blow it across the valley. Since the surface is nearly flat, there isn't much to slow down the wind until it reaches the Sangre de Cristo Mountains. There, the air is pushed heavenward by the steep mountain flanks, and it is swirled around by a bend in the line of peaks. As the wind rises, it slows and drops its load of sand at the foot of the range.

Frequently, in late winter and spring, the wind switches direction and blows from the north through Music, Medano, and Mosca Passes, pushing the sand back onto itself in big piles. Snowmelt streams pick up sand in the Sangre de Cristos and carry it to the dunes as well.

Only about one-tenth of the sand at the foot of the mountains is visible in the dune field itself. Most of it lies beneath scrubby bushes and grasses on the surrounding sand sheet, or cemented by minerals brought to the surface in the springs of the sabkha. Together, these two less-obvious sandy regions cover nearly 300 square miles.

Plants and Wildlife: Neighborhoods

Great Sand Dunes National Park and Preserve has several components, all knitted together, creating conditions for an amazing variety of life. From the steep, high peaks on the east to the marshy wetlands out on the valley floor, the plants and animals that live under National Park Service protection here function in a huge connected system.

The spine of the Sangre de Cristo Mountains stretches the length of the national preserve. The alpine, subalpine, montane, and piñon-juniper life zones here provide a cool, restful alternative to lower-elevation glare.

Alpine Tundra Life Zone

Within the preserve, eight peaks scratch the clouds with altitudes over 12,000 feet above sea level. At this height, the wind screams more often than it whispers, and the snowpack can last most of the year. Nighttime temperatures are likely to drop below freezing even in the summer. The climate in this alpine life zone is too harsh for trees to survive, and the plants that do thrive are similar to those found in the arctic tundra.

Cushion plants, such as moss campion and dwarf phlox, hug the ground, where they can soak up warmth from the rocks and soil and hide from the wind. Look also for purple fringe, snow buttercup, bistort, and alpine primrose. Horned larks nest in the tundra in the summer and white-crowned sparrows feed on the ground or survey the tundra from trees at the edge of timberline. Surprisingly, white-throated swifts and violet-green swallows hunt for insects at this altitude as well. Look for rock wrens with their cute little curvy beaks hopping among the rocks. Here, also, endearing little pikas dash through the rock piles, gathering grasses like hay for the winter and issuing their sharp

Bison   © Wendy Shattil/Bob Rozinski

little "Eee!" calls. Once in a while, a coyote will venture here to search for supper. Visitors frequently spot yellow-bellied marmots and bighorn sheep in alpine areas as well.

Subalpine Forest Life Zone

At about 11,000 feet above sea level, trees are able to survive and create the subalpine life zone. Stunted, even to the point of growing flat along the ground right at timber-line, the trees become taller and thicker as elevation drops. Heavy snowfall provides enough moisture for subalpine forests to grow thick with Engelmann and blue spruce trees, subalpine fir trees, and aspen and willows along the watercourses and seeps. In sunny patches, the short summer growing season explodes with wildflowers such as rock primrose, shooting stars, columbine, penstemon, and paint-brush. Violets grow in the grassy meadows while wild iris live in wet meadows.

Bobcat
© Wendy Shattil/Bob Rozinski

Club moss thrives along streams where Rio Grande cutthroat trout have been reintro-duced. These fish feed on aquatic insects like stone-, caddis-, and mayflies. Crane flies and mosquitoes also like this area, and big fat bumblebees dance among the wildflowers. Wild turkeys are sometimes seen walking through the forest understory. Gray jays and Steller's jays scold in the trees and try to steal snacks from picnickers. Watch for red-naped sapsuckers and American robins. Diminutive flyers in this forest include mountain chickadees, cordilleran flycatchers, and ruby-crowned kinglets. Northern harriers hunt low over marshy meadow areas by day, while the twilight sky is home to nighthawks dipping and soaring in their evening hunt.

Birds are joined in the sky by little brown bats, who also search for insects at nightfall. Just below in the treetops, pine martens hunt in the darkness for their favorite food, chickarees (also known as pine squirrels). Cousins of the martens, short-tail ermine prowl the forest floor at night, looking for mice, voles, and other tasties. Long-tailed weasels, which closely resemble ermine except for the length of the tail, are more likely to be seen since they hunt by day. A favorite food of theirs is also a common resident of the preserve's subalpine areas: pocket gophers. Both ermine and long-tailed weasels change color with the seasons, turning white when the snow flies, just like the snow-shoe hares found in the area. Red foxes, bobcats, and black bears rummage through the woods here, while beaver work the streams. Visitors are very likely to see elk and mule deer grazing and browsing on the meadow edges.

Montane and Piñon-Juniper Woodland Life Zones

The montane forest and piñon-juniper woodlands occupy about the same elevation, the difference being the availability of water. Drainages and shady north-facing slopes that hold more snowfall tend to have animals and plants typical of the montane life zone. A few yards away, on sunnier, drier slopes, the piñon-juniper life zone dominates. Thus, this elevation holds a wonderful variety of living things.

Trees include Douglas fir, white fir, ponderosa pine, aspen, Rocky Mountain maple, and thinleaf alder in the wetter, shadier areas. Narrow-leaf cottonwoods grow along the watercourses as do stinging nettles and the native Parry's thistle. Look also for wax currants (bears think they are yummy), virgin's bower (a type of clematis), and shooting stars blooming in the early summer. Other wildflowers in the montane areas include groundsel (little sunflowers) and verbenas. Parry's oat grass and mountain muhly grow there as well.

Piñon pine and juniper trees, of course, dominate the piñon-juniper life zone. Grasses are more common here, including blue grama grass and ring muhly, which grows in circles, sprouting on the outside of last year's dead grasses. Mountain mahogany and rabbitbrush blossom in the piñon-juniper life zone, as does mountain spray. This member of the rose family has a misty pink inflorescence with a pungent scent. Other wildflowers include claret cup cactus, paintbrush, Apache plume, fringe sage (artemisia), pussytoes, one-sided penstemon, and firecracker penstemon. Purple asters bloom profusely at the end of August.

Spider wasps zip about at this elevation, while lots of ants till the forest soils. Families are likely to see butterflies such as tigerswallows dancing among the flowers, and the cute, clumsy ochre ringlets bouncing around on their creamy yellow wings in early in June. Hummingbird moths sip primrose nectar here as well. Dead and dying trees attract longhorn beetles, named for their huge antennae. These mottled chocolate iridescent insects bore into the wood with their sizable chompers, preferring trees that are already dead or nearly so. The Ips beetle, however, attacks live trees. A native, this bug responds to distress signals caused by drought or other circumstances in piñon trees. It is responsible for large swaths of dead trees in the southwest part of the state.

Garter snakes slither through the undergrowth at this elevation, and tiger salamanders like the wetter areas in the montane. Skink lizards, bullsnakes, and woodhouse toads reside in the piñon-juniper woodlands, and rattlesnakes may be there, although they are not common. Rio Grande suckers and Rio Grande cutthroat trout, rainbow trout, and brook trout swim in the creeks.

Lush montane forests are home to many bird species, including pine siskins, juncos, downy woodpeckers, western tanagers, mountain bluebirds, violet-green swallows, robins, green-tailed towhees, warbling vireos, and ravens. The drier piñon-juniper areas see mountain bluebirds as well, plus piñon jays, Clark's nutcrackers, northern flickers, Lewis' woodpeckers, bushtits, Townsend's solitaires, olive-sided flycatchers, white- and red-breasted nuthatches, pine grosbeaks, and broad-tailed hummingbirds. Nighthawks call in the twilight and observant kids might spot a great horned owl looking like a stick as it sleeps in a tree by day.

Snowshoe hares seem to prefer areas of downed wood in the montane life zone, while cottontails hop through both montane and piñon-juniper forests. Other mammals traveling between the two life zones include deer mice, rock squirrels, Abert's squirrels, chickarees, bobcats, and black bears. Drier areas are more likely to see piñon mice, chipmunks, and golden-mantled ground squirrels. Mule deer are almost ubiquitous in the piñon-juniper life zone, and it follows that mountain lions hunt the area, too.

Although you aren't likely to see a mountain lion, it makes sense to follow safety measures with your kids here. Big brown bats and Townsend's big-eared bats flit over the piñon-juniper come evening. The lush montane area sees more skunks, porcupines, and raccoons. Beavers dam Medano Creek to make their ponds, a favorite hangout of water shrews. Bats flying over this area include long-legged bats and hoary bats.

Dune Field Life Zone

Although daytime air temperatures seldom reach higher than 85 degrees on the sand dunes, their surface can reach 140 degrees. In the winter, temperatures drop to 20 degrees below zero. And the wind just blows and blows, no matter what time of year it is. Not a lot of life can survive out here, so you develop a certain respect for those creatures that do.

Plants include scurfpea, Indian rice grass, blowout grass, prairie sunflower, skeletonweed, sand dropseed, and occasionally rabbitbrush. Most of them seem pretty used to getting beat up by the flying sand, and have developed root systems that help them hang on.

More insects live on the dunes than any other kind of life. The list includes noctuid moths, Great Sand Dunes tiger beetles, circus beetles, ant-like flower beetles, hister beetles, and giant

Kangaroo rat © Wendy Shattil/Bob Rozinski

sand treader camel crickets. Seven of the insect species in the dune field are so well adapted to this place that they're considered endemic and live nowhere else in the world.

Spadefoot toads also have been seen on the dunes. National Park Service biologist Phyllis Pineda Bovin has heard horned larks in the winter, with their "squeaky call, like crinkling cellophane." Doves inhabit the edges of the dunefield, while red-tailed hawks and occasionally turkey vultures and ravens soar overhead. While coyotes, bobcats, weasels, and even elk will sometimes venture into the dunes, only Ord's kangaroo rats make a living there. Humans are the most common visitor, and you are likely to sight them most times of the year.

Sand Sheet Life Zone

Surrounding the main dune field are the vast, open fields of the sand sheet. Windy and exposed to the elements, this life zone exists on a sandy base, with transient dunes moving across it and seasonal streams flowing through it. This is the life zone you hike through on the trail that leads from the campground to the dunes.

Ponds, many of which have disappeared in the past several decades, dot the sand sheet's eastern edge. Of about 80 ponds photographed in the 1930s and 1940s, only five were left at the turn of the 21st century. A few other ponds have formed in the past few years, however, apparently due to the way the creeks cut down through the sand.

Grasses dominate the sand sheet and anchor the grains. Common grasses include blue grama grass, wheatgrass, Indian rice grass, squirreltail, needle-and-thread grass, sand bluestem, and foxtail barley. A member of the pea family grows here, its pods inflated, mottled, and looking like a spotted pot. Its species name is *ceramicus*. Prickly pear cactus and yucca do well in this dry, sandy landscape, as do rabbitbrush and wild oregano. Look for the tall stalks and fuzzy leaves of mullein growing singly or in groups. Wildflowers include sand verbena, prairie sunflower, low lupine, firecracker red penstemon, narrow-leaf penstemon, and wild iris in the wet meadows. Baltic rushes and bulrushes grow along the waterways, and a rare beauty also grows the in wetlands: the slender spider-flower. According to park biologist Bovin, when the buckwheat bloom in late August they smell just like someone's stinky bare feet.

Wolf spiders hunt insects such as the mosquitoes, small wasps, rabbitbrush beetles, and bees that live in the sand sheet. Robber flies catch their prey in mid-air, stab their victims in the back, and then suck out the juices. Moths flit about at night, pollinating the desert plants. Short-horned lizards, many-lined skinks, garter snakes, and bullsnakes sneak around underneath the shady branches of the shrubs. Although rattlesnakes may potentially live here, they are not commonly reported in the park.

Short-horned lizard   © Wendy Shattil/Bob Rozinski

Say's phoebes, violet-green swallows, and white-throated swifts hunt insects over the sand sheet, while American kestrels hover and dive for small rodents or insects. Sage sparrows are seen here in the San Luis Valley, without much broader distribution in any other parts of the state. Often, they will run on the ground rather than fly away. Birds of prey commonly seen in the sand sheet include red-tailed hawks, burrowing owls, and ferruginous hawks.

These hunting birds often look for jackrabbits, Gunnison's prairie dogs, silky pocket mice, and northern grasshopper mice to eat for supper. The bunnies and rodents also must keep an eye out for weasels, coyotes, and badgers. Mountain lions make it out onto the sand sheet, where pronghorn, elk, and bison are common. (Surveys of bison DNA show the animals here actually have a little bit of cow in them, although you wouldn't know it to look at them.)

Sabkha Life Zone

An unusual life zone, the sabkha brings surprises to the desert of the San Luis Valley. Water that flows out of the Sangre de Cristo Mountains sinks into the ground underneath the sand dunes, but it keeps flowing along underground layers of sand and rock.

As the surface elevation drops, the water seeps to the surface in spring-fed lakes and marshes. As it rises, the water brings alkalinity to the surface, and although they are not caustic, sabkha ponds have a high pH. The minerals cement the sandy soils into a thin, whitish crust.

Few plants can survive the alkalinity. Among them are four-wing saltbrush, saltgrass, sueada (a little succulent), and willows. Baltic rush, also called wiregrass, grows in damp areas, as does a small, reddish-orange mallow.

Circus beetles live here, as do robber flies and mosquitoes. Short-horned lizards join them, plus many-lined skinks, garter snakes, and bullsnakes. Although there is archaeological evidence that humans fished the lakes of the sabkha region, the ponds in the park are so ephemeral today that no fish live there.

Shorebirds are attracted to the water and observers see snowy plovers, American avocets, greater sandhill cranes, and American white pelicans in the sabkha lakes. Red-winged blackbirds and yellow-headed blackbirds like the marshy areas, while sage sparrows hop around in the nearby scrub. Golden eagles soar overhead and bald eagles often fly through in the wintertime. While kangaroo rats burrow under the saltbrush, bison and elk will wander through the sabkha as well.

In Great Sand Dunes National Park and Preserve, volcanic crumbs, layers of sediment, soaring peaks, freezing snowpack, corrosive chemicals, ever-flowing water, and wind all push each other around, back and forth, bumping and tugging, digging and grinding, sifting and sticking, in one of the most fragile and complex dune systems in the world. And within this chaotic system lives an amazing variety of life forms, all interacting with one another as well. It is a huge and complicated net, woven with strands of many colors and sizes, all pulling together to keep the dunes a rare and spectacular natural wonder.

Human History

When deep glaciers gouged mountainsides, turning rocks into sand, and the dunes at the edge of the rift were younger, great Ice Age mammals roamed across the plains of the San Luis Valley. The wet environment at the end of the Pleistocene created marshes and lakes, and giant mammoths were fond of such spots. Paleontologists have uncovered mammoth bones in several locations near the Great Sand Dunes. In one of those sites, evidence suggests that Clovis hunters, the earliest universally accepted culture in the New World, may have killed mammoths there.

As huge mammals such as mammoths began to decline, the culture of the people in the valley changed as well. The Folsom people hunted with fluted projectile points, while adapting with more foraging. Several Clovis and Folsom points have been found lying on the surface of the San Luis Valley. If you are lucky enough to discover an arrowhead or other artifact, leave it *exactly* as you find it and contact a park ranger. Its location and position may lend great insight into the ancient folks who made their livings in the area.

Evidence of Folsom cultural presence in the valley fades out after about 5000 BC, although humans still made their mark. A research team from the Smithsonian Institution has discovered what are possibly pit houses and attendant hearths near

Mount Herard is named after a 19th-century rancher in the area.

springs in the sand sheet area. At nearly 5,000 years old, they date from the Archaic period. And pictographs and petroglyphs ranging in age from 3000 BC to the late 19th century adorn boulders and rock faces in several places around the San Luis Valley.

More recently, modern American Indians have expressed various connections to the dunes area. Some of the Pueblo tribes along the Rio Grande speak of the sabkha region's lakes as their people's place of emergence into this world. The Navajo hold Blanca Peak as one of their four sacred mountains, and the San Luis Valley was a hunting ground for the southern Utes and Jicarilla Apaches. Within Great Sand Dunes National Park, large ponderosa pine trees stand with bark partially stripped off by American Indians. This Indian Grove is listed on the National Register of Historic Places.

The first people of European descent to explore in and around the San Luis Valley were Spanish colonists. Folks on hunting trips or herding stock may have come this far north around AD 1600 or so. It wasn't until nearly a hundred years later that the oldest known record of exploration into the San Luis Valley was made. Territorial governor Don Diego de Vargas kept a diary as he explored to a point about 35 miles south of the sand dunes. The names in his diary suggest that Spanish-speaking people had already seen and named the places he visited. Another territorial governor, Juan Bautista de Anza, kept a journal of his travels past the western edge of what is now Great Sand Dunes National Park and Preserve in 1779.

While neither de Vargas nor de Anza mentioned the dunes in their writings, Zebulon Pike left us a nice description when he ventured through the Sangre de Cristos and onto the dune field one January day in 1807.

Trade roads through the San Luis Valley and past the dunes saw significant use in the 19th century. What became known as the Old Spanish Trail, from Santa Fe to Los Angeles, saw heavy use from 1829 to 1848, as trade in furs, woven goods, and mostly horses and mules increased. Other historical documents and oral histories indicate that local people were captured as slaves and transported along the Old Spanish Trail as well.

In 1853, Captain John W. Gunnison explored the sand dunes while trying to discover an economical railway route to the Pacific. He ventured partway up Mosca and Medano Passes from the west, and then skirted the dune field to the south and west, heading north toward Saguache from there.

In 1871, Frank Hastings opened the Mosca Pass Toll Road, called "the lifeline of the San Luis Valley," as a stagecoach and mail route. Near the base of the pass, the town of Montville sprung up, with cabins, a store, a post office, and an orchard near the corrals and tollgate of the road. Other homesteaders settled in the area, including Ulysses Herard who built a ranch along Medano Creek in 1875. Mount Herard, the 13,297-foot peak that rises prominently to the northwest of the dunes, is named after him.

In the 1930s, a gold mill was built to recover gold from the sand of the dunes, but the quantities were so minute that it was never profitable. By that time, a local movement emerged to protect the dunes and support grew for designation of the Great Sand Dunes as a national monument. It finally achieved that status on March 17, 1932. The Great Sand Dunes were designated a National Wilderness Area in October of 1976, with wilderness designation for the surrounding Sangre de Cristo Mountains following in August of 1993. Authorization to expand the national monument and change it to a national park came in November of 2000. When land with a sufficient diversity of resources was acquired in September of 2004, the monument and surrounding mountains officially became Great Sand Dunes National Park and Preserve.

Restaurants and Picnic Areas

There are **no restaurants** within the park or preserve. However, four **picnic areas** offer lunch spots with spectacular views. The **Mosca Creek Picnic Area** is accessible via a paved road and offers picnic tables, drinking water, raised fire grills for charcoal only, and restrooms. The others, **Ponderosa Point, Sand Pit,** and **Castle Creek,** lie along the four-wheel-drive Medano Pass Primitive Road and provide picnic tables.

Lodging and Camping

No hotel lodging is available inside of the park. Just outside the park boundary, however, you'll find the **Great Sand Dunes Lodge.** This small motel offers a deck with barbecue grills, beautiful views of the mountains and dunes, and an indoor heated swimming pool. Contact them at 719-378-2900 or www.gsdlodge.com.

The **Piñon Flats Campground** has 88 sites and is open year-round. Reservations are not accepted. The fee is $14 per night, and includes a site with a fire grate and a picnic table. Drinking water, flush toilets, and a trash dumpster are available. You can buy firewood at the visitor center or in the campground. Sites will accommodate RVs and tents, and many have spectacular views of the sand dunes and the surrounding Sangre de Cristo Mountains. On busy weekends, such as Memorial Day or the Fourth of July, rangers recommend arriving several nights early to ensure a spot.

Backcountry primitive camping permits can be obtained from the visitor center.

The **Great Sand Dunes Oasis,** located on US 150 just outside the park boundary, runs a campground with showers. It has 100 non-hookup sites, 20 hookup sites, camping cabins, and group tent sites. Families can buy gas there and shop at the convenience store for necessities and souvenirs. The shop offers not only ice for your cooler and firewood, but a restaurant that serves breakfast, lunch, and dinner. They claim their homemade pies and old-fashioned milk shakes are famous. You can also wash a load of clothes at their laundromat. The Oasis rents two motel rooms in a duplex building at that location as well. For information, call 719-378-2222.

The Piñon Flats Campground looks out over
the dunes and surrounding mountains.

Nearby Towns

Tiny **Mosca,** 23 miles southeast of the visitor center on Colorado State Route 17, has a gas station, a restaurant, a post office, and a motel. Colorado Gators, a "family oriented, recreational, and educational farm," raises and shows live alligators between Mosca and Hooper, the next town to the north. Contact Colorado Gators at 719-378-2612 or www.gatorfarm.com.

Hooper, 7 miles north of Mosca, has a gas station with a convenience store and a restaurant, called My Sister's Place, plus a park with a playground and a post office. Less than 1 mile north of town, the Sand Dunes Swimming Pool and RV Park offers swimming in artesian hot springs water. Call 719-378-2807 for information or visit the website at www.sanddunespool.com.

Just over 34 miles south and east of the national park's visitor center, the town of **Alamosa** lies at the junction of US 285 and US 160. With a population of nearly 8,500 people and the San Luis Valley Regional Airport, it is the hub of this southern Colorado breadbasket. The Spanish word *alamosa* means "full of cotton-wood trees" and shady Cole Park along the Rio Grande has its share. The park is home to a big modern playground, skate park, picnic tables, restrooms with drinking water, a library, and a post office. Alamosa Tourism's Visitor Center is located in the

The dunes yell, "Come play!"

little train depot here. A variety of fast-food and sit-down restaurants offers families several choices for grabbing a bite, while private and chain motels provide showers and pillows for your heads. Safeway, City Market, and a Wal-Mart Supercenter have groceries and other necessities. The San Luis Valley Regional Medical Center, located at 106 Blanca Avenue in Alamosa, features valley-wide ambulance service and a Level III trauma center. Museums in town include the San Luis Valley Museum, featuring ranch life, narrow-gauge train, and history exhibits; and the Luther E. Bean Museum, located at Adams State College, which features Native American, Hispanic, and other local art. For information, contact the chamber of commerce at 719-589-3681 or online at www.alamosachamber.com, or call the Alamosa Visitor Center at 800-258-7597.

Special Considerations for Families

As beautiful as the sand dunes are, remember they are here due to a combination of rather harsh elements. Sand, of course, is the big element. It is gritty and tiny, and finds its way into everything.

The next biggest harsh element is invisible—but it is what piled the dunes so high in the first place. Great Sand Dunes National Park and Preserve is a windy, windy place. And what does the wind blow around? Sand. Now those little grains are in even more places than they were before. You and your kids just have to learn to live with it in shoes and sleeping bags and food. But eyes are a bit more sensitive. Bring saline solution for irrigating eyes, and a box of tissues for blowing noses. On the other hand, all that moving air and open space make for fantastic kite flying. Tuck some string and a collapsible kite in your pack before you head out.

The San Luis Valley is a desert and there aren't often clouds to provide shade. Not only that, but at 8,500 feet above sea level, there is less atmosphere to filter the ultraviolet rays. When they bounce off the dunes and water, it's sunburn city. Lay the sunblock on thickly and often. Tie wide-brimmed hats to your kids' heads and threaten them with no TV for their entire visit if they take them off. Slather on lip balm and encourage them to drink lots of water to keep them hydrated. Although bathing suits are practical for grubbing around in Medano Creek, hiking on the dunes dressed like Sahara traders isn't a bad idea. Don't forget good shoes or boots and socks for venturing into the dune field. Burned feet are no fun.

Despite the potential for heat, the park and preserve are pretty high in elevation, and the wind can be cold, even in the summertime. Bring coats, hats, and long pants for chilly days. Also be aware that sand, especially blowing sand, will eat your camera's insides before you can say, "Scoot together a little more." Keep cameras off the sandy surface, and if it is windy, just put it away. Think twice about throwing it in the bottom of your daypack—sand likes to hang out there, too. Zip-closure plastic bags can help protect photographic equipment (and anything else you want to keep sand out of).

If you are here when Medano Creek is running, warn your kids to be careful about getting the water in their mouths. The water quality is high, but dogs, deer, and toddlers are walking around in it, and it isn't drinking water. Families who like to build sand castles should bring their own pails and scoops as the visitor center doesn't sell them.

Medano Creek, at the base of the dunes, and the dune field are very resilient ecosystems. It is one of the few places in Colorado's national parks where you can run all over in wild abandon without worrying about messing up the landscape for future generations. Even throwing your sweaty, sunblock-covered body in the stream is pretty harmless. The water just soaks into the sand downstream and is well filtered by the time it comes up in the sabkha, years later.

The rest of the park and preserve are a bit more fragile, however. Rangers ask folks to stay on the trails when hiking in the mountains or across the sand sheet. The hike from the campground to the creek follows a well-beaten path through this wildlife community, and it can be pretty interesting, but please watch your step.

What Makes Great Sand Dunes National Park and Preserve Special

This is one tricky national park. Families can have more bald-faced fun playing at the Great Sand Dunes than just about anywhere else in the whole state. And you can plunk your kids down for a day of splashing and running and digging and climbing right in the midst of some of Colorado's most spectacular scenery. Children won't even notice they are doing important hands-on (really, whole bodies-on) experiential learning. They cannot help but get curious about why the dunes are there and what makes them like that. Next thing you know, your youngsters are grasping high-powered explanations about one of the most complex geological and biological systems in the world. Pretty good for a giant sandbox.

Cooling down after playing in the sand

Prairie

Stretched, windblown, and full of sky, Colorado's high plains host national grasslands and historic trails and sites, but no national parks or monuments. That would lead some people to think that eastern Colorado's only draw is the story of those who crossed these vast open spaces. Those people would be wrong.

A hawk uses a windmill as a perch. Several hawk species hunt over the prairie at Sand Creek.

The trails and sites do have fascinating histories, of course, yet they are even more valuable because they get visitors out of their cars and onto the subtle, gorgeous monotony of the grasslands. Once you look beyond and below the surface, you realize the wildlife, geology, and wildness of the region make historical stops a deeply enriching experience.

Colorado's Eastern Plains have been the location of many historical events.
© John Fielder

ENTRY

NATIONAL PARK SERVICE PASSPORT STAMP

Bird's-Eye View:
Rolling and Stretching to the Horizon

In eastern Colorado, 115 miles east of I-25 and 50 miles south of I-70, the wind blows unhindered across the high plains. Big Sandy Creek drains a huge swath of this area, from just east of Colorado Springs to the Arkansas River near Lamar. Near Limon, Big Sandy Creek begins to trend southeast for about 75 or 80 miles. Then it bends and goes almost straight south. The Sand Creek Massacre took place in the vicinity of this big bend.

The massacre didn't happen all at once, however, and its events didn't happen in one specific spot. At one spot, the U.S. military first viewed the Arapaho and Cheyenne camps strung out along the creek. At other places, American Indian women dug pits in the sand from which they defended the camps. At Chief Black Kettle's lodge, he flew the American flag and a white flag of surrender. The troops engaged in a running battle, chasing people along the waterway and across the prairie. Finally, the military set up their own camp. All of these spots, significant to the massacre's history, are planned for inclusion in the Sand Creek Massacre National Historic Site, which will be open to the public when the Park Service acquires enough land.

Within the historic site boundaries, the prairie rolls and stretches toward the horizons, while Big Sandy Creek carves gentle bluffs here and there. Dry much of the year, it runs with spring meltwater once in a while or after a rain. This makes it hard to find, even when you are driving right over it. Head east on

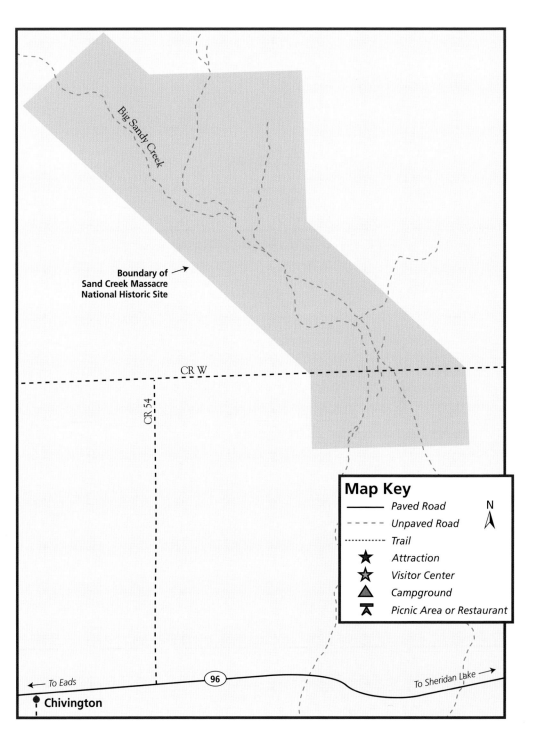

Big Sandy Creek

Boundary of
Sand Creek Massacre
National Historic Site

CR W

CR 54

Map Key

—— *Paved Road*

- - - *Unpaved Road*

.... *Trail*

★ *Attraction*

☆ *Visitor Center*

▲ *Campground*

☗ *Picnic Area or Restaurant*

N

← *To Eads*

96

To Sheridan Lake →

📍 **Chivington**

CO 96 to just before Chivington, nearly a ghost town. Turn north on County Road 54 and travel across the prairie to CR W. Turn east again; the road crosses a low spot and then climbs a small bluff in the landscape. The creek here is near where the events of the Sand Creek Massacre took place.

Attractions

The historic site is not yet open. There are no facilities or interpretive structures.

Programs and Activities

The National Park Service offers **no scheduled programs** or **Junior Ranger Program** at Sand Creek.

Natural History

Geology: Grassy Ocean

During the time of the dinosaurs, a large, shallow sea covered much of eastern Colorado with a thick layer of mud. When the Rockies grew, sands and gravels that eroded off their slopes came to rest on top of the former sea bottom. The climate is dry and most streams are dry except when a spring snow is melting or after a summer rainsquall. The creeks have eroded rolling dips in the prairie, like gentle swells on a grassy ocean. Winds have piled the dry sands into low hills, which are now covered in prairie grasses. Here and there a waterway chews into a sand hill to form a one-sided gully.

Plants and Wildlife: Farm Meets Prairie

Mostly devoted to agriculture, the plains near the Sand Creek Massacre National Historic Site produce sunflowers and some sorghum, and offer grazing for cattle. Cottonwood clumps, willows, and chokecherries dot the drainages. Uncultivated land near the stream supports sand sagebrush and grama grass. Wild roses, tansy asters, and prairie sunflowers bloom in the spring and summer.

Wildlife watching is surprisingly rich in these parts. I saw a pronghorn, western box turtles basking in the middle of the roads—drive carefully!—several ring-necked pheasants, dozens of hawks sitting on roadside fence posts, a porcupine, and a feral hog. Prairie rattlesnakes rub their bellies on the ground, while meadowlarks sing from the tops of shrubs above. Deer step daintily along the creek bed, while foxes and coyotes follow their noses in the brush. Flickers,

Ring-necked pheasant
© Wendy Shattil/Bob Rozinski

OUR EXPERIENCE: COTTONWOOD SHADOWS

Mustard-colored grasses jostle each other, making hissing sounds in the gentle yet relentless breeze. A grainy scent like underdone toast wafts from the fields, and my eyes and lungs feel stretched by the distances and the cleanness of the air. The prairie is beautiful. I gaze over the landscape, soothed by the loveliness that contrasts with ugly thoughts of terror and death and torn families. I keep thinking, "Where would we hide? How would we hide?"

My heart is heavy on this trip. Yet there is a strength, a growing-up that happens when we face this evil. The emptiness of the prairie, the cleansing breeze, and the absence of clutter allow us to sit down and be with the events. We conjure them in our minds, we take a walk with the spirits, we cry, we regret, we soothe. And we are soothed—by the wind, the grasses, the deer in the cottonwood shadows, and by the hawks that sail overhead.

Many called it a battle; today it is called a massacre. But here, now, I face the pain and am surprised to find peace.

juncos, goldfinches, and lazuli buntings fly through tree branches and brush, while owls hunt for mice by night. By day, red-tailed hawks soar overhead.

Human History

Paleo-Indians, as long as 10,500 years ago, were busy hunting bison on the plains near Sand Creek. One nearby archaeological site exposes a place where nearly 200 bison were driven into an arroyo and killed. Projectile points found buried with the bones suggest they were the instruments of death for many of the animals.

Pronghorn antelope
© Wendy Shattil/Bob Rozinski

Through the years the culture of the plains people shifted, showing influence from the plains woodlands people in the east. Archaeologists date the presence of Apachean folks in the area from around 1350. Of Athapascan stock, the Apaches are linguistically related to some Pacific Northwest tribes and the Bloods of Canada. Whether they migrated into the area via the plains or along a mountain route is open for some debate. In the mid-1700s, the Utes were occupying the mountainous areas of Colorado. As they got more horses, they expanded out onto the plains and joined with a linguistically related group, the Comanches, to push the Apaches south.

Around 1800, Colorado saw the arrival of another group from the north. The Arapaho people were migrating into the area from North Dakota or Montana, after breaking with their kin, the Atsina. Another Algonkian-speaking group, the Cheyenne, were hunting in South Dakota and northern Wyoming.

In the late 1820s and early 1830s, Ceran St. Vrain and Charles and William Bent built trading posts along the Front Range and eastern prairies. They invited the Cheyenne and the Arapaho to come to southeastern Colorado to trade. The Cheyenne split, some staying put to become the Northern Cheyenne while others headed down to the Arkansas River and eventually became the Southern Cheyenne. As the Arapaho and Cheyenne moved south, the Comanche migrated out of the area to Oklahoma and southern Kansas.

During the second half of the 1800s, conflict between European-American migrants and local natives increased, with misunderstandings, skirmishes, raids, and violence. While the Civil War dragged on in the east, fighting and negotiations alternated in the west. After several American Indian chiefs met with President Abraham Lincoln in Washington, D.C., in 1863, a Cheyenne chief named Black Kettle became convinced that peace was the only viable alternative. Cheyenne chiefs subsequently met with Colorado governor John Evans and with Colonel John Chivington, who instructed them to return with their people to the area near Sand Creek.

Meanwhile, Northern Cheyenne Dog Soldiers, working without tribal sanction, increasingly raided Denver supply routes and murdered a family of settlers near Denver, mutilating their bodies. The *Rocky Mountain News* ran editorials filled with incendiary rhetoric. Governor Evans issued a proclamation to all the citizens of Colorado to pursue, kill, and destroy all Indians wherever they were found, as enemies of the country. Colonel Chivington, who was eyeing a position on Colorado's congressional delegation, took up the quest. In a Denver speech, he vowed to "kill and scalp all, big and little."

At dawn on November 29, 1864, about 500 Arapaho and Cheyenne were camped along a stretch of Big Sandy Creek. Chivington and his troops attacked with artillery and gunfire. Most of the able-bodied Indian men were off hunting, but the few left behind tried to hold off the soldiers. Black Kettle raised the American flag and a white flag of surrender and told his people to gather around it. Many were killed there, but Black Kettle escaped. Most people were able to run away onto the frozen prairies, making their way north to relatives encamped along the Smokey Hill Trail. By afternoon, more than 150 people were dead. Most had been easy targets—elders, pregnant women, and toddlers. U.S. troops mutilated many of the victims' bodies, later parading the parts through Denver.

Sand Creek Massacre National Historic Site at a Glance

Location: Eastern Colorado, about 20 miles northeast of Lamar

Address: P.O. Box 249, Eads, CO 81036

Telephone: 719-438-5916

Website: www.nps.gov/sand

Size: 12,500 acres authorized, 920 of which the National Park Service has acquired and 1,465 acres of which have been acquired by the Cheyenne and Arapaho tribes of Oklahoma

Elevation: 4,200 feet above sea level

Major Activities: History, archaeology, education, and commemoration

Weather: Summer highs from 80 to 105 degrees; winter temperatures range from 0 to 65 degrees; occasional rain or snow throughout the year, mostly in the spring.

Best Season: Fall

Hours: Not applicable

Closures: Sand Creek Massacre National Historic Site is closed to the public until the official establishment is complete.

Cost: Not applicable

Facilities: There are no facilities at Sand Creek Massacre National Historic Site, which is not yet open to the public.

Accessibility: The site is not accessible according to ADA standards.

About 500 Cheyenne and Arapaho people camped along a section of Big Sandy Creek.

The day after the massacre, an Indian Bureau interpreter, John Smith, sat in the military camp. His son, Jack, had joined him while the Arapaho and Cheyenne were being killed. When Smith was called away for a moment, soldiers shot the interpreter's son dead because his mother was an Indian.

The Sand Creek Massacre was a turning point in Colorado history. Black Kettle and his band retreated to the Washita River, in Indian Country in what is now Oklahoma. Almost exactly four years after Sand Creek, the band was attacked again, this time by George A. Custer and his men. At Washita, Black Kettle and his wife were killed.

After Sand Creek, the Arapaho and Cheyenne formed an alliance with the Comanche, Kiowa, and Lakota tribes. They made war, attacking settlers and supply shipments, traders and telegraphs. Eventually, a coalition of Lakota Sioux, Cheyenne, and Arapaho defeated George A. Custer and his troops at the Battle of the Little Bighorn. However, within a year, most of the Indians present at Little Bighorn were forced to surrender. By the 1880s, the Arapaho and the Cheyenne people were gone from Colorado, moved to reservations in Oklahoma, Wyoming, and Montana.

The land Big Sandy Creek flows across was homesteaded. Memories of the massacre's exact locations faded. A stone marker was erected at what was guessed to be the site in 1950. On November 7, 2000, Congress authorized a national historic site and directed the park service to acquire enough land from willing sellers to appropriately preserve, commemorate, and interpret the massacre. In a site study, 12,500 acres were identified for the historic site, about 2,500 of which have subsequently been acquired by the National Park Service or the Cheyenne and Arapaho tribes. When enough land has been acquired, the historic site will be opened to the public, and about 30,000 visitors a year are expected.

Restaurants and Picnic Areas

Currently, Sand Creek Massacre National Historic Site offers **no restaurants or picnic facilities.**

Lodging and Camping

Currently, Sand Creek Massacre National Historic Site offers **no hotel lodging or camping.**

Nearby Towns

Eads, the Kiowa County seat, is located at the intersection of US 287 and Colorado State Route 96. With three convenience stores, a small grocery store, two gas stations, and three restaurants, it offers visitors the essentials. Families looking to spend the night can find lodging at the Econolodge in town. A town park, right on CO 96, offers ornate cement picnic tables, restrooms, and a historical marker. The Weisbrod Memorial Hospital and Nursing Home has emergency facilities. In the summer, the city pool gives kids a place to cool off and splash around. Private landowners in the area run guided tours of part of the massacre site, just west of the National Park Service lands. See www.sandcreektours.com for details.

Other nearby attractions include the Kiowa County Historical Museum and a transcontinental bike trail that passes through town. The Great Plains Reservoirs, a cluster of lakes a few miles south of Eads, have been designated an Important Bird Area by the Colorado Audubon Society. The organization claims that the Great Plains Reservoirs have "Hosted almost every species ever recorded in Colorado," and "The southern point of Neenoshe Reservoir is unique in the interior U.S. for hosting seven species of terns: Least, Black, Forster's, Common, Arctic, Caspian, and Royal." Indeed, the area around Eads offers some of the best birding in the state.

The roadside park in Eads displays a beautiful sculpture of the women who have lived on the prairie.

Lamar, 30 to 40 miles south of the Sand Creek Massacre site, has nearly 9,000 residents and is home to the Colorado Welcome Center. Four city parks offer playgrounds, restrooms, and a place for the kids to run around. Several locally owned and chain restaurants and hotels provide sustenance and shelter in this town near the eastern end of the Santa Fe Trail in Colorado.

Special Considerations for Families

When this historic site does open, it may be an emotionally difficult place to visit with children. The sheer violence of the event is hard enough for adults to fathom, much less explain to innocents. The first impulse is to protect them from such atrocity. Many families will opt to save Sand Creek for when their children are much older.

Yet the violence that is a part of Sand Creek is a part of the world our kids will inherit. If we can face it with them—and be there to support them and help them learn from it—then perhaps when they grow up, they will answer violence and hate with strength, wisdom, maturity, and grace.

What Makes Sand Creek Massacre National Historic Site Special

Sand Creek treats the senses with its vast skyline, its wild plants and animals, its unsurpassed sunrises and sunsets, its morning chorus of birdsong, its buffeting gusts, and its whiffs of fresh-turned earth and baking grasses. It challenges the brain and the heart, and forces us to ponder. It sobers us, as well as lifts us up. And it is not ready for visitors. The best we can do is drive lonely county roads and wonder if we are close to where the events occurred. So while Sand Creek is a special place, it isn't time to go there yet.

ENTRY

NATIONAL PARK SERVICE PASSPORT STAMP

Bird's-Eye View: Walk Back in Time

A key feature of the Santa Fe National Historic Trail, Bent's Old Fort hunkers down on the banks of the Arkansas River, about two-and-a-half hours southeast of Colorado Springs. Take I-25 to Pueblo, then US 50 to La Junta. From there, travel north about 1 mile on Colorado State Route 109 across the Arkansas River. Turn east on Colorado State Route 194 and go about 6 miles to Bent's Old Fort. Signs make finding it easy.

Rebuilt on the original foundations, the fort's adobe walls both blend in and rise above eastern Colorado's arid plains. The parking lot is hidden in a prairie low spot. From there, the fort itself is 0.25 mile away—and 160 years back in time.

Attractions

Guides in Period Garb

Trek past tepees and free-roaming mules to the front gate where piñon smoke and characters from the fort's past greet you. Passing through the massive mud walls, you'll emerge in an open courtyard. Four times a day during the summer and twice a day the rest of the year, expert historians conduct tours and discussions here about the fort and its denizens. You'll begin to feel the struggle, savvy, and talent of the people who lived here.

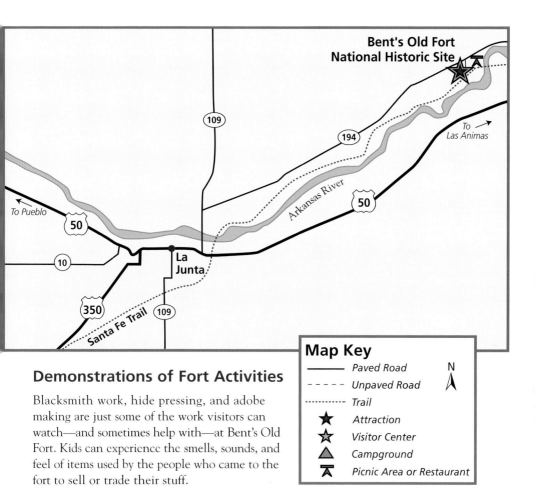

Demonstrations of Fort Activities

Blacksmith work, hide pressing, and adobe making are just some of the work visitors can watch—and sometimes help with—at Bent's Old Fort. Kids can experience the smells, sounds, and feel of items used by the people who came to the fort to sell or trade their stuff.

Map Key

		N
———	Paved Road	
- - - - -	Unpaved Road	⋀
··········	Trail	
★	Attraction	
☆	Visitor Center	
△	Campground	
⋔	Picnic Area or Restaurant	

Programs and Activities

Through **guided tours,** the living history staff is excellent at helping visitors understand the fort, its builders, its customers, and their role in history. The tours are held twice a day, at 10:30 a.m. and 1 p.m., September through May.

Kids' Quarters, held in June, features great hands-on activities for 7- to 11-year-old historians. The **Traditional Holiday Celebration** is held at the beginning of December and includes games, toy making, wagon rides, candlelight tours, and foods of the frontier. Check the website for schedules and to make reservations.

If kids complete parts of the Bent's Old Fort Adventure Guide, view the video, **Castle of the Plains,** and go on either a guided or self-guided tour, they can become eligible to earn a **Junior Ranger badge** from Bent's Old Fort National Historic Site. Pick up the free pamphlet at the fort entrance.

Guided tours deepen visitors' understanding of Bent's Old Fort.

School tours are available for classes wishing to make a field trip to the site. Staff will also take 40-minute, off-site programs to local schools. Additionally, teachers can check out a traveling trunk, which brings items and activities illustrating Santa Fe Trail life to schoolchildren around the state.

Natural History

Geology: Floodplain

The land that is now eastern Colorado once lay beneath the Western Interior Seaway, a large, shallow, prehistoric sea that stretched across much of what is now America's Midwest. Detritus from the waters settled to the bottom in a thick layer of muck. Huge animals, like the pointy-toothed and impossibly long-necked plesiosaurs, also sank when they died, only to be covered by even more silty deposits. An intact skeleton was discovered south of Bent's Old Fort, in Baca County, and two casts of this beautiful specimen now hang in the atrium of the Denver Museum of Nature & Science.

As the land began to rise when the mountains developed, the Interior Seaway retreated, leaving beach sand behind at its edges. Gravel then washed down from the rising mountains, covering the sands in more sedimentary layers that spread out in a wide sheet as far as Kansas.

High in the Rockies, the Arkansas River begins as snowmelt and flows through the northern part of a deep rift in the continent, the Rio Grande Rift. The Arkansas would keep flowing south to join the Rio Grande, except that volcanoes erupted and diverted its path to the east. As the Arkansas pours out of the mountains and across the plains, smaller streams run to join it, eroding rolling dips and small gullies in the surrounding prairies.

The Arkansas River slowly digs a wide floodplain in the sedimentary layers of the plains. Where the sandstone is harder, the river gouges narrower canyons with cliffy sides. In other places it spreads out, braiding around islands and watering long bosques (cottonwood forests) as it goes.

OUR EXPERIENCE:
HOT SPOT

When I first visited Bent's Old Fort as a wee child, it was little more than an ankle-high, nubby outline of mud bricks in the prairie. When I venture there now, with my own children, it is completely restored, featuring towers, balconies, and furniture. The adobe walls, costumed guides, and artifacts capture my imagination, helping me grasp the thinking of the folks who built the original fort in an empty land. Their stories, fragmented and full of holes, give me insight into the historian's quandary and mission. If only we could find out more about these people, what they thought, and how they felt, then maybe we could see our own lives with better perspective.

This was William Bent's home and business—until it exploded and burned under mysterious circumstances. You wonder if its ghosts swirled around him in the smoke. Or maybe he felt relieved. It's a mystery. Bent's Old Fort National Historic Site gives you the chance to talk to those ghosts, and to get a feel for life in one of the Old West's early hot spots.

The walk from the parking lot to the fort takes you back 160 years in time.

Plants and Wildlife: A Bend in the River

The fort is located on a bend of the Arkansas River, near a ford where the Santa Fe Trail crossed the water. The Bent brothers and their business partner, Ceran St. Vrain, picked the spot because it would serve their customers well. Not only was it on the trail route, but it also offered water and grazing for the ponies and other livestock the visitors had with

Wild turkeys
© Wendy Shattil/Bob Rozinski

them. There was timber nearby, as well as good hunting in the bosques near the river. In the mid-19th century, enough buffalo and deer lived here for hunters to supply the fort with food.

Visitors are not encouraged to roam around the property of the site, but instead to tour the fort itself. However, if you wander down toward the river, you can enjoy a wide variety of prairie plants that inhabit the floodplain of the Arkansas River. Most obvious are the huge cottonwood trees, but there are also willows and ground cherries. Pretty wildflowers also bloom there, including wild roses, tansy asters, and prairie sunflowers.

This area is home to coyotes, red foxes, and swift foxes. Mule deer were noted historically, and they and their cousins, the white-tailed deer, still inhabit the site. You may also see (or smell) signs of skunks, raccoons, and badgers. Several different species of squirrels live at the site, and beaver have been viewed venturing into this section of the Arkansas River as well.

More than 130 species of birds have been sighted at Bent's Old Fort. Nesting birds include red-tailed and ferruginous hawks, wild turkeys, great horned owls, western meadowlarks, and lazuli buntings.

Also be sure to look for Great Plains toads, green-collared lizards, coachwhip and western ribbon snakes, and prairie rattlesnakes.

Badgers
© Wendy Shattil/Bob Rozinski

Bent's Old Fort National Historic Site at a Glance

Location: Southeast Colorado, about 70 miles east of Pueblo

Address: 35110 Highway 194 East, La Junta, CO 81050-9523

Telephone: 719-383-5010

Website: www.nps.gov/beol

Size: 799 acres

Elevation: 4,000 feet above sea level

Major Activities: History of the Old West, photography, and picnicking

Weather: Summer highs from 80 to 105 degrees; winter temperatures from 0 to 65 degrees; occasional rain or snow throughout the year, mostly in the spring

Best Seasons: Summer and fall

Hours: The site is open from 8 a.m. to 5:30 p.m. in June, July, and August, and 9 a.m. to 4 p.m. the remainder of the year.

Closures: The site is closed on Thanksgiving, Christmas, and New Year's Days.

Cost: Fees are $3 per person for ages 13 and up, $2 per person for ages 6 to 12, and free for kids 5 and younger.

Facilities: The Bent's Old Fort Information Center has a bookstore as well as exhibits. A 20-minute video shown in the fort is a good introduction to the site. Restrooms with diaper-changing stations are located in the fort and in the parking lot.

Accessibility: A shuttle is available to take those who are unable to walk from the parking lot to the fort. The bathrooms and some of the rooms on the first floor of the fort are wheelchair accessible.

The Arapaho and the Cheyenne were very important customers of the Bent–St. Vrain Company.

Human History

Bent's Old Fort was the Santa Fe Trail's cosmopolitan border crossing with Mexico, and its business was global in nature. Built in 1833 to serve commerce in the region and on the trail itself, the fort's thick walls guarded a warehouse of 19th-century riches. Its clients were sophisticated and complex. They traded buffalo hide for Chinese face paint and Czechoslovakian beads, silver for iron tools, and labor for adventure.

Bent's Old Fort harbors a poignant story of wealth, love, political influence, and circumstances beyond anyone's control. In 1847, William Bent's brother was killed, his wife died, and his best customers were driven away. Bent's efforts to sell the fort failed. Sometime later, a group of travelers miles away heard an explosion and the fort burned.

As you climb over doorframes and unlatch heavy wooden shutters, you begin to feel as if you are peeking into the lives of the fort's occupants, chatting with their spirits. B-movie images of the Old West melt away as you begin to understand the depth of the people who lived here. Designated a national historic site in 1960, the fort still holds its secrets close. Today, no one knows why there was an explosion or if William Bent set it off. The 30,000 visitors each year can only let their fingers trace the plaster of the old gunpowder storeroom and wonder.

Restaurants and Picnic Areas

There are **no restaurants** at the site. However, **a picnic area** offers tables in the shade of large poplar trees.

Lodging and Camping

No hotel lodging is available at the site, but there are several motels in La Junta and Las Animas.

No campgrounds are located at Bent's Old Fort itself. The closest campgrounds are a KOA that is just west of La Junta, at Holbrook Reservoir State Wildlife Area, and at John Martin Reservoir State Park.

Guides dressed in period garb bring the fort back to life.

A broad, 0.25-mile path starts out from the parking lot, crosses a rise in the prairie, and leads to the front gate of Bent's Old Fort. The walk lets families approach the building on foot—the way traders did 160 years ago.

Nearby Towns

La Junta, a town of about 7,500 people, is 8 miles west of Bent's Old Fort. The town offers seven parks, including Potter Park featuring an outdoor swimming pool, and a new skateboard park, billed a "most excellent gathering place" by the *Pueblo Chieftain*. A big, new playground lies right next to it in the shady City Park. Hospital services are provided at the Arkansas Valley Regional Medical Center at 1100 Carson Avenue. Numerous restaurants and several hotels are also located in La Junta. In spite of its name, we found the Hog's Breath Saloon to be a kid-friendly and fairly tasty place to eat on a Sunday evening. The Koshare Indian Museum in La Junta houses an impressive collection of Native American artifacts and art.

Special Considerations for Families

Kids are naturally pretending to be someone else all the time. Bent's Old Fort is a fantastic place for them to do their pretending right. Once they get a feel for the place and what happened there, it is perfect for trying the Old West on for size. Bring a bandanna, a hat, or any object that will serve as enough costume to get them into the role. Then, get busy being workers or business people of the mid-19th century.

Be sure to watch kids carefully on the second floor plazas—they have no guardrails and kids can fall off if they aren't careful. Also, many of the furnishings in the fort's rooms should not be touched or sat upon. Once kids know the limits, however, they can have a ball here.

What Makes Bent's Old Fort Special

Bent's Old Fort offers an antidote to traditional Old West stereotypes. The costumed guides are good at showing kids and adults how similar we are to the folks who came to the fort so long ago. The fort helps kids understand a significant piece of Colorado and American history in a way books never can.

Trip Log

Trip Dates: _____

Destination: _____

Who went: _____
_____

What we did: _____
_____
_____
_____

What we saw: _____
_____
_____
_____

Something I learned: _____
_____
_____
_____

Surprises: _____
_____
_____

The worst part was: _____
_____
_____

The best part was: _____
_____
_____
_____

Trip rating: ☆ ☆ ☆ ☆ ☆

(Color in the number of stars to rate the trip.)

Comments:

_____

_____

_____

_____

_____

_____

Artwork:

Leave No Trace Principles

As outdoor recreation became increasingly popular in the middle of the 20th century, managers of our wild lands and outdoor enthusiasts began to see the impact recreationists were having on nature. At first, regulations were put in place to limit the damage, but managers soon realized that education was a more pleasant and more effective way of getting people to take care of the outdoors. Research into nature-friendly practices eventually lead to the development of the following Principles of Outdoor Ethics. Find out more at www.lnt.org.

If you plan to adventure into the outdoors, whether for a short hike or for an extended overnight backpacking trip, keep the following guidelines in mind.

Plan Ahead and Prepare
- Know the regulations and special concerns for the area you'll visit.
- Prepare for extreme weather, hazards, and emergencies.
- Schedule your trip to avoid times of high use.
- Visit in small groups. Split larger parties into groups of four to six.
- Repackage food to minimize waste.
- Use a map and compass to eliminate the use of marking paint, rock cairns, or flagging.

Travel and Camp on Durable Surfaces
- Durable surfaces include established trails and campsites, rock, gravel, dry grasses, or snow.
- Protect riparian areas by camping at least 200 feet from lakes and streams.
- Good campsites are found, not made. Altering a site is not necessary.
- In popular areas:
  - Concentrate use on existing trails and campsites.
  - Walk single file in the middle of the trail, even when wet or muddy.
  - Keep campsites small. Focus activity in areas where vegetation is absent.
- In pristine areas:
  - Disperse use to prevent the creation of campsites and trails.
  - Avoid places where impacts are just beginning.

Dispose of Waste Properly
- Pack it in, pack it out. Inspect your campsite and rest areas for trash or spilled foods. Pack out all trash, leftover food, and litter.
- Deposit solid human waste in catholes dug 6 to 8 inches deep at least 200 feet from water, camp, and trails. Cover and disguise the cathole when finished.
- Pack out toilet paper and hygiene products.
- To wash yourself or your dishes, carry water 200 feet away from streams or lakes and use small amounts of biodegradable soap. Scatter strained dishwater.

Leave What You Find

- Preserve the past: examine, but do not touch, cultural or historic structures and artifacts.
- Leave rocks, plants, and other natural objects as you find them.
- Avoid introducing or transporting non-native species.
- Do not build structures or furniture, or dig trenches.

Minimize Campfire Impacts

- Campfires can cause lasting impacts to the backcountry. Use a lightweight stove for cooking and enjoy a candle lantern for light.
- Where fires are permitted, use established fire rings, fire pans, or mound fires.
- Keep fires small. Only use sticks from the ground that can be broken by hand.
- Burn all wood and coals to ash, put out campfires completely, then scatter cool ashes.

Respect Wildlife

- Observe wildlife from a distance. Do not follow or approach them.
- Never feed animals. Feeding wildlife damages their health, alters natural behaviors, and exposes them to predators and other dangers.
- Protect wildlife and your food by storing rations and trash securely.
- Control pets at all times, or leave them at home.
- Avoid wildlife during sensitive times: mating, nesting, raising young, or winter.

Be Considerate of Other Visitors

- Respect other visitors and protect the quality of their experience.
- Be courteous. Yield to other users on the trail.
- Step to the downhill side of the trail when encountering pack stock.
- Take breaks and camp away from trails and other visitors.
- Let nature's sounds prevail. Avoid loud voices and noises.

Essential Gear for Family Hiking

Must-Have Items

- Hiking boots or sturdy shoes
- Daypacks for everyone in the family (who isn't in a backpack baby carrier)
- Drinking water bottle (one for each person in the family)
- Sun protection (sunblock, hats with brims, sunglasses, lip balm)
- Jackets and extra clothes for the weather (raingear, knit hats, mittens)
- Lunch and snacks
- Map and compass (know how to use them and do it often, so the kids can learn, too)
- First aid kit
- Poop-in-the-woods kit (small trowel, toilet paper, plastic bags for packing out TP) and diaper kit (if your kids are that age)
- Plastic tarp and foam pad for nap time or emergency bivouac
- Whistles (each person carries his or her own for use only when truly lost)
- Waterproof matches and fire starter for emergencies
- Flashlight
- Pocket knife

Extra Items

- Camera and film
- Tissues for runny noses
- Insect repellant
- Guidebooks (birds, wildflowers, etc.)
- Notebook or sketchbook and pencils

For little tykes, a baby backpack carrier can be just the ticket.

Guides and Outfitters

1. Dinosaur National Monument

River Outfitters
- *Adrift Adventures, 800-824-0150, www.adrift.com
- Adventure Bound, 800-423-4668, www.raft-colorado.com
- American River Touring Association, 800-323-2782, www.arta.org
- Dinosaur River Expeditions, 800-345-7238, www.dinoadv.com
- *Don Hatch River Expeditions, 800-342-8243, www.hatchriver.com
- Eagle Outdoor Sports, 801-451-7238, www.eagle5.com
- Holiday River Expeditions, 800-624-6323, www.bikeraft.com
- National Outdoor Leadership School, 307-332-6973 or 800-346-6277, www.oars.com
- Sheri Griffith Expeditions, 800-332-2439, www.griffithexp.com

These companies offer one-day trips.

2. Colorado National Monument

Driving Tours Along Rim Rock Drive
- American Spirits Shuttle, 888-226-5031, www.gisdho.com

Rock Climbing Guides
- Colorado Alpine and Desert Adventures, 970-248-8513 or 970-216-2953, www.coloradoadventures.net

3. Canyons of the Ancients National Monument

Hiking and Educational Trips
- Crow Canyon Archaeology Center, 800-422-8975, www.crowcanyon.org
- Far Out Expeditions, 435-672-2294, www.faroutexpeditions.com
- Kelly Place, 800-745-4885, www.kellyplace.com

Horseback Rides
- Canyon Trails Ranch, 970-565-1499
- Dolores River Outfitters, 970-882-3099, www.djoutfitting.com
- San Juan Outfitters, 970-259-6259, www.sanjuanoutfitting.com

Hunting Guides
- Dolores River Outfitters, 970-882-3099, www.djoutfitting.com

Mountain Bike Tours
- Western Spirit Cycling, 800-845-2453, www.westernspirit.com

5. Mesa Verde National Park

Bus Tours
- ARAMARK, 800-449-2288, www.visitmesaverde.com

7. Rocky Mountain National Park

Backpacking

- Outward Bound Wilderness, 720-497-2453, www.outwardboundwilderness.org
- Overland Trails, Inc., 800-458-0588, www.overlandsummers.com
- The Road Less Traveled, Inc., 800-939-9839, www.theroadlesstraveled.com

Bicycle Touring

- Colorado Bicycling Adventures, 970-586-4241, www.coloradobicycling.com

Day Hiking

- Longs Peak Mountain Guides, 303-520-7949
- New England Hiking Holidays, 800-869-0949, www.nehikingholidays.com
- The Sierra Club, 415-977-5626, www.sierraclub.org
- The World Outdoors, 800-488-8483, www.theworldoutdoors.com
- YMCA of the Rockies, 970-586-3341, www.ymcarockies.org

Fly-Fishing Instruction

- Estes Angler, 970-586-2110
- Estes Park Mountain Shop, 970-586-6548, www.estesparkmountainshop.com
- Front Range Anglers, 866-994-1375, www.frontrangeanglers.com
- Kinsley Outfitters, 800-442-7420, www.kinsleyoutfitters.com
- Kirk's Flyshop, 877-669-1859, www.kirksflyshop.com
- Rocky Mountain Adventures, 800-858-6808, www.shoprma.com
- Rocky Mountain Outfitters, 303-447-2400, www.rockymtanglers.com
- Scot's Sporting Goods, 970-586-2877, www.scotssportinggoods.com

Livery Operations

- Aspen Lodge and Guest Ranch, 800-332-6867, www.aspenlodge.net
- Glacier Creek Stables, 970-586-3244
- Meeker Park Lodge, 303-747-2266
- Moraine Park Stables, 970-586-2327
- National Park Gateway Stables, 970-586-5269, www.nationalparkgatewaystables.com
- Silver Lane Stables, 970-586-4695, www.silverlanestables.com
- Sombrero Ranch, Allenspark, 303-747-2551, www.sombrero.com
- Sombrero Ranch, Estes Park, 970-586-4577, www.sombrero.com
- Sombrero Ranch, Glen Haven, 970-586-2669, www.sombrero.com
- Sombrero Ranch, Grand Lake, 970-627-3514, www.sombrero.com
- Winding River Resort, 970-627-3215, www.windingriverresort.com
- YMCA of the Rockies, 970-586-3341, www.ymcarockies.org

Llama Packing

- Kirk's Flyshop, 877-669-1859, www.kirksflyshop.com

Mountain Climbing Instruction and Guides

- Colorado Mountain School, 888-267-7783, www.cmschool.com

Photography Workshops

- James Frank Photography, 970-586-3418, www.jamesfrank.com
- The Nature Workshops, 303-828-3210, www.natureworkshops.com
- Weldon Lee's Rocky Mountain Photo Adventures, 303-747-2074, www.rockymountainphotoadventures.com

9. Black Canyon of the Gunnison National Park

Horseback Rides

- Elk Ridge Trail Rides, 970-240-6007, www.elkridgetrailrides.com

Rock Climbing

- San Juan Mountain Guides, 970-325-4925, www.ourayclimbing.com
- Skyward Mountaineering, 970-209-2985, www.skywardmountaineering.com

10. Curecanti National Recreation Area

Guided Fishing

- Adaptive Sports Center, 866-349-2296, www.adaptivesports.org
- Ferro's Blue Mesa Outfitters, 970-641-4671
- Gunnison Fish and Raft, 877-559-3474, www.floatfish.com
- High Mountain Drifters, 800-793-4243
- Scenic River Tours, 970-641-3131, www.scenicrivertours.com
- Three Rivers Outfitting, 888-761-3474, www.3riversoutfitting.com
- Troutfitter Sports Co., 866-349-1323, www.troutfitter.com

Kayaking, Canoeing, and Rafting

- Adaptive Sports Center, 866-349-2296, www.adaptivesports.org
- Scenic River Tours, 970-641-3131, www.scenicrivertours.com
- Three Rivers Outfitting, 888-761-3474, www.3riversoutfitting.com

Lake Tours

- Adaptive Sports Center, 866-349-2296, www.adaptivesports.org
- Ferro's Blue Mesa Outfitters, 970-641-4671

Winter Activities

- Adaptive Sports Center, 866-349-2296, www.adaptivesports.org
- Gunnison Fish and Raft, 877-559-3474, www.floatfish.com

11. Great Sand Dunes National Park and Preserve

Four-Wheel-Drive Tours

- Great Sand Dunes Oasis, 719-378-2222

Hiking

- Cottonwood Gulch Foundation, 800-246-8735, www.cottonwoodgulch.org
- Outward Bound West, 888-837-5205, www.cobs.org
- Trailhead Wilderness School, 303-569-0767, www.trailheadwildernessschool.com

Bring a kite to Great Sand Dunes National Park and Preserve to take advantage of the steady winds.

11. Great Sand Dunes National Park and Preserve (continued)

Horseback Riding and Pack Trips
- Bear Basin Pack Trips, 719-783-2519, www.bearbasinpacktrips.com
- Red Mountain Outfitters, 719-589-4186, www.jimflynn-redmountainoutfitters.com

Hunting
- R&R Outfitters, 888-255-0211, www.randroutfitters.com
- Sangre de Cristo Outfitters, 719-783-2265, www.sangreoutfitters.com

Photography Workshops
- The Nature Workshops, 303-828-3210, www.natureworkshops.com

12. Sand Creek Massacre National Historic Site

Archaeological and Historical Tours
near the National Historic Site
- Sand Creek Tours, 719-336-5082, www.sandcreektours.com

Recommended Reading

Families who want to learn more may wish to check out the following books.
I have found them to be extremely helpful references.

Armstrong, David M. *Rocky Mountain Mammals: A Handbook of Mammals of Rocky Mountain National Park and Shadow Mountain National Recreation Area, Colorado*. Estes Park, CO: Rocky Mountain Nature Association, 1975.

Bernard, Ernest S., ed. *Isabella Lucy Bird's "A Lady's Life in the Rocky Mountains": An Annotated Text*. Norman, OK: University of Oklahoma Press, 1999.

Cassells, E. Steve. *The Archeology of Colorado*, Revised Edition. Boulder, CO: Johnson Books, 1997.

Chronic, Halka and Felicie Williams. *Roadside Geology of Colorado*. Missoula, MT: Mountain Press Publishing Company, 2002.

Fielder, John. *John Fielder's Best of Colorado*. Englewood, CO: Westcliffe Publishers, 2002.

Folsom, Gil. *Colorado Campgrounds: The 100 Best and All the Rest*. Englewood, CO: Westcliffe Publishers, 2000.

Gray, Mary Taylor. *Colorado Wildlife Viewing Guide*. Helena and Billings, MT: Falcon Press, 1992.

———. *The Guide to Colorado Birds*. Englewood, CO: Westcliffe Publishers, 1998.

Kessler, Ron. *Old Spanish Trail North Branch and Its Travelers*. Santa Fe: Sunstone Press, 1998.

Weber, William A. *Rocky Mountain Flora: A Field Guide for the Identification of Ferns, Conifers, and Flowering Plants of the Southern Rocky Mountains from Pikes Peak to Rocky Mountain National Park and from the Plains to the Continental Divide*. Boulder, CO: Colorado Associated University Press, 1976.

Young, Mary Taylor (formerly Mary Taylor Gray). *Land of Grass and Sky: A Naturalist's Prairie Journey*. Englewood, CO: Westcliffe Publishers, 2002.

Index

Note: Citations followed by the letter "p" denote photos.

A

Abert's squirrel, 140p
Alamosa, Colorado, 195
Alcove Nature Trail, 43, 50p
alpine tundra life zone, 123–124, 186–187
Alpine Visitor Center, 112
altitude sickness, 12
Anasazi Heritage Center, 54, 63
artifacts, ancient, 16
Aspenglen Campground, 128

B

badger, 212p
Balcony House, 9p, 86
Barksdale Picnic Area, 142
Bear Lake, 113
Beaver Creek Picnic Area, 173
Beaver Meadows Visitor Center, 110
Bent's Old Fort National Historic Site
    attractions, 208–209
    at a glance, 213
    hike for little legs, 215
    human history, 214
    lodging and camping, 214
    map, 209
    natural history, 210, 212
    nearby towns, 215
    overview of, 208, 215
    programs and activities, 209–210
    restaurants and picnic areas, 214
    special considerations for families, 215
bighorn sheep, 33p
bison, 186p
black bear, 170p
Black Canyon of the Gunnison Nat'l Park
    at a glance, 149
    guides and outfitters, 223
    hike for little legs, 152
    human history, 154–155
    lodging and camping, 155
    map, 145
    natural history, 153–154
    nearby towns, 156
    North Rim attractions, 150–151
    overview of, 144, 157
    programs and activities, 151–153
    restaurants and picnic areas, 155
    South Rim attractions, 148, 150
    special considerations for families, 156
BLM (Bureau of Land Management) national monuments, 19
bluebird, 140p
blue flax, 142p
Blue Mesa Recreational Ranch, 174
Blue Mesa Reservoir, 159, 160, 160p
bobcat, 187p

C

Cajon Ruins, 70
Canyon Area Visitor Center, 29, 36
Canyon Overlook Picnic Area, 36
Canyons of the Ancients Nat'l Monument
    attractions, 54, 56, 58–59
    at a glance, 57
    guides and outfitters, 221
    hike for little legs, 62
    human history, 61–63
    lodging and camping, 63
    map, 53
    natural history, 60–61
    nearby towns, 64
    overview of, 52, 65
    programs and activities, 59
    restaurants and picnic areas, 63
    special considerations for families, 64–65
Castle Creek Picnic Area, 193
Chapin Mesa Archaeological Museum, 82, 87
Chasm View Overlook, 148, 148p
Chasm View Trail, 151
children, adventuring with
    gear, 12, 220
    keys for success, 11
    national park services for families, 15

park manners, 15–18
safety considerations, 12–13, 17–18
trip logs, 216–217
chipmunk, 91p
Cimarron Campgrounds, 174
Cimarron Canyon Railroad Exhibit, 162, 164
Cliff Palace, 84, 84p, 93
Colorado, map of, 6–7
Colorado National Monument
  attractions, 43–44
  at a glance, 45
  guides and outfitters, 221
  hike for little legs, 46
  human history, 49
  lodging and camping, 50
  map, 41
  natural history, 47–49
  nearby towns, 50–51
  overview of, 40, 51
  programs and activities, 44, 46
  restaurants and picnic areas, 50
  special considerations for families, 51
Colorado National Monument Visitor
  Center, 43
Colorado River, 118p
Columbus Canyon, 46p
Cortez, Colorado, 64, 78, 94, 103
coyote, 47p
Craig, Colorado, 38
Crawford, Colorado, 156
crow, 100p
cryptobiotic soil, 49p
Crystal Creek Trail, 173–174
Crystal Reservoir, 159, 162
Curecanti National Recreation Area
  attractions, 160, 162, 164
  at a glance, 163
  guides and outfitters, 223
  hike for little legs, 165
  human history, 171–173
  lodging and camping, 174
  map, 158–159
  natural history, 166–171
  nearby towns, 174–175
  overview of, 159, 175

programs and activities, 164
restaurants and picnic areas, 173–174
special considerations for families, 175
Cutthroat Castle, 70

D
Deadhorse Trail, 151
Deerlodge Park Campground, 37
dehydration, 12–13
Desert Voices Nature Trail, 4p, 28–29
Devil's Kitchen Picnic Area, 50
Dillon Pinnacles, 168p
Dinosaur, Colorado, 38
Dinosaur National Monument
  attractions, 26, 28–30
  at a glance, 27
  guides and outfitters, 221
  hike for little legs, 32
  human history, 34–36
  lodging and camping, 37
  map, 22–23
  natural history, 31–33
  nearby towns, 38
  overview of, 23–24, 39
  programs and activities, 30
  restaurants and picnic areas, 36
  special considerations for families, 38–39
Dinosaur Quarry Visitor Center, 26, 26p
dogs, 16
Dolores, Colorado, 64
dune field life zone, 189
Durango, Colorado, 94–95

E
Eads, Colorado, 206–207
East Elk Creek Group Campground, 174
East Portal, 164
Echo Park, 30
Echo Park Campground, 37
Echo Park Overlook, 36
Echo Rock, 39p
elk, 109p
Elk Creek Campground, 174
Elk Creek Marina, 162
Elk Creek Picnic Area, 173

Ely Creek, 37
equipment, 12, 220
Escalante Interpretive Trail and Pueblo, 54
Estes Park, Colorado, 129–130
Exclamation Point, 150–151

F
Fall River Visitor Center, 110, 110p
Far View Lodge, 93
Far View Ruins, 95p
Far View Terrace, 93
Far View Visitor Center, 82
Florissant, Colorado, 142
Florissant Fossil Beds Nat'l Monument
    attractions, 134, 136
    at a glance, 137
    hike for little legs, 138
    human history, 141–142
    lodging and camping, 142
    map, 133
    natural history, 139–141
    nearby towns, 142–143
    overview of, 132, 143
    programs and activities, 136
    restaurants and picnic areas, 142
    special considerations for families, 143
Florissant Fossil Beds National Monument
    Visitor Center, 134
fossils, 16
Fruita, Colorado, 50

G
Gates of Lodore, 28p, 36p
Gates of Lodore Campground, 37
gear, 12, 220
giant sequoia tree, 135p
Glacier Basin Campground, 128
golden eagle, 74p
Goodman Point Ruins, 72
Grand Junction, Colorado, 51
Grand Lake, Colorado, 130
great blue heron, 61p
great horned owl, 61p
Great Sand Dunes Lodge, 193

Great Sand Dunes Nat'l Park and Preserve
    attractions, 179–180, 182
    at a glance, 183
    guides and outfitters, 223–224
    hike for little legs, 184
    human history, 191–193
    lodging and camping, 193–194
    map, 177
    natural history, 185–191
    nearby towns, 195
    overview of, 176–177, 197
    programs and activities, 182
    restaurants and picnic areas, 193
    special considerations for families, 196
Great Sand Dunes Oasis, 194
Great Sand Dunes Visitor Center, 180
Green River, 26–27
Green River Campground, 37
Green River mud, 25p
Gunnison, Colorado, 174–175

H
Hackberry Ruins, 70
Harpers Corner Drive, 24p, 29
Harpers Corner Trail, 29
Herard, Mount, 192p
Hermits Rest Picnic Area, 173
High Point Picnic Area, 155
Hog Canyon Hike, 29
Holly Ruins, 70
Holzwarth Historic Site, 115
Hooper, Colorado, 195
Hornbek Homestead, 134, 134p
Horseshoe Ruins, 70
Hovenweep Campground, 77
Hovenweep Castle, 76p
Hovenweep National Monument
    attractions, 67, 69–70, 72
    at a glance, 71
    hike for little legs, 72
    human history, 75–76
    lodging and camping, 77
    map, 67
    natural history, 73–75
    nearby towns, 78

overview of, 66–67, 79
programs and activities, 73
restaurants and picnic areas, 77
special considerations for families, 78
hummingbird, 121p

I
Indian Arts and Culture Festival, 87p
Indian paintbrush, 51p
Iola Picnic Area, 173

J
jackrabbit, 75p
Jones Hole, 30
Josie Bassett Morris Homestead, 28, 36

K
kangaroo rat, 189p
Kawuneeche Valley, 118p
Kawuneeche Visitor Center, 114–115

L
La Junta, Colorado, 215
Lake Fork Campgrounds, 174
Lake Fork Marina, 162
Lake George, Colorado, 143
Lamar, Colorado, 207
Leave No Trace, 218–219
Little Ruin Canyon, 72p
Little Ruin Canyon Trail, 67
Long House, 84
Longs Peak, 114, 115p
Longs Peak Campground, 128
Lowry Pueblo, 56, 56p, 63
lupine, 155p

M
Mancos, Colorado, 94
Mancos Valley Overlook, 93
manners, park, 15–18
map, Colorado, 6–7
McPhee Campground, 63
Medano Creek, 179–180, 179p, 180p
Mesa Top Loop Drive, 82, 84

Mesa Verde National Park
attractions, 82, 84, 86
at a glance, 85
guides and outfitters, 221
hike for little legs, 89
human history, 91–92
lodging and camping, 93–94
map, 81
natural history, 88, 90–91
nearby towns, 94–95
overview of, 80, 95
programs and activities, 87
restaurants and picnic areas, 93
special considerations for families, 95
Metate Room, 93
montane life zone, 120–122, 187–189
Montezuma Valley Overlook, 93
Montrose, Colorado, 156
Montville Nature Trail, 182
Monument Canyon, 44p
Monument Canyon Trail, 43–44
Moraine Park, 129p
Moraine Park Campground, 128
Moraine Park Museum, 114
Morefield Campground, 93p, 94
Morefield Village, 86
Morrow Point Reservoir, 159, 160, 162
Mosca, Colorado, 195
Mosca Creek Picnic Area, 193
Mosca Pass Trail, 180, 182
mule deer, 17p, 60p

N
national historic sites, 14
national monuments, 14, 19
national parks, 14
national preserves, 14
national recreation areas, 14
Never Summer Mountain Range, 130p
northern flicker, 153p
North Rim Campground, 155
North Rim Road, 150
North Vista Trail, 150–151, 150p
Nymph Lake, 126p

O

Old Fall River Road, 112

P

Painted Hand Pueblo, 19p, 54p, 56, 58
Painted Wall Overlook, 148
Pappy's Restaurant, 173
penstemon, 120p
Petrified Forest Loop, 136
petrified wood, 138p
pika, 124p
Pine Creek Trail, 1p, 165p
Piñon Flats Campground, 194, 194p
piñon-juniper woodland life zone,
   187–189
Pioneer Point Picnic Area, 173
Plug Hat Butte Picnic Area, 36
Ponderosa Campground, 173p
Ponderosa Point Picnic Area, 193
porcupine, 123p
prairie dog, 169p
pronghorn antelope, 203p
Pueblo Ruins, 93

R

Rainbow Park, 37
Rangely, Colorado, 38
Red Creek Group Campground, 174
red fox, 102p
Rim Rock Drive, 43
ring-necked pheasant, 202p
Rocky Mountain National Park
   attractions, 110, 112–115
   at a glance, 111
   guides and outfitters, 222–223
   hike for little legs, 117
   human history, 125–126
   lodging and camping, 128–129
   map, 106–107
   natural history, 116–124
   nearby towns, 129–130
   overview of, 106, 108, 131
   programs and activities, 116
   restaurants and picnic areas, 127
   special considerations for families,
      130–131

S

sabkha life zone, 190–191
Saddlehorn Campground, 50
Saddlehorn Picnic Area, 50
safety, outdoor, 12–13, 17–18
Sand Canyon Pueblo, 58
Sand Canyon Trail, 57p, 58–59, 58p, 62p
Sand Creek Massacre Nat'l Historic Site
   attractions, 202
   at a glance, 205
   guides and outfitters, 224
   human history, 203–204, 206
   lodging and camping, 206
   map, 201
   natural history, 202–203
   nearby towns, 206–207
   overview of, 200, 202, 207
   programs and activities, 202
   restaurants and picnic areas, 206
   special considerations for families, 207
Sand Pit Picnic Area, 193
sand sheet life zone, 189–190
Sawmill Trail, 136
short-horned lizard, 190p
skunk, 154p
Sleeping Ute Mountain, 55p, 77p, 79p,
   100
South Rim Campground, 155
South Rim Road, 148
South Rim Visitor Center, 148
Split Mountain Campground, 37, 37p
Split Mountain Picnic Area, 36
Sprague Lake, 113
Spruce Canyon Trail, 89p, 93
Spruce Tree House, 82, 82p
Stevens Creek Campground, 174
subalpine forest life zone, 187
subalpine life zone, 122–123
sun protection, 12
Sunset View Picnic Area, 155

T

temperature change, 13
Tilted Rocks, 28, 34p
Timber Creek Campground, 128–129

Trailhead Restaurant, 127
Trail Ridge Road, 112
Trail Ridge Snack Bar, 127
trip logs, 216–217
turkey vulture, 90p

V
Vernal, Utah, 38
violet-green swallow, 48p
volcanic palisades, 161p

W
Walk Through Time Trail, A, 134
Warner Point Nature Trail, 148, 150
weather, 12–13
Wetherill Mesa, 93
Wetherill Mesa Tram, 84
Whirlpool Canyon, 32p
Wild Basin, 114
wildlife safety, 13, 17–18
wild turkey, 212p
Window Rock Nature Trail, 42p
Woodland Park, Colorado, 143

Y
Yampa River, 26–27
Yucca House National Monument
    attractions, 98
    at a glance, 101
    hike for little legs, 100
    human history, 102
    lodging and camping, 102
    map, 97
    natural history, 100
    nearby towns, 103
    overview of, 96–98, 103
    programs and activities, 100
    restaurants and picnic areas, 102
    special considerations for families, 103

About the Author/Photographer

At the age of three, Carolyn Sutton snuggled into a big Coleman sleeping bag in the campground at the Great Sand Dunes. Looking up, she found herself face to face with the Milky Way in party mode. Her family was camping out during the annual Perseid meteor shower, and Carolyn still hasn't recovered from the experience.

Together with her Mom, Dad, and big sister, she went on to visit nearly all of Colorado's national parks. Today she loves hiking, cross-country skiing, and especially camping with her husband and kids all across the state.

A Colorado native, she received her bachelor's degree and a diploma in education from the University of Colorado at Boulder. Later, she taught junior high and high school science and eventually went into business. Now she is a mom and a freelance travel writer, scribbling about her family's travel adventures.

Carolyn's work has been published in *Sunset*, *Frontier*, *Camping Life*, and *Arthur Frommer's Budget Travel*, among other magazines. Her first book, *The Preschooler's Guide to Denver—Best Outings for Kids Under 6 Years Old*, received abundant praise from the media and moms alike. It placed in the top 2% of Amazon.com rankings the summer it was released. Carolyn is the current editor of a travel planning website, www.FamilyTravelWest.com.

Carolyn, age two-and-a-half, visiting Mesa Verde